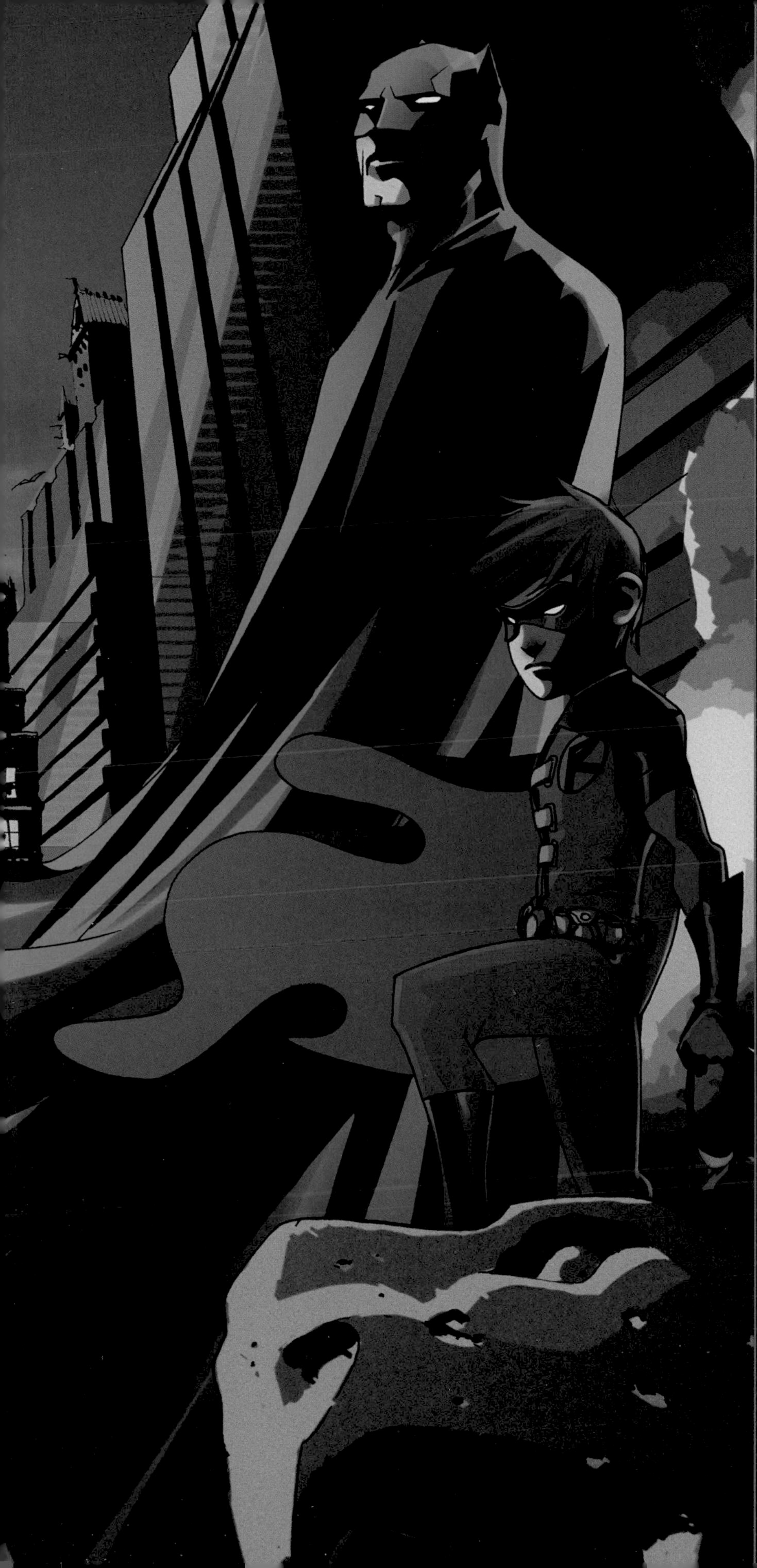

BATMAN
HEART OF HUSH

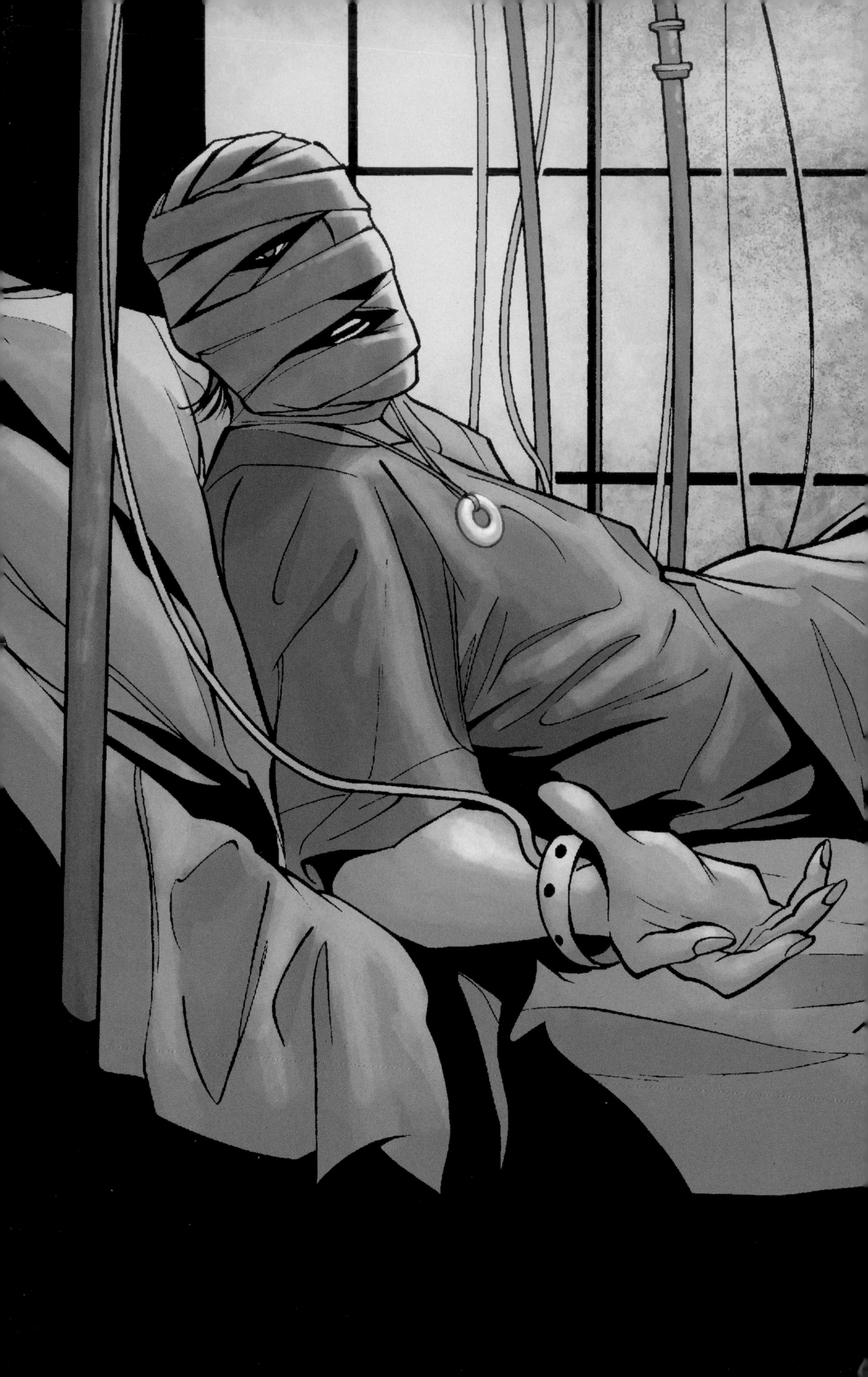

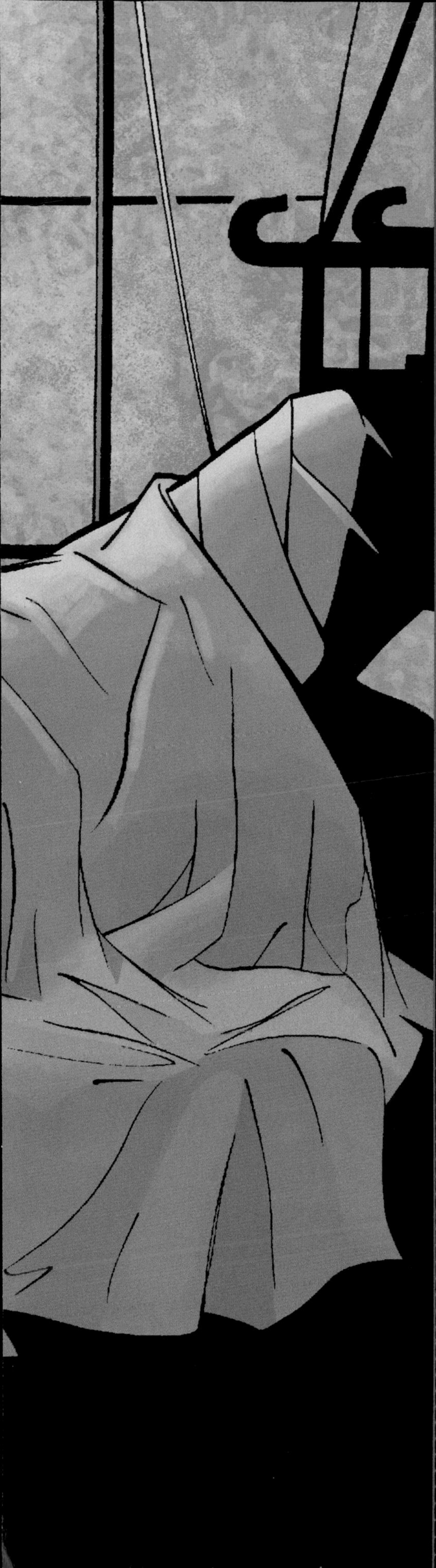

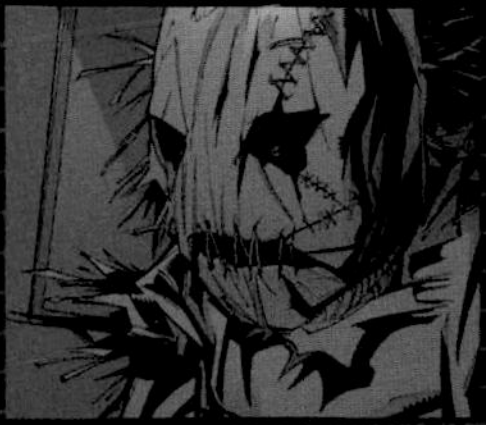

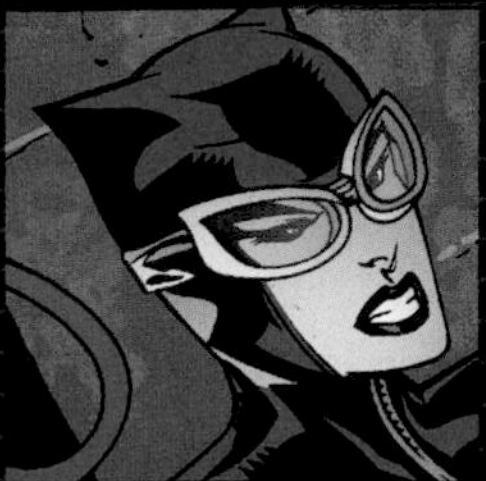

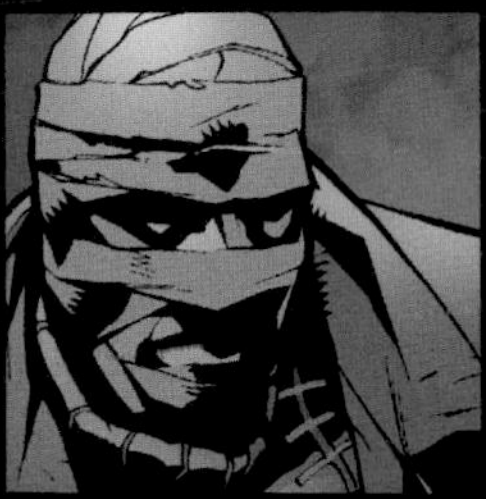

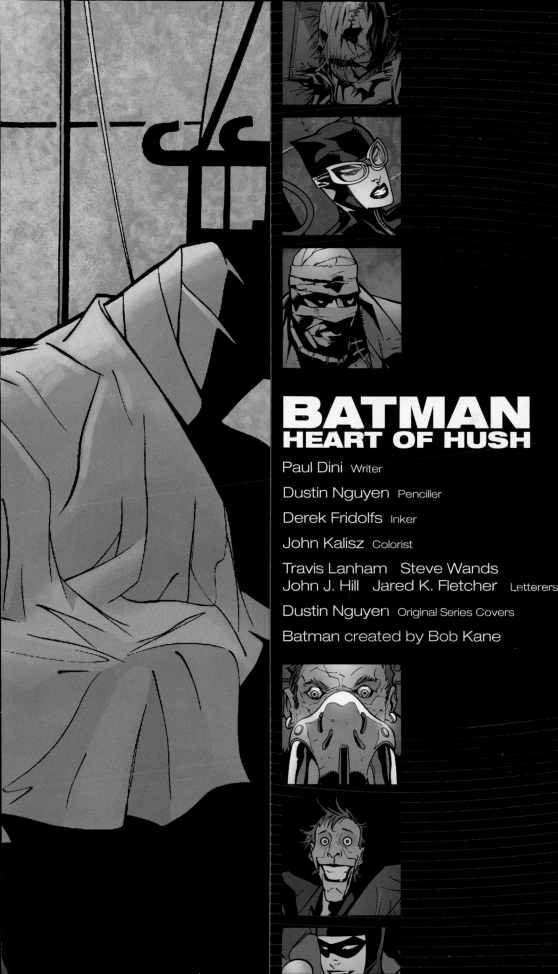

BATMAN
HEART OF HUSH

Paul Dini Writer

Dustin Nguyen Penciller

Derek Fridolfs Inker

John Kalisz Colorist

Travis Lanham Steve Wands
John J. Hill Jared K. Fletcher Letterers

Dustin Nguyen Original Series Covers

Batman created by Bob Kane

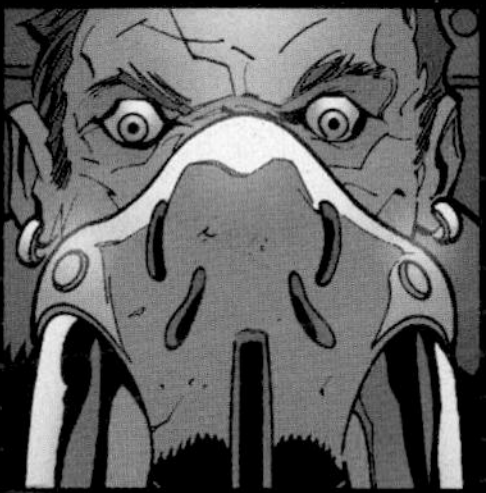

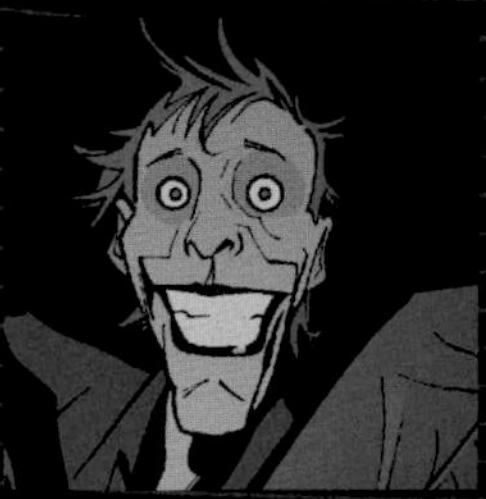

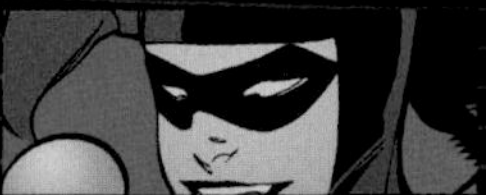

Dan DiDio Senior VP-Executive Editor   Mike Marts Editor-original series   Jeanine Schaefer Associate Editor-original series   Janelle Siegel Assistant Editor-original series   Scott Nybakken
Editor-collected edition   Robbin Brosterman Senior Art Director   Paul Levitz President & Publisher   Georg Brewer VP-Design & DC Direct Creative   Richard Bruning Senior VP-Creative Director
Patrick Caldon Executive VP-Finance & Operations   Chris Caramalis VP-Finance   John Cunningham VP-Marketing   Terri Cunningham VP-Managing Editor   Amy Genkins Senior VP-Business &
Legal Affairs   Alison Gill VP-Manufacturing   David Hyde VP-Publicity   Hank Kanalz VP-General Manager, WildStorm   Jim Lee Editorial Director-WildStorm   Gregory Noveck Senior VP-Creative
Affairs   Sue Pohja VP-Book Trade Sales   Steve Rotterdam Senior VP-Sales & Marketing   Cheryl Rubin Senior VP-Brand Management   Alysse Soll VP-Advertising & Custom Publishing   Jeff Trojan
VP-Business Development, DC Direct   Bob Wayne VP-Sales

Cover art by **Dustin Nguyen.** Publication design by **Robbie Biederman.**

BATMAN
HEART OF HUSH

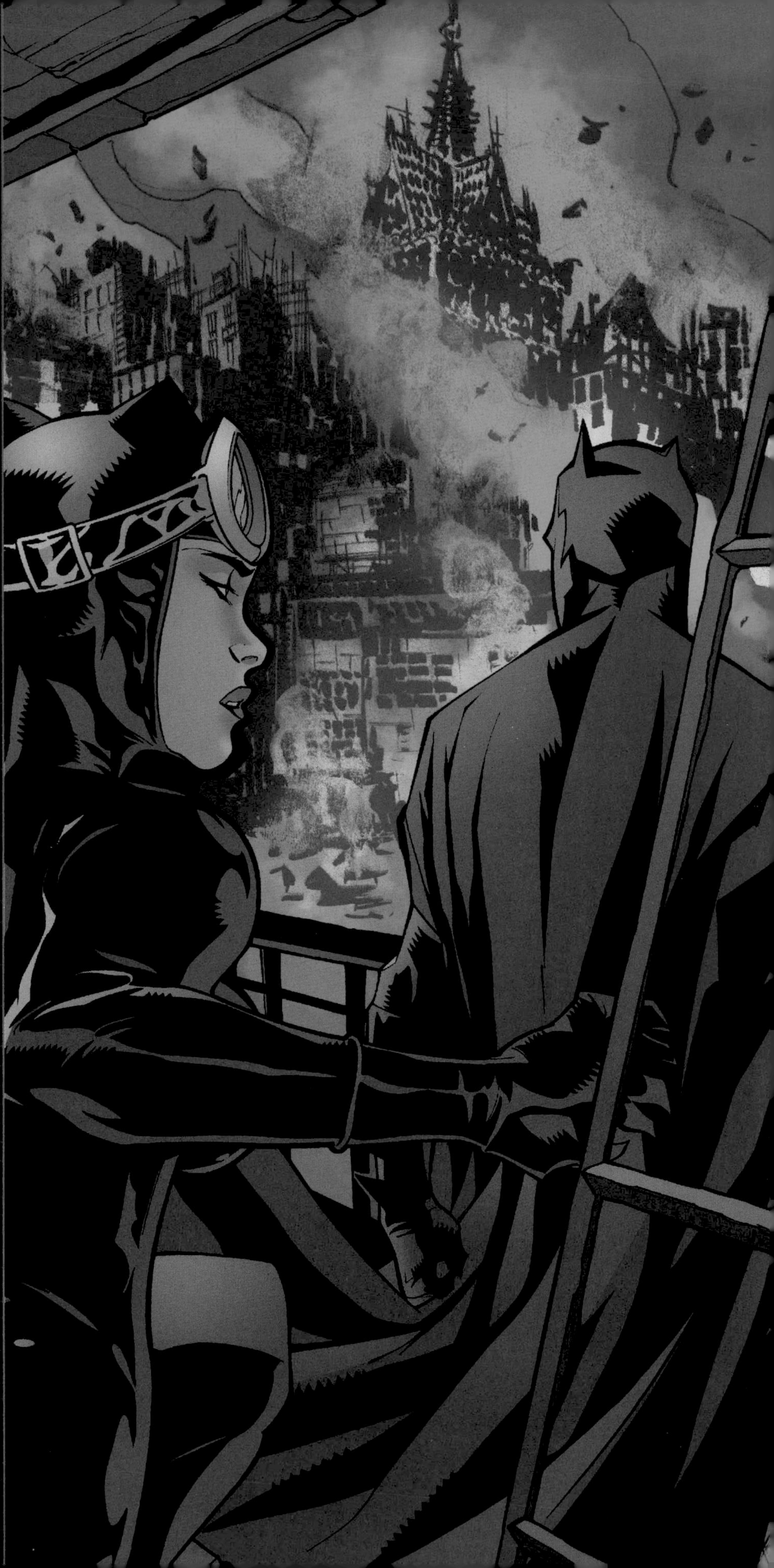

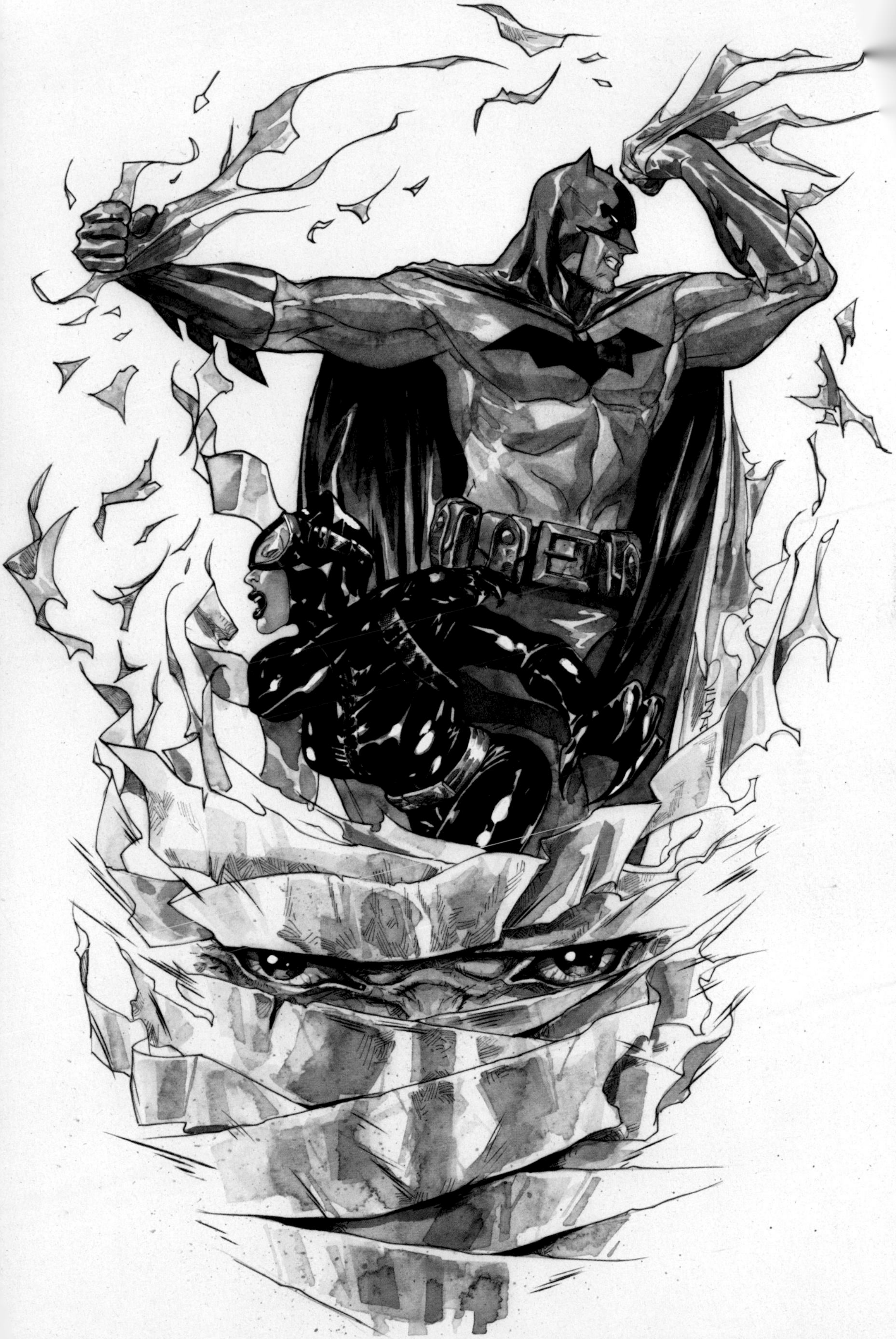

"Beware the man who can strike from a distance."

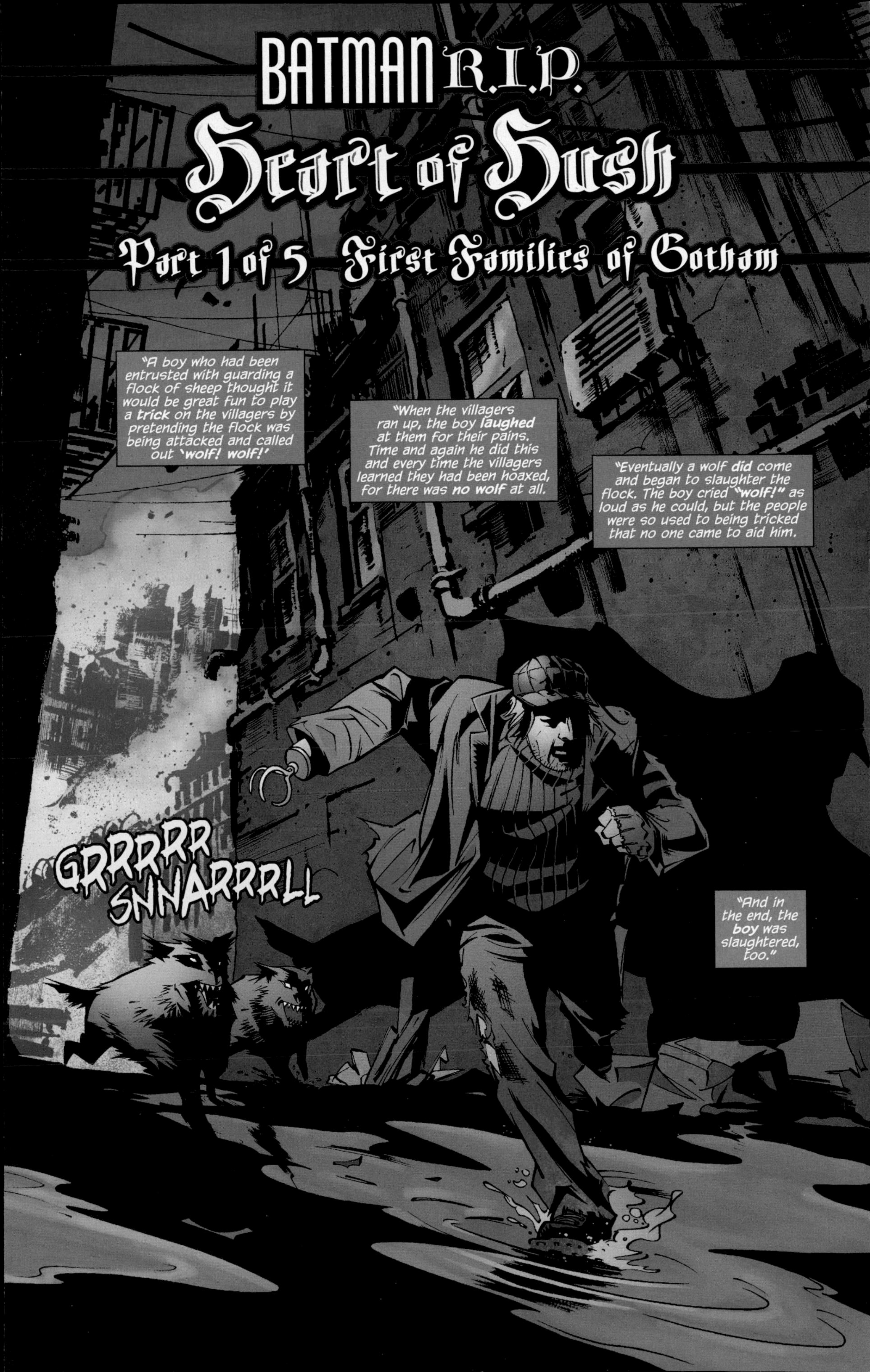
BATMAN R.I.P.
Heart of Hush
Part 1 of 5 First Families of Gotham
"A boy who had been entrusted with guarding a flock of sheep thought it would be great fun to play a trick on the villagers by pretending the flock was being attacked and called out 'wolf! wolf!'
"When the villagers ran up, the boy laughed at them for their pains. Time and again he did this and every time the villagers learned they had been hoaxed, for there was no wolf at all.
"Eventually a wolf did come and began to slaughter the flock. The boy cried "wolf!" as loud as he could, but the people were so used to being tricked that no one came to aid him.
GRRRRR SNNARRRLL
"And in the end, the boy was slaughtered, too."

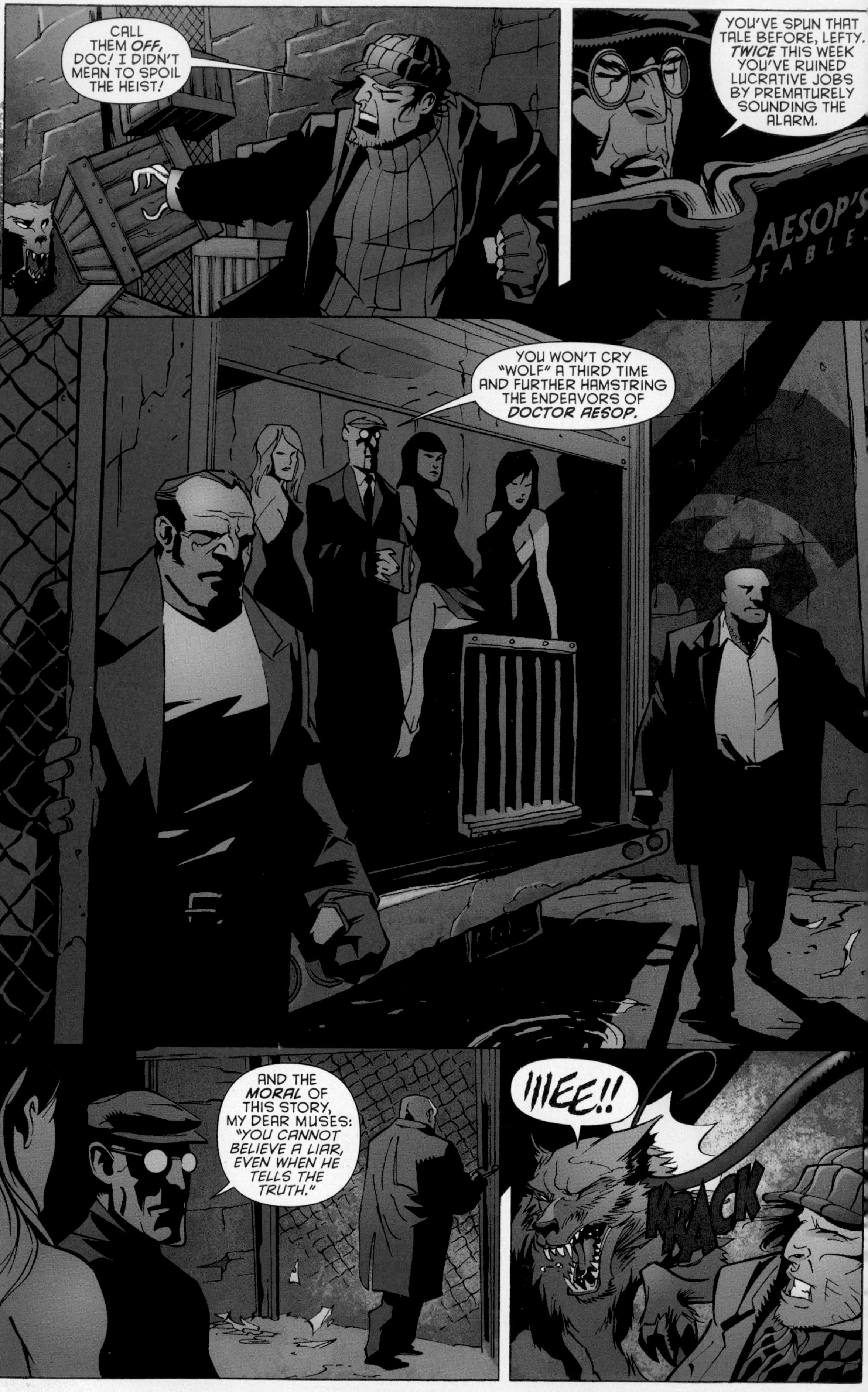
CALL THEM OFF, DOC! I DIDN'T MEAN TO SPOIL THE HEIST!
YOU'VE SPUN THAT TALE BEFORE, LEFTY. TWICE THIS WEEK YOU'VE RUINED LUCRATIVE JOBS BY PREMATURELY SOUNDING THE ALARM.
AESOP'S FABLES
YOU WON'T CRY "WOLF" A THIRD TIME AND FURTHER HAMSTRING THE ENDEAVORS OF DOCTOR AESOP.
AND THE MORAL OF THIS STORY, MY DEAR MUSES: "YOU CANNOT BELIEVE A LIAR, EVEN WHEN HE TELLS THE TRUTH."
IIIEE!!
KRACK

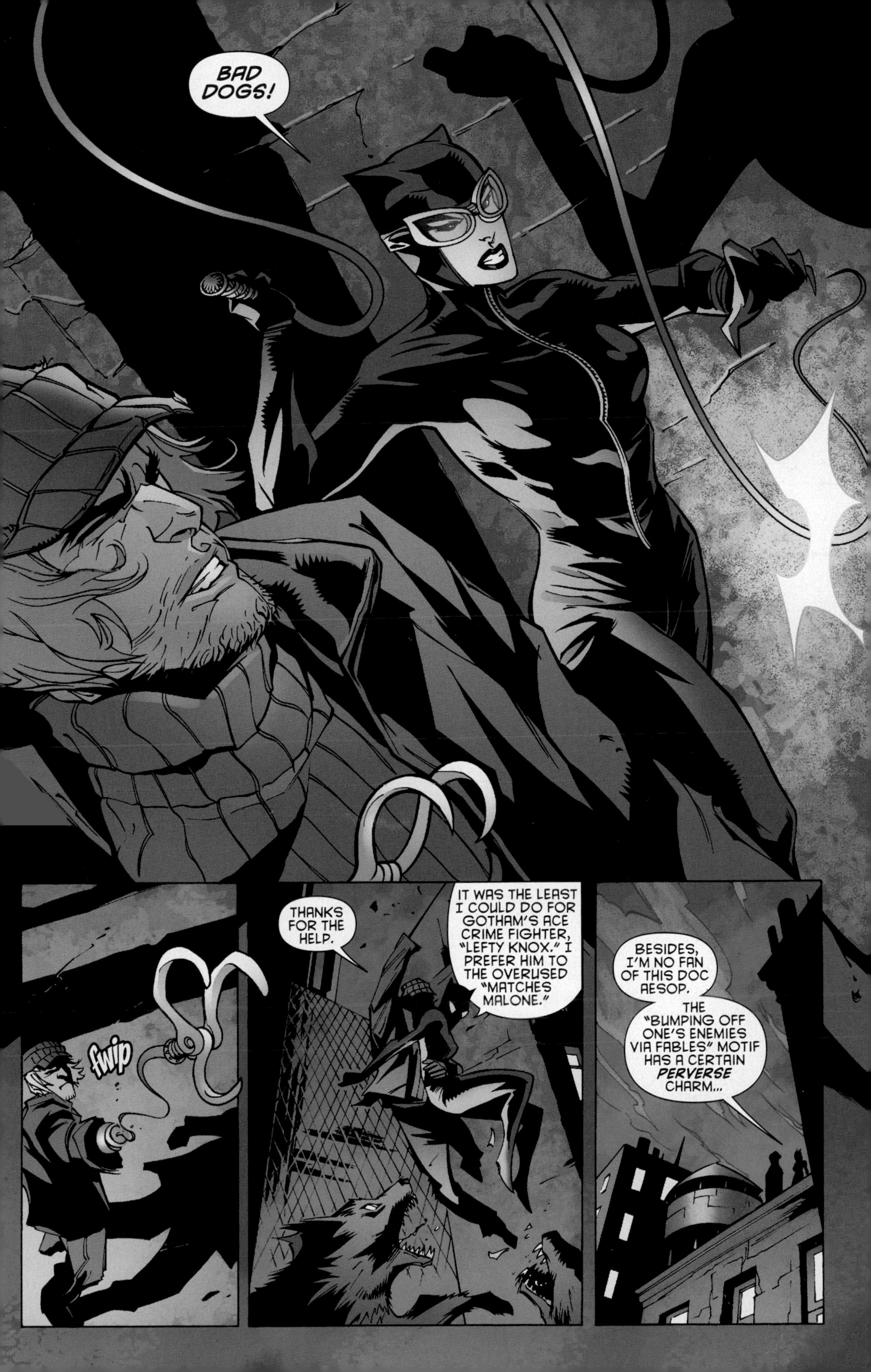
BAD DOGS!
fwip
THANKS FOR THE HELP.
IT WAS THE LEAST I COULD DO FOR GOTHAM'S ACE CRIME FIGHTER, "LEFTY KNOX." I PREFER HIM TO THE OVERUSED "MATCHES MALONE."
BESIDES, I'M NO FAN OF THIS DOC AESOP.
THE "BUMPING OFF ONE'S ENEMIES VIA FABLES" MOTIF HAS A CERTAIN PERVERSE CHARM...

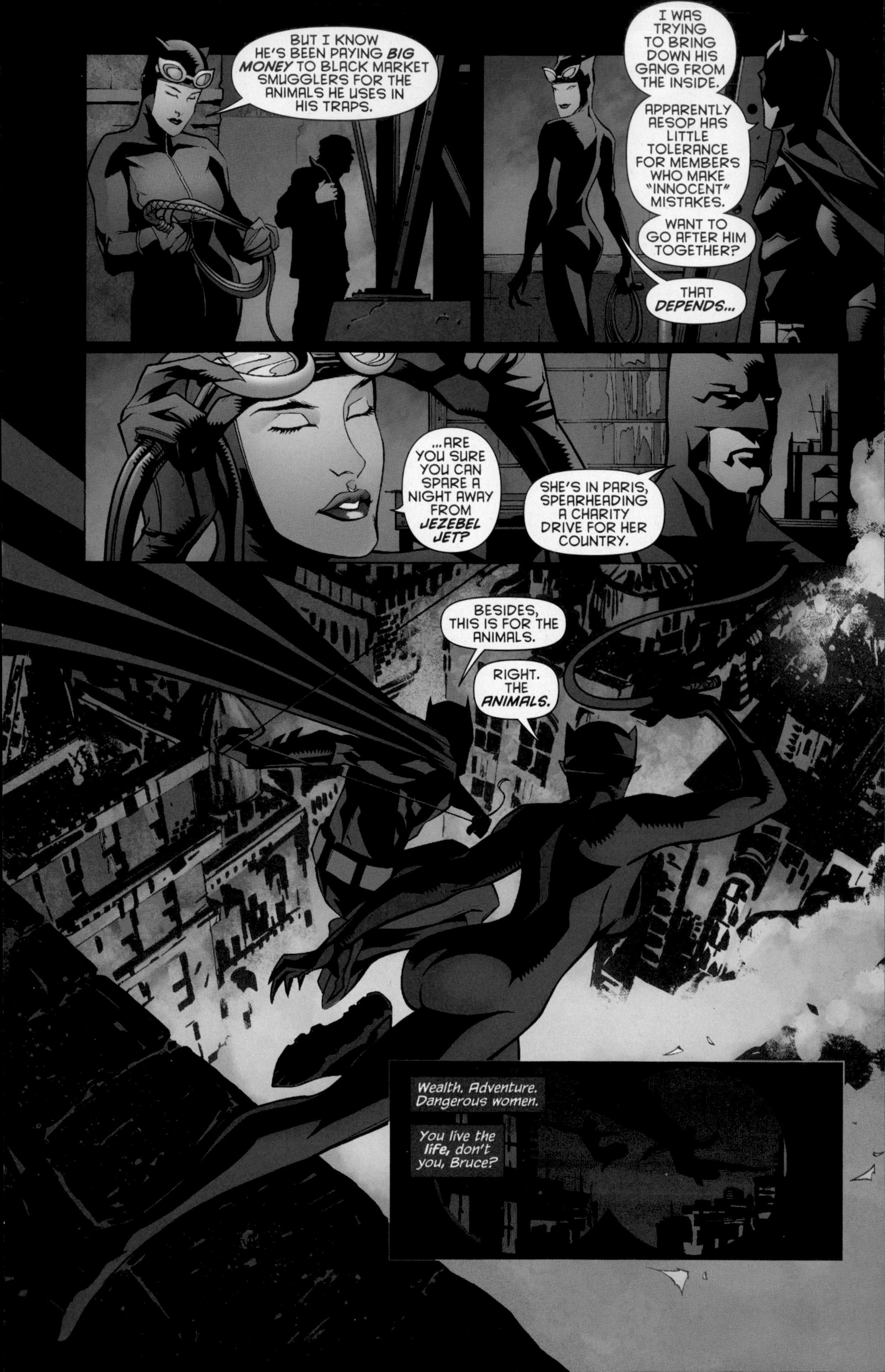
BUT I KNOW HE'S BEEN PAYING BIG MONEY TO BLACK MARKET SMUGGLERS FOR THE ANIMALS HE USES IN HIS TRAPS.
I WAS TRYING TO BRING DOWN HIS GANG FROM THE INSIDE.
APPARENTLY AESOP HAS LITTLE TOLERANCE FOR MEMBERS WHO MAKE "INNOCENT" MISTAKES.
WANT TO GO AFTER HIM TOGETHER?
THAT DEPENDS...
...ARE YOU SURE YOU CAN SPARE A NIGHT AWAY FROM JEZEBEL JET?
SHE'S IN PARIS, SPEARHEADING A CHARITY DRIVE FOR HER COUNTRY.
BESIDES, THIS IS FOR THE ANIMALS.
RIGHT. THE ANIMALS.
Wealth. Adventure. Dangerous women.
You live the life, don't you, Bruce?

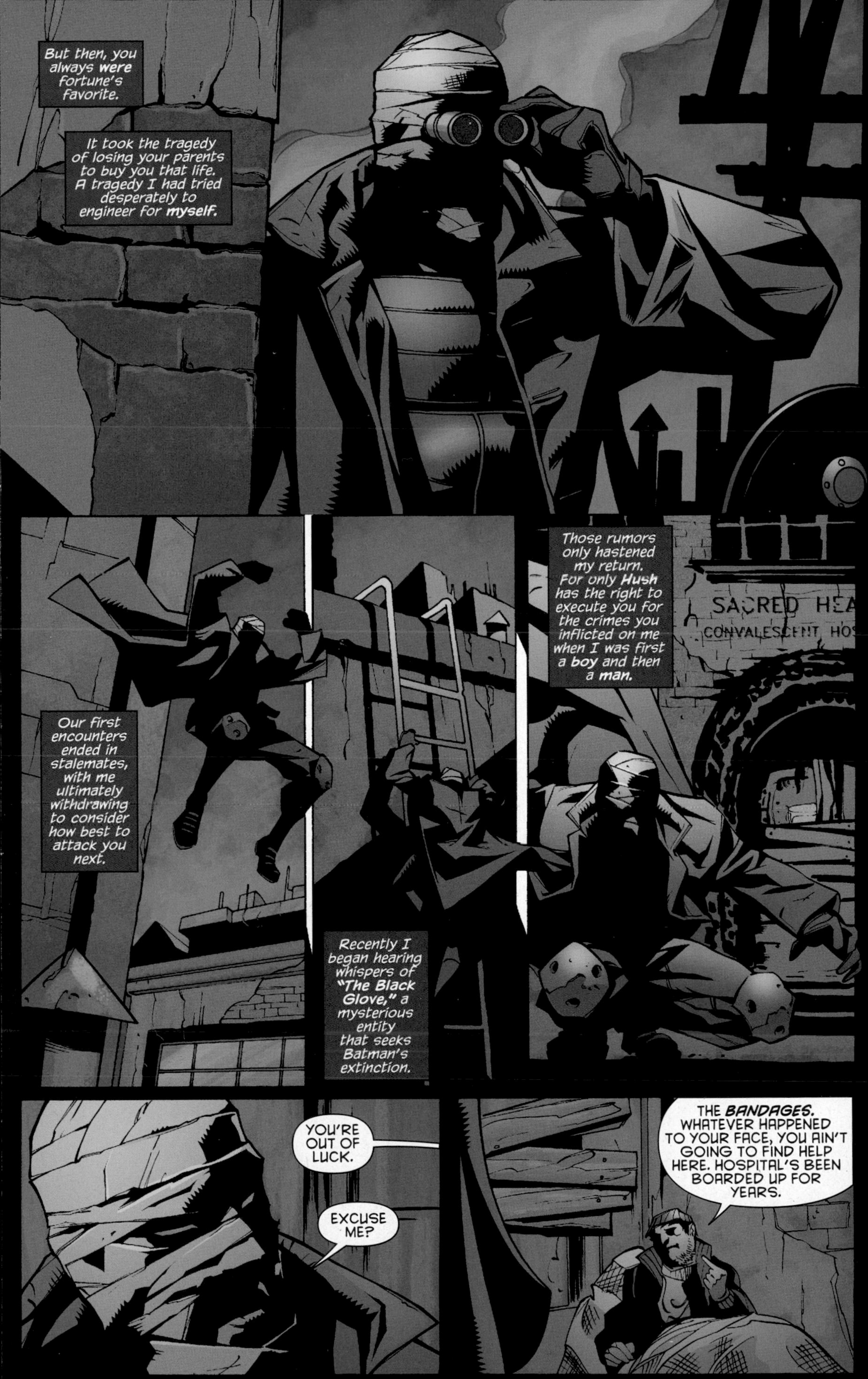
But then, you always were fortune's favorite.
It took the tragedy of losing your parents to buy you that life. A tragedy I had tried desperately to engineer for myself.
Our first encounters ended in stalemates, with me ultimately withdrawing to consider how best to attack you next.
Recently I began hearing whispers of "The Black Glove," a mysterious entity that seeks Batman's extinction.
Those rumors only hastened my return. For only Hush has the right to execute you for the crimes you inflicted on me when I was first a boy and then a man.
SACRED HEA
CONVALESCENT HOS
YOU'RE OUT OF LUCK.
EXCUSE ME?
THE BANDAGES. WHATEVER HAPPENED TO YOUR FACE, YOU AIN'T GOING TO FIND HELP HERE. HOSPITAL'S BEEN BOARDED UP FOR YEARS.

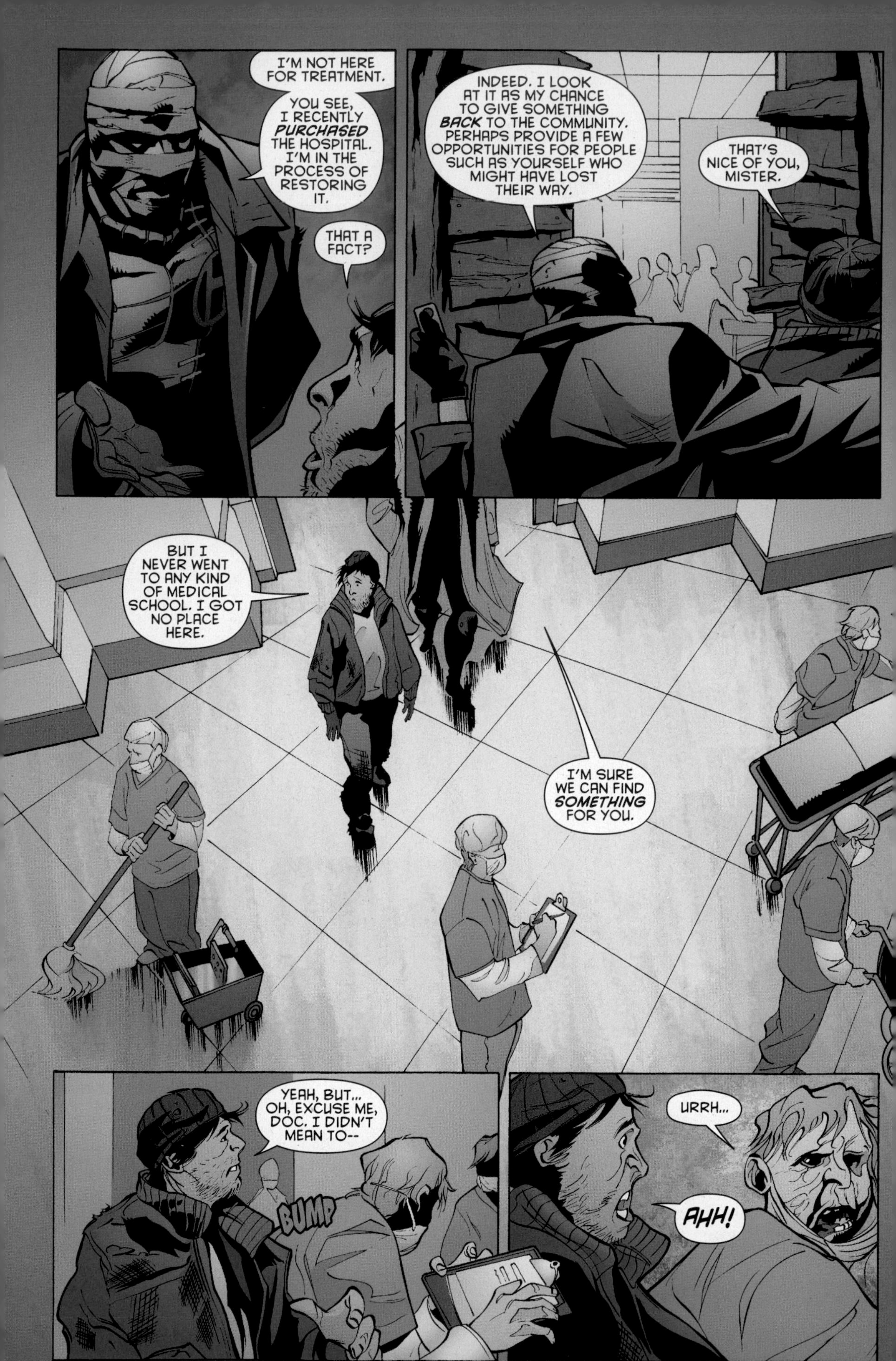
I'M NOT HERE FOR TREATMENT.
YOU SEE, I RECENTLY *PURCHASED* THE HOSPITAL. I'M IN THE PROCESS OF RESTORING IT.
THAT A FACT?
INDEED. I LOOK AT IT AS MY CHANCE TO GIVE SOMETHING *BACK* TO THE COMMUNITY. PERHAPS PROVIDE A FEW OPPORTUNITIES FOR PEOPLE SUCH AS YOURSELF WHO MIGHT HAVE LOST THEIR WAY.
THAT'S NICE OF YOU, MISTER.
BUT I NEVER WENT TO ANY KIND OF MEDICAL SCHOOL. I GOT NO PLACE HERE.
I'M SURE WE CAN FIND *SOMETHING* FOR YOU.
YEAH, BUT... OH, EXCUSE ME, DOC. I DIDN'T MEAN TO--
BUMP
URRH...
AHH!

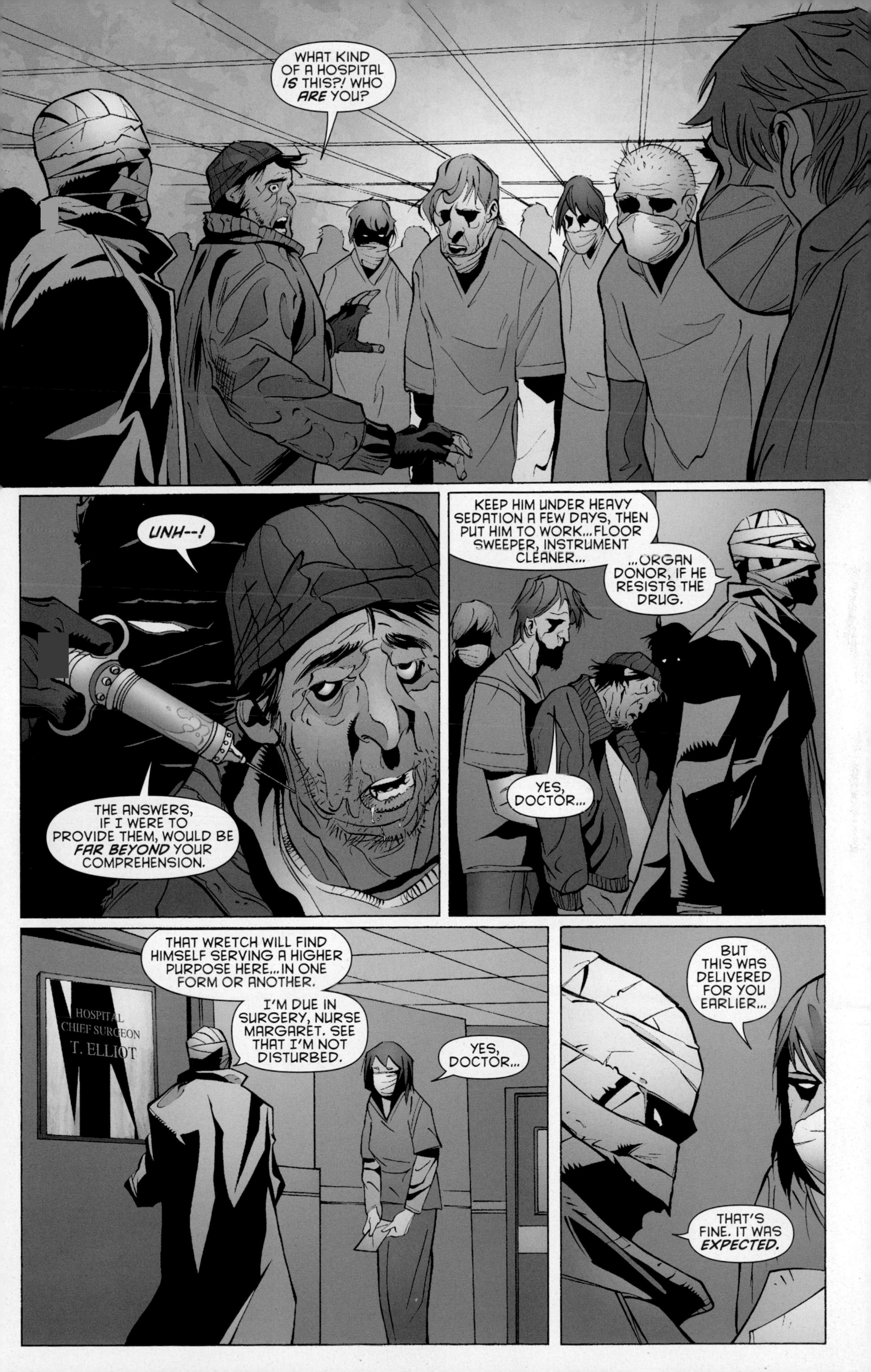
WHAT KIND OF A HOSPITAL IS THIS?! WHO ARE YOU?
UNH--!
THE ANSWERS, IF I WERE TO PROVIDE THEM, WOULD BE FAR BEYOND YOUR COMPREHENSION.
KEEP HIM UNDER HEAVY SEDATION A FEW DAYS, THEN PUT HIM TO WORK... FLOOR SWEEPER, INSTRUMENT CLEANER...
...ORGAN DONOR, IF HE RESISTS THE DRUG.
YES, DOCTOR...
HOSPITAL CHIEF SURGEON
T. ELLIOT
THAT WRETCH WILL FIND HIMSELF SERVING A HIGHER PURPOSE HERE... IN ONE FORM OR ANOTHER.
I'M DUE IN SURGERY, NURSE MARGARET. SEE THAT I'M NOT DISTURBED.
YES, DOCTOR...
BUT THIS WAS DELIVERED FOR YOU EARLIER...
THAT'S FINE. IT WAS EXPECTED.

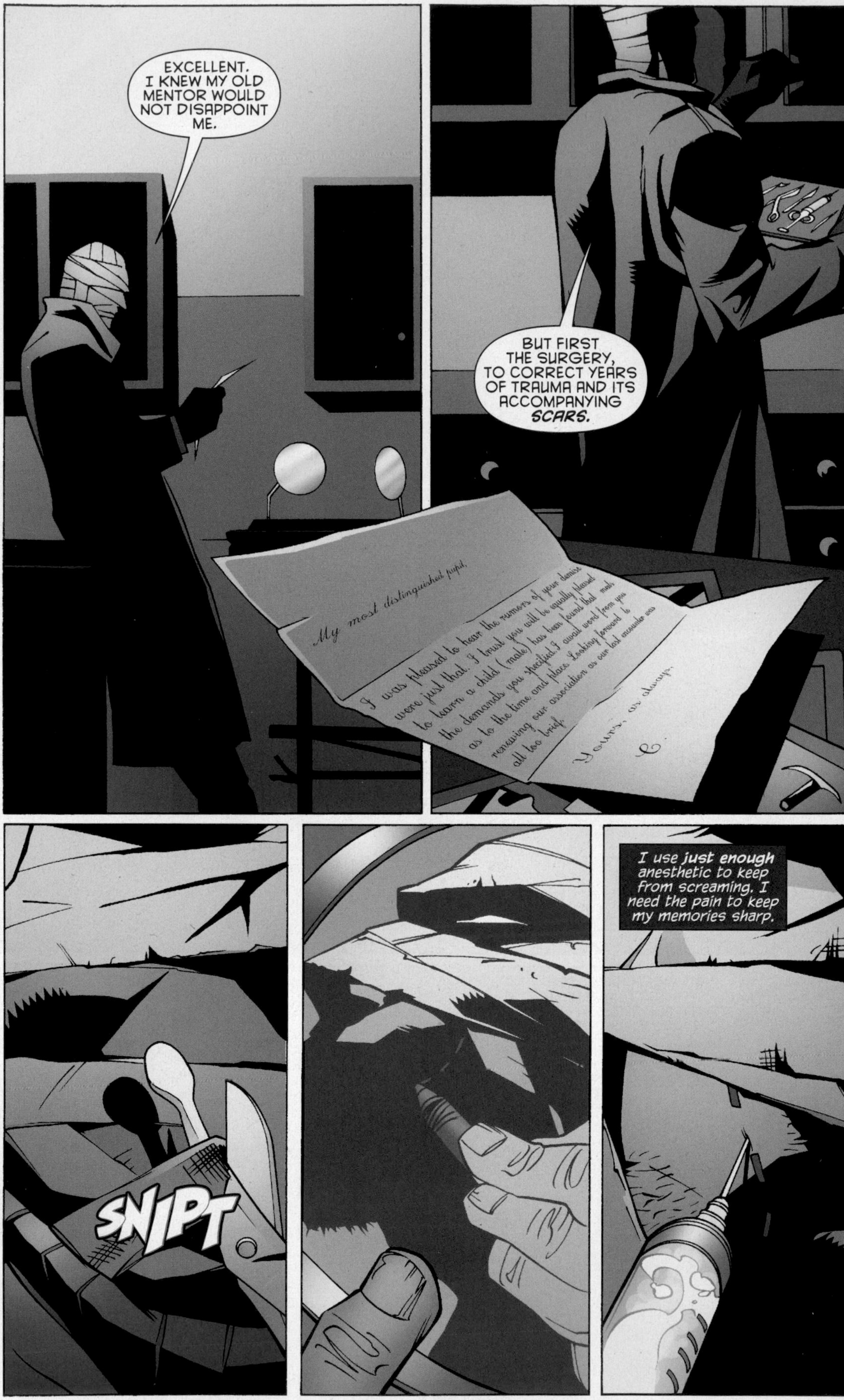
EXCELLENT. I KNEW MY OLD MENTOR WOULD NOT DISAPPOINT ME.
BUT FIRST THE SURGERY, TO CORRECT YEARS OF TRAUMA AND ITS ACCOMPANYING *SCARS.*
My most distinguished pupil,
I was pleased to hear the rumors of your demise were just that. I trust you will be equally pleased to learn a child (male) has been found that meets the demands you specified. I await word from you as to the time and place. Looking forward to renewing our association as our last encounter was all too brief.
Yours, as always,
C.
SNIPT
I use **just enough** anesthetic to keep from screaming. I need the pain to keep my memories sharp.

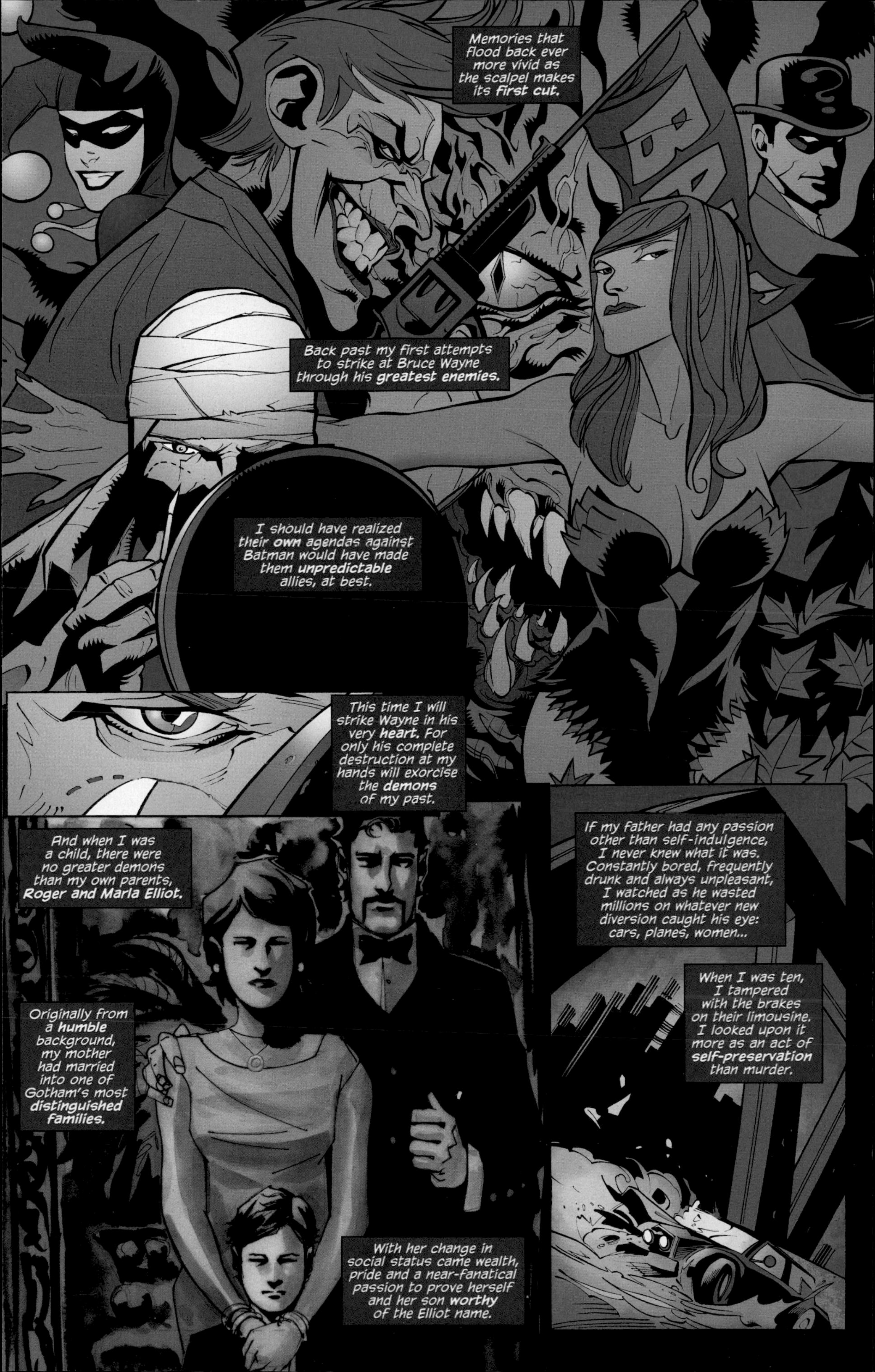

Memories that flood back ever more vivid as the scalpel makes its **first cut.**
Back past my first attempts to strike at Bruce Wayne through his **greatest enemies.**
I should have realized their **own** agendas against Batman would have made them **unpredictable** allies, at best.
This time I will strike Wayne in his very **heart.** For only his complete destruction at my hands will exorcise the **demons** of my past.
And when I was a child, there were no greater demons than my own parents, **Roger and Marla Elliot.**
Originally from a **humble** background, my mother had married into one of Gotham's most **distinguished families.**
With her change in social status came wealth, pride and a near-fanatical passion to prove herself and her son **worthy** of the Elliot name.
If my father had any passion other than self-indulgence, I never knew what it was. Constantly bored, frequently drunk and always unpleasant, I watched as he wasted millions on whatever new diversion caught his eye: cars, planes, women...
When I was ten, I tampered with the brakes on their limousine. I looked upon it more as an act of **self-preservation** than murder.

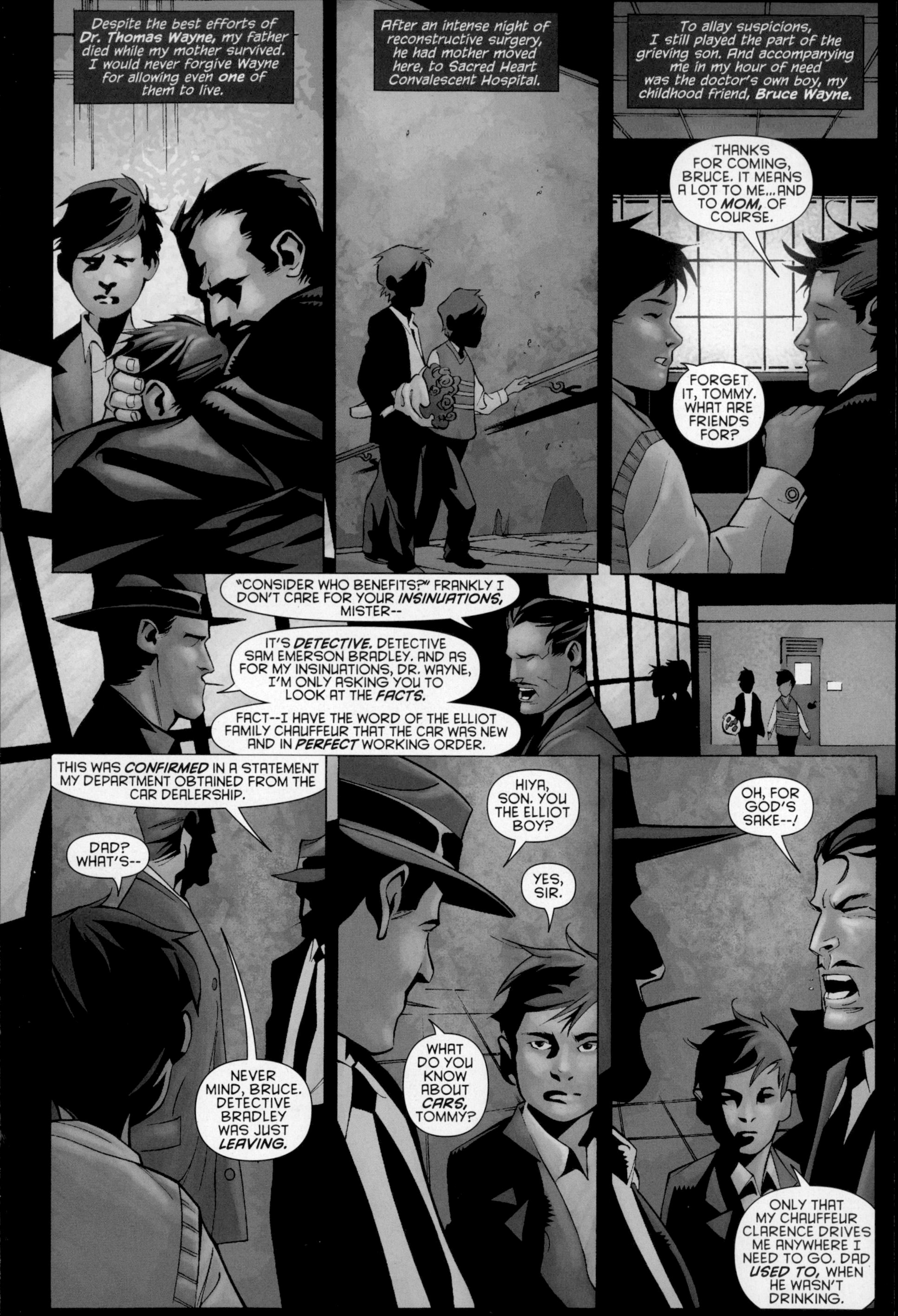
Despite the best efforts of Dr. Thomas Wayne, my father died while my mother survived. I would never forgive Wayne for allowing even one of them to live.
After an intense night of reconstructive surgery, he had mother moved here, to Sacred Heart Convalescent Hospital.
To allay suspicions, I still played the part of the grieving son. And accompanying me in my hour of need was the doctor's own boy, my childhood friend, Bruce Wayne.
THANKS FOR COMING, BRUCE. IT MEANS A LOT TO ME... AND TO MOM, OF COURSE.
FORGET IT, TOMMY. WHAT ARE FRIENDS FOR?
"CONSIDER WHO BENEFITS?" FRANKLY I DON'T CARE FOR YOUR INSINUATIONS, MISTER--
IT'S DETECTIVE. DETECTIVE SAM EMERSON BRADLEY. AND AS FOR MY INSINUATIONS, DR. WAYNE, I'M ONLY ASKING YOU TO LOOK AT THE FACTS.
FACT--I HAVE THE WORD OF THE ELLIOT FAMILY CHAUFFEUR THAT THE CAR WAS NEW AND IN PERFECT WORKING ORDER.
THIS WAS CONFIRMED IN A STATEMENT MY DEPARTMENT OBTAINED FROM THE CAR DEALERSHIP.
DAD? WHAT'S--
NEVER MIND, BRUCE. DETECTIVE BRADLEY WAS JUST LEAVING.
HIYA, SON. YOU THE ELLIOT BOY?
YES, SIR.
WHAT DO YOU KNOW ABOUT CARS, TOMMY?
OH, FOR GOD'S SAKE--!
ONLY THAT MY CHAUFFEUR CLARENCE DRIVES ME ANYWHERE I NEED TO GO. DAD USED TO, WHEN HE WASN'T DRINKING.

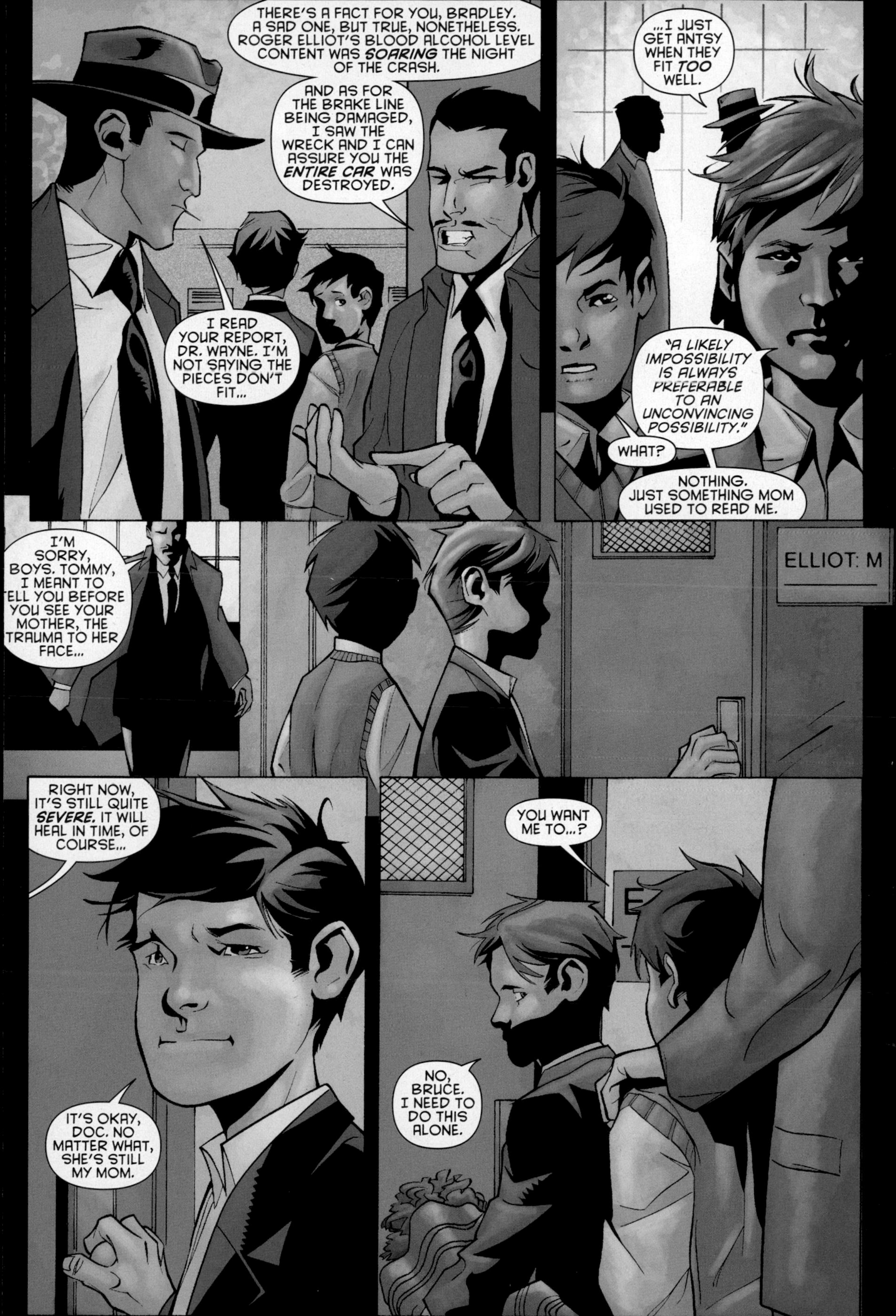
THERE'S A FACT FOR YOU, BRADLEY. A SAD ONE, BUT TRUE, NONETHELESS. ROGER ELLIOT'S BLOOD ALCOHOL LEVEL CONTENT WAS SOARING THE NIGHT OF THE CRASH.
AND AS FOR THE BRAKE LINE BEING DAMAGED, I SAW THE WRECK AND I CAN ASSURE YOU THE ENTIRE CAR WAS DESTROYED.
I READ YOUR REPORT, DR. WAYNE. I'M NOT SAYING THE PIECES DON'T FIT...
...I JUST GET ANTSY WHEN THEY FIT TOO WELL.
"A LIKELY IMPOSSIBILITY IS ALWAYS PREFERABLE TO AN UNCONVINCING POSSIBILITY."
WHAT?
NOTHING. JUST SOMETHING MOM USED TO READ ME.
I'M SORRY, BOYS. TOMMY, I MEANT TO TELL YOU BEFORE YOU SEE YOUR MOTHER, THE TRAUMA TO HER FACE...
ELLIOT: M
RIGHT NOW, IT'S STILL QUITE SEVERE. IT WILL HEAL IN TIME, OF COURSE...
IT'S OKAY, DOC. NO MATTER WHAT, SHE'S STILL MY MOM.
YOU WANT ME TO...?
NO, BRUCE. I NEED TO DO THIS ALONE.

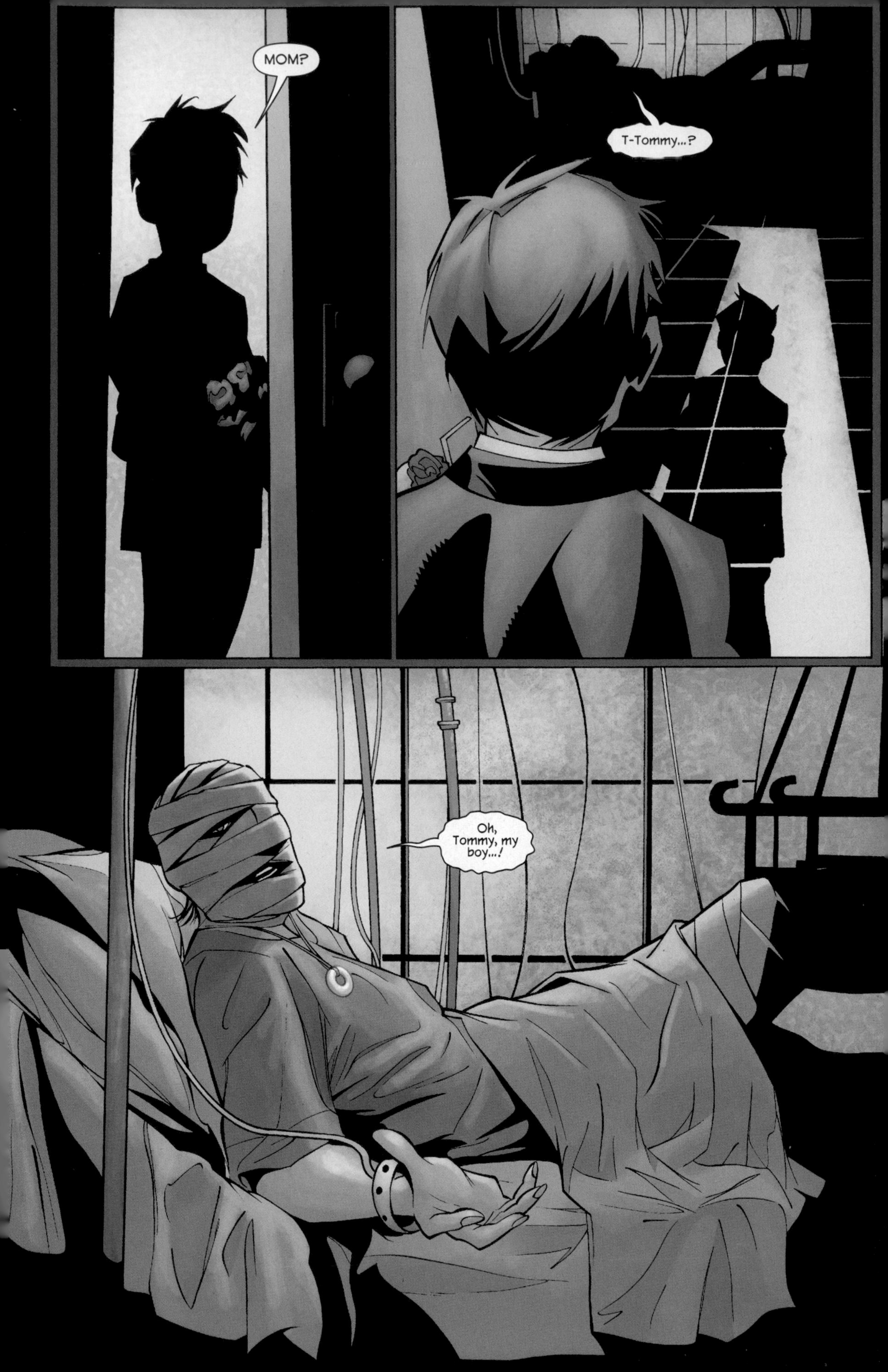
MOM?
T-Tommy...?
Oh, Tommy, my boy...!

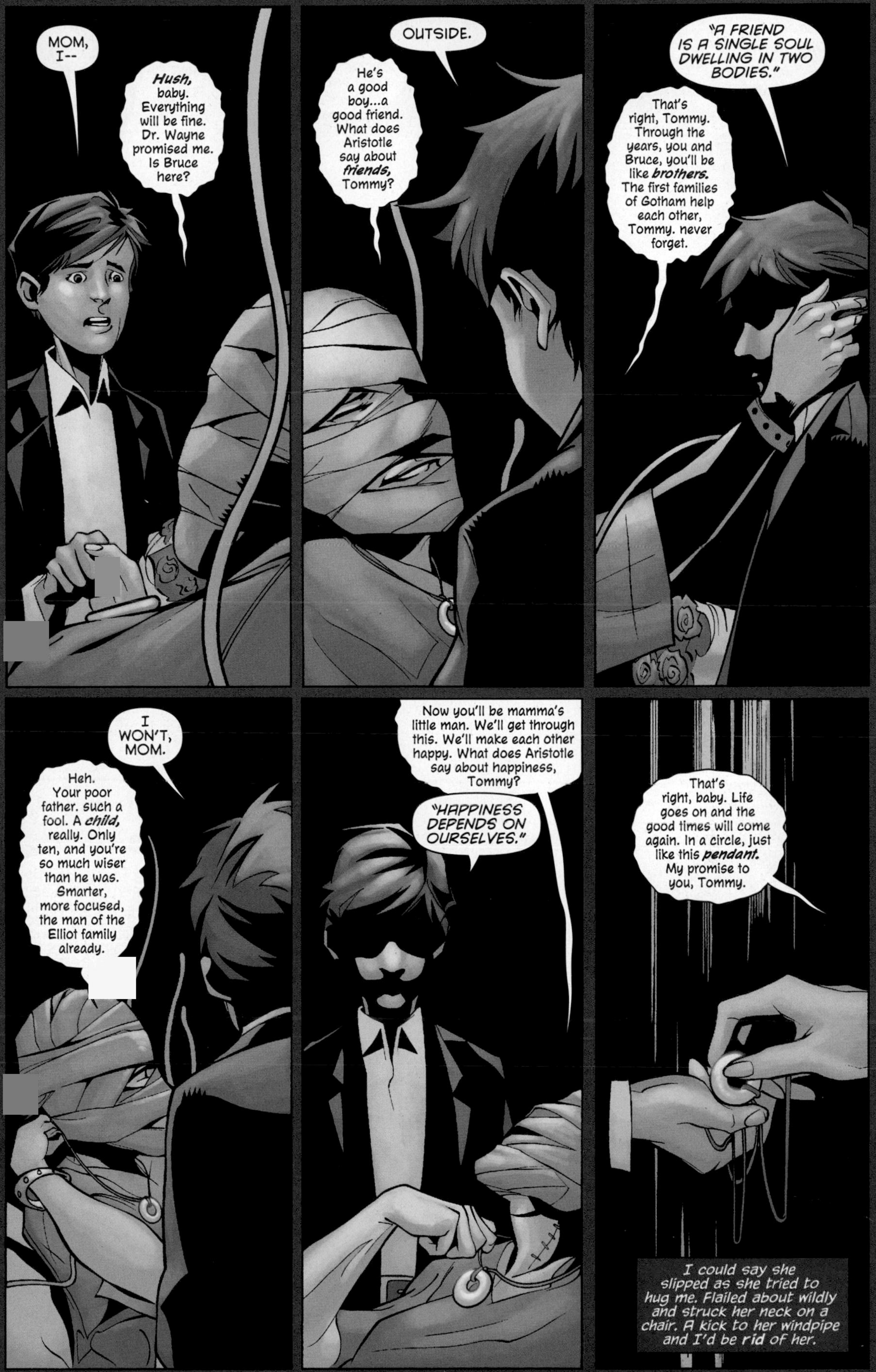
MOM, I--
Hush, baby. Everything will be fine. Dr. Wayne promised me. Is Bruce here?
OUTSIDE.
He's a good boy...a good friend. What does Aristotle say about *friends,* Tommy?
"A FRIEND IS A SINGLE SOUL DWELLING IN TWO BODIES."
That's right, Tommy. Through the years, you and Bruce, you'll be like *brothers.* The first families of Gotham help each other, Tommy. never forget.
I WON'T, MOM.
Heh. Your poor father. such a fool. A *child,* really. Only ten, and you're so much wiser than he was. Smarter, more focused, the man of the Elliot family already.
Now you'll be mamma's little man. We'll get through this. We'll make each other happy. What does Aristotle say about happiness, Tommy?
"HAPPINESS DEPENDS ON OURSELVES."
That's right, baby. Life goes on and the good times will come again. In a circle, just like this *pendant.* My promise to you, Tommy.
I could say she slipped as she tried to hug me. Flailed about wildly and struck her neck on a chair. A kick to her windpipe and I'd be **rid** of her.

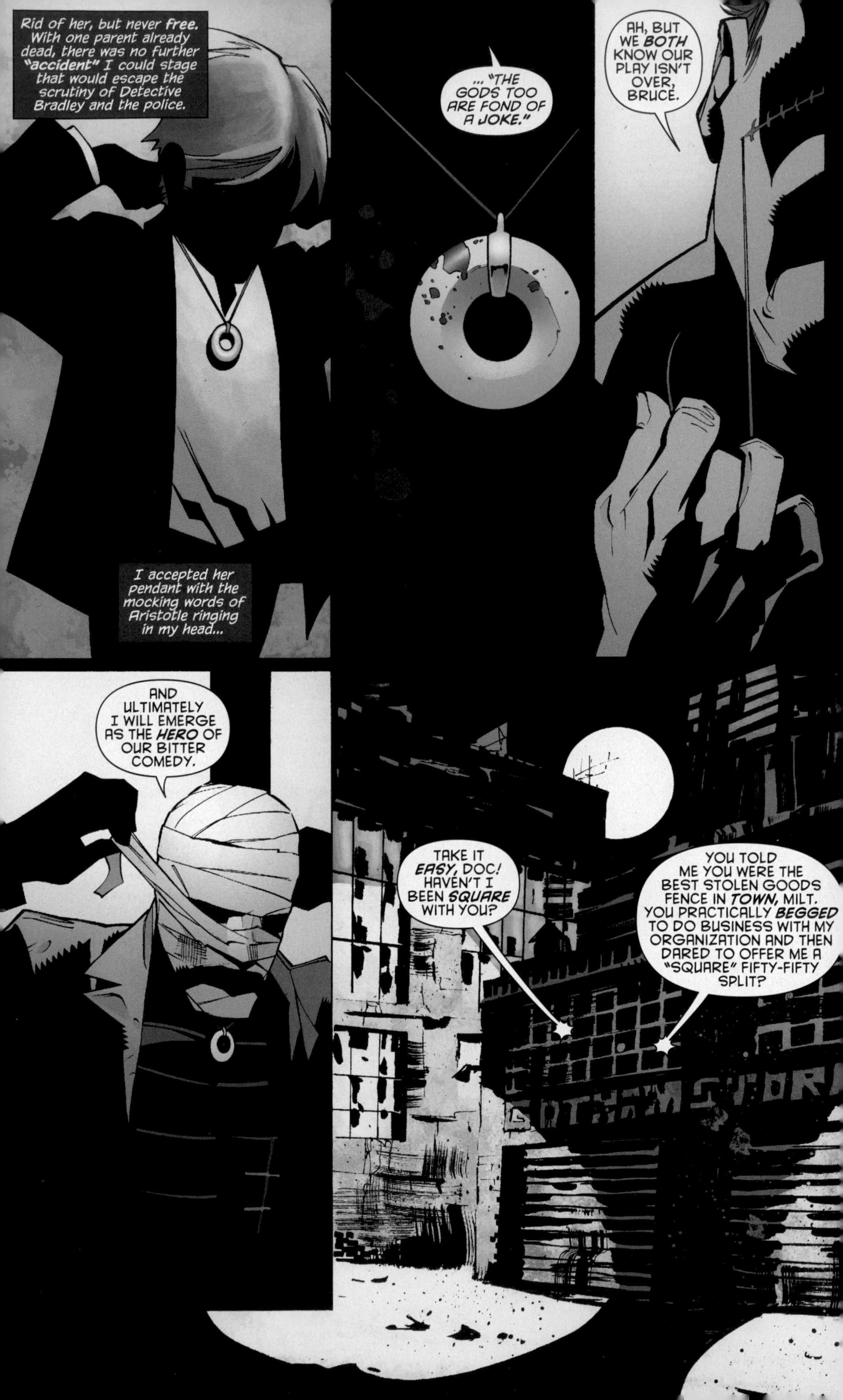
Rid of her, but never free. With one parent already dead, there was no further "accident" I could stage that would escape the scrutiny of Detective Bradley and the police.
I accepted her pendant with the mocking words of Aristotle ringing in my head...
..."THE GODS TOO ARE FOND OF A JOKE."
AH, BUT WE BOTH KNOW OUR PLAY ISN'T OVER, BRUCE.
AND ULTIMATELY I WILL EMERGE AS THE HERO OF OUR BITTER COMEDY.
TAKE IT EASY, DOC! HAVEN'T I BEEN SQUARE WITH YOU?
YOU TOLD ME YOU WERE THE BEST STOLEN GOODS FENCE IN TOWN, MILT. YOU PRACTICALLY BEGGED TO DO BUSINESS WITH MY ORGANIZATION AND THEN DARED TO OFFER ME A "SQUARE" FIFTY-FIFTY SPLIT?

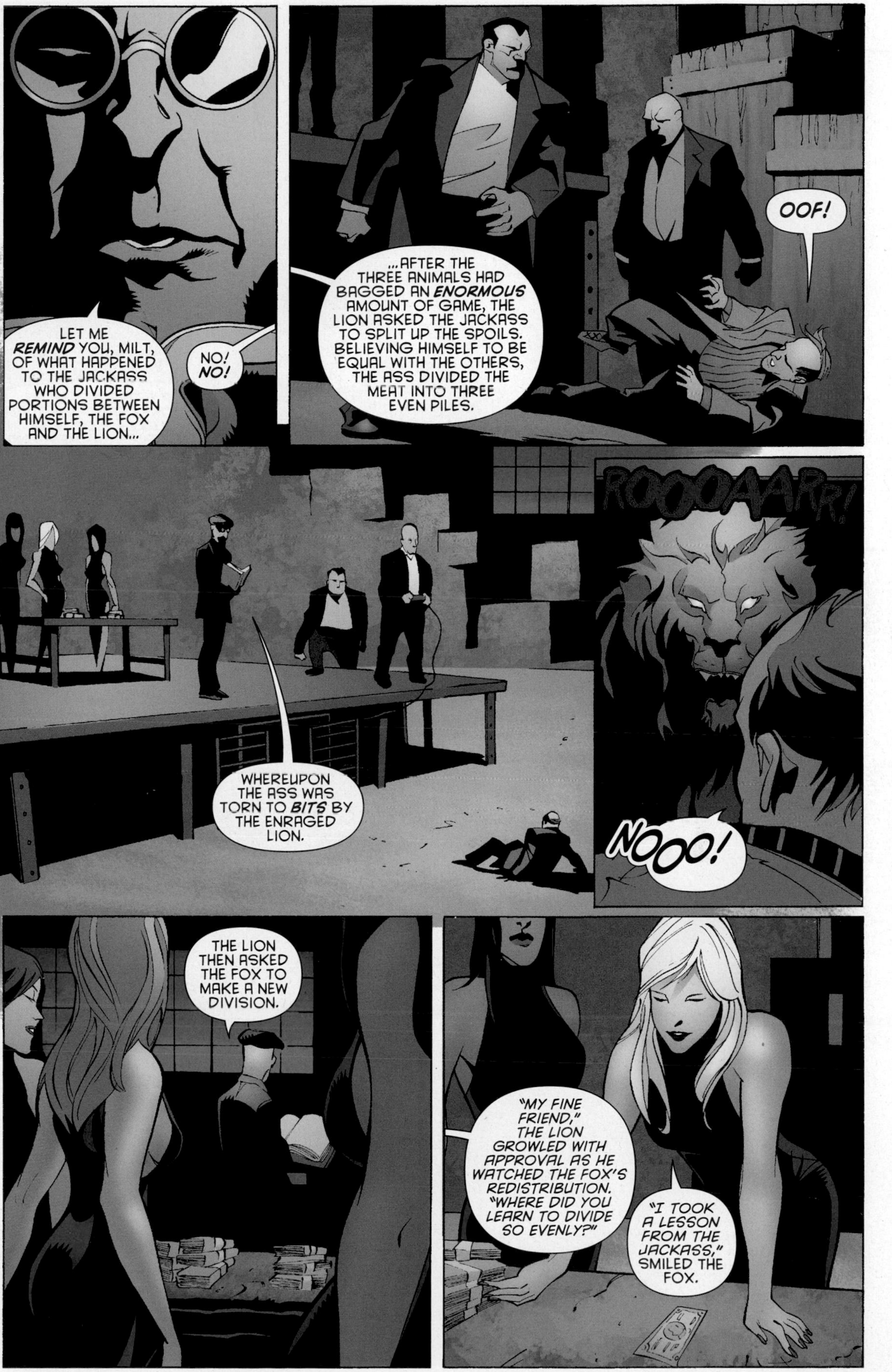
LET ME *REMIND* YOU, MILT, OF WHAT HAPPENED TO THE JACKASS WHO DIVIDED PORTIONS BETWEEN HIMSELF, THE FOX AND THE LION...
NO! *NO!*
...AFTER THE THREE ANIMALS HAD BAGGED AN *ENORMOUS* AMOUNT OF GAME, THE LION ASKED THE JACKASS TO SPLIT UP THE SPOILS. BELIEVING HIMSELF TO BE EQUAL WITH THE OTHERS, THE ASS DIVIDED THE MEAT INTO THREE EVEN PILES.
OOF!
WHEREUPON THE ASS WAS TORN TO *BITS* BY THE ENRAGED LION.
ROOOAARR!
NOOO!
THE LION THEN ASKED THE FOX TO MAKE A NEW DIVISION.
"MY FINE FRIEND," THE LION GROWLED WITH APPROVAL AS HE WATCHED THE FOX'S REDISTRIBUTION. "WHERE DID YOU LEARN TO DIVIDE SO EVENLY?"
"I TOOK A LESSON FROM THE JACKASS," SMILED THE FOX.

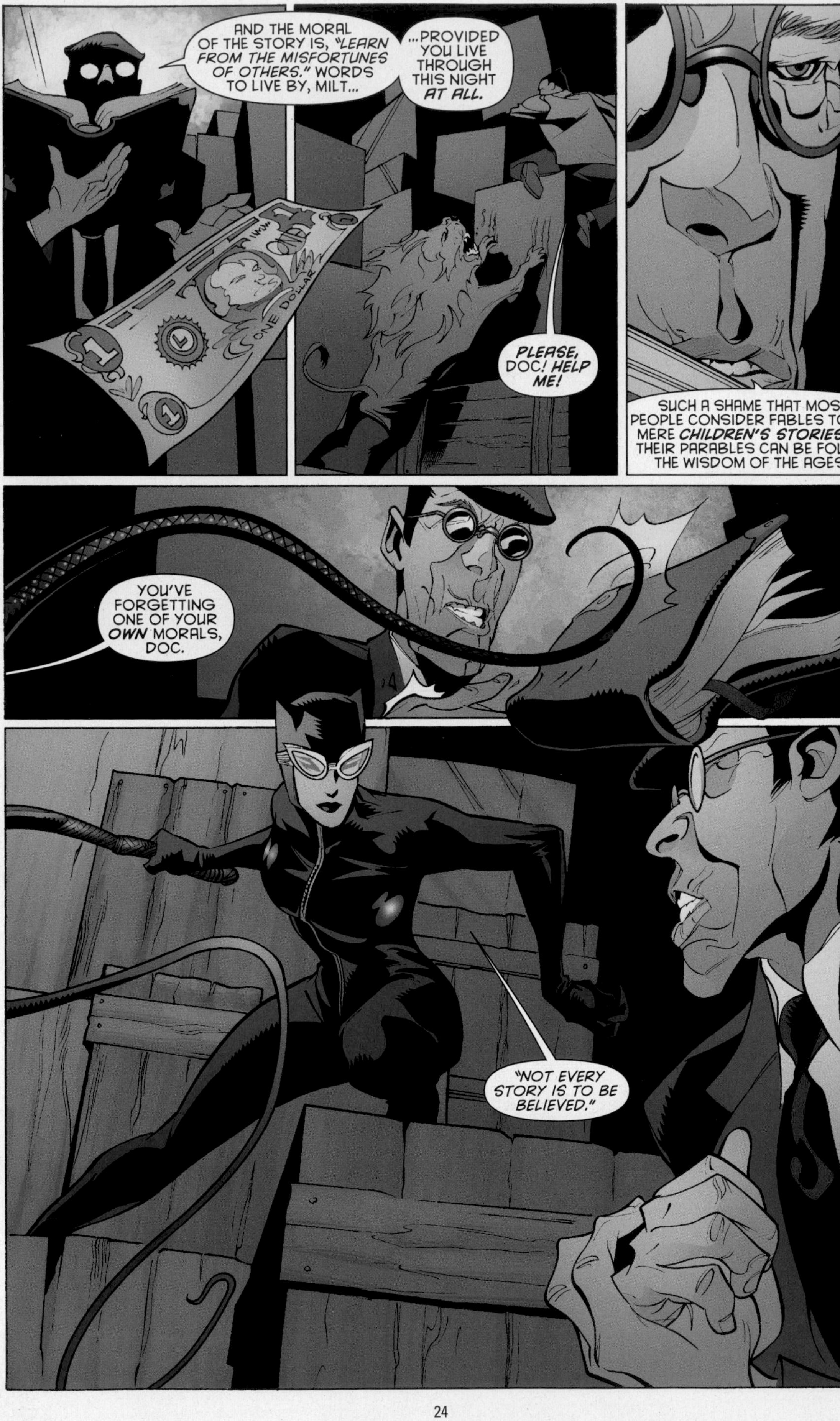
AND THE MORAL OF THE STORY IS, "LEARN FROM THE MISFORTUNES OF OTHERS." WORDS TO LIVE BY, MILT...
...PROVIDED YOU LIVE THROUGH THIS NIGHT AT ALL.
PLEASE, DOC! HELP ME!
SUCH A SHAME THAT MOST PEOPLE CONSIDER FABLES TO BE MERE CHILDREN'S STORIES. IN THEIR PARABLES CAN BE FOUND THE WISDOM OF THE AGES.
YOU'VE FORGETTING ONE OF YOUR OWN MORALS, DOC.
"NOT EVERY STORY IS TO BE BELIEVED."

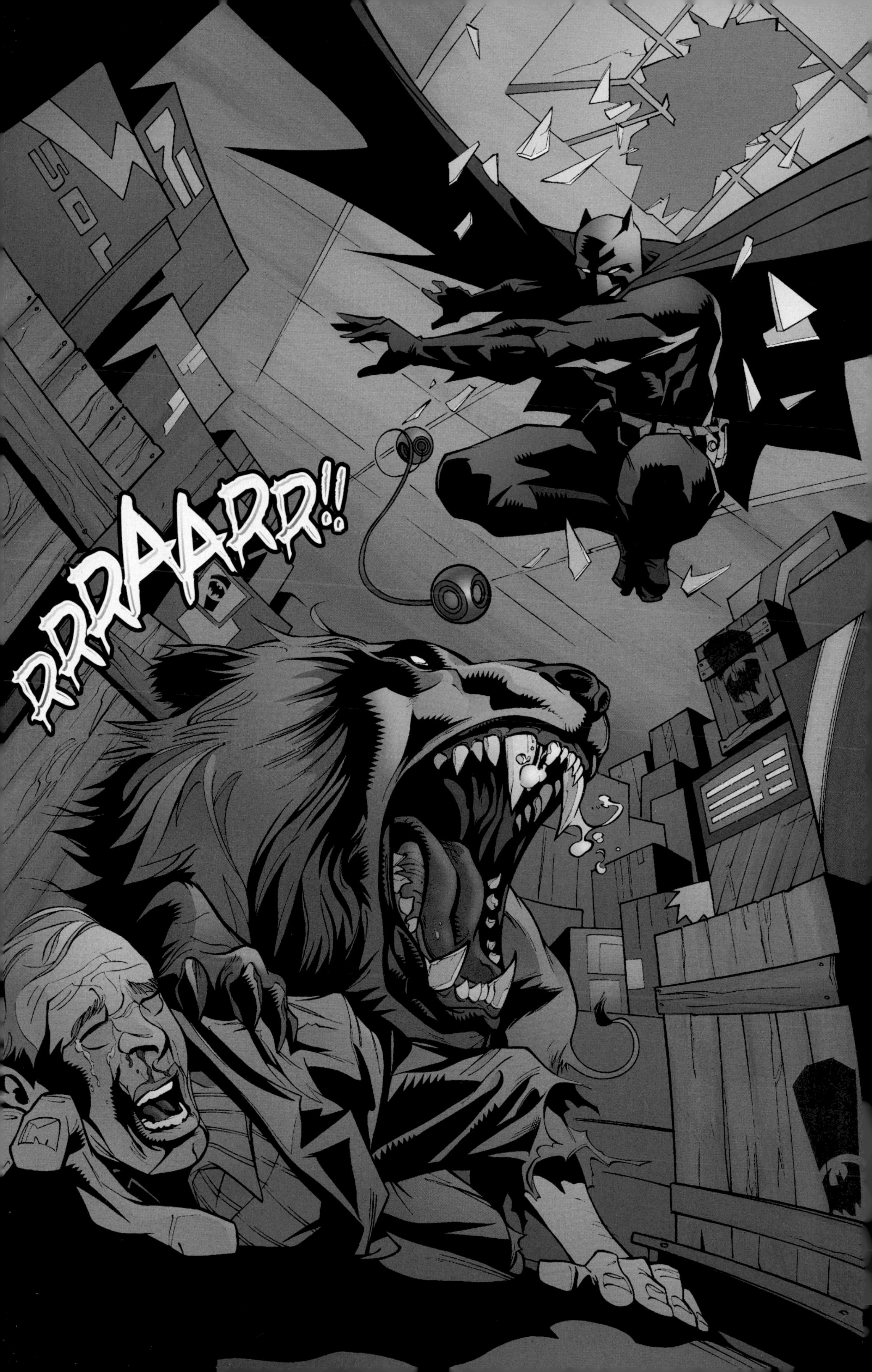
RRRAARR!!

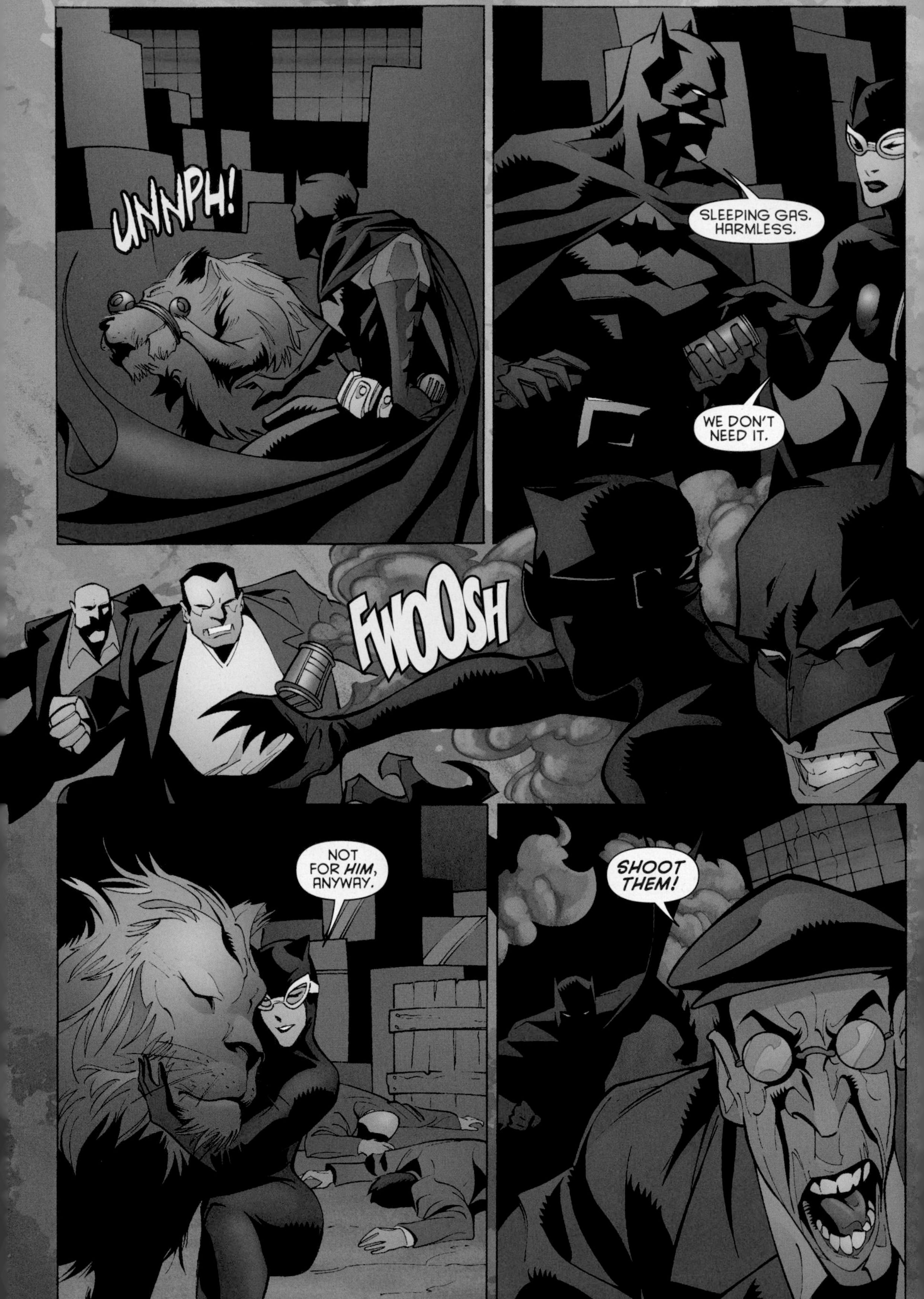
UNNPH!
SLEEPING GAS. HARMLESS.
WE DON'T NEED IT.
FWOOSH
NOT FOR *HIM*, ANYWAY.
SHOOT THEM!

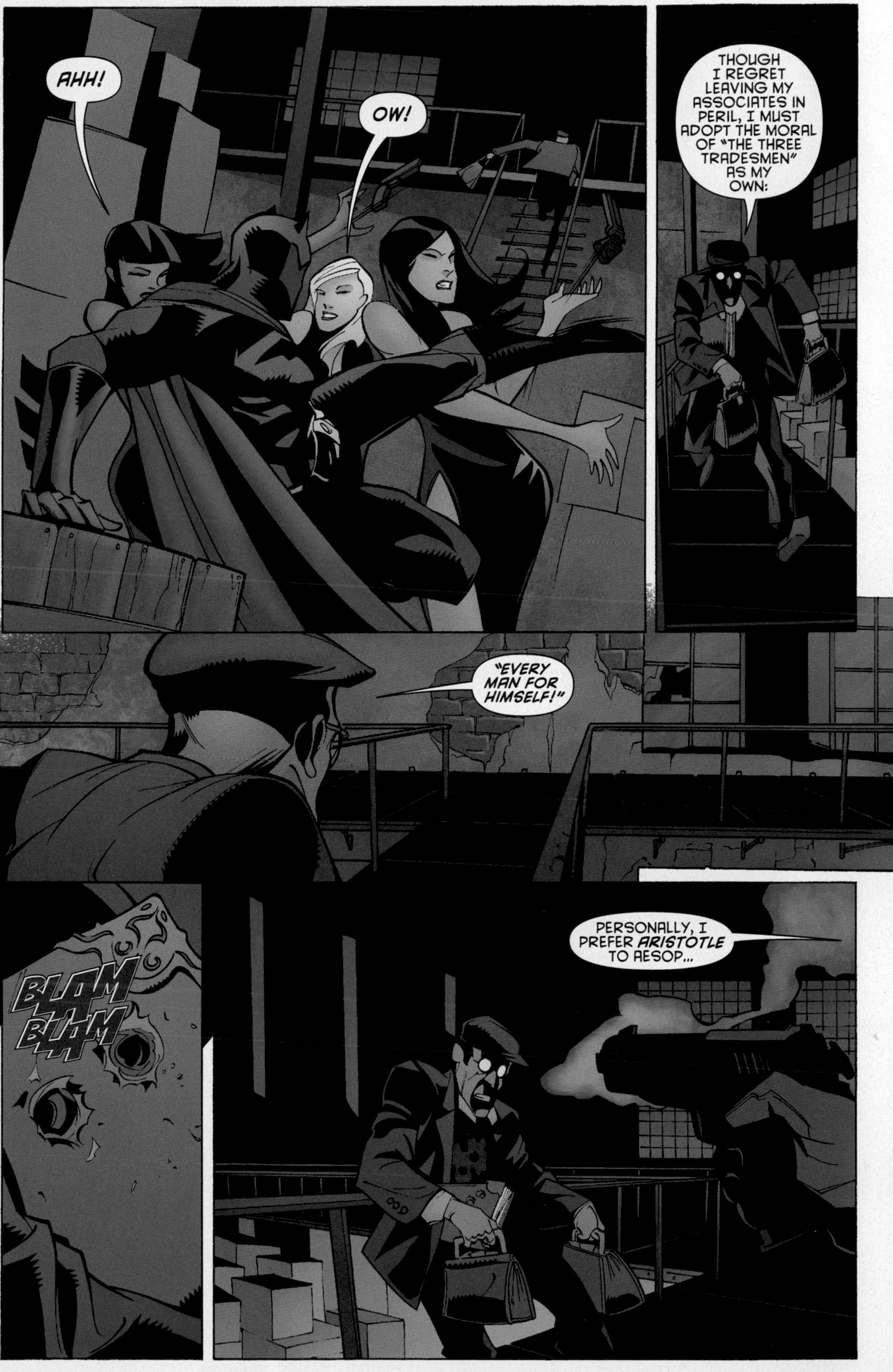
AHH!
OW!
THOUGH I REGRET LEAVING MY ASSOCIATES IN PERIL, I MUST ADOPT THE MORAL OF "THE THREE TRADESMEN" AS MY OWN:
"EVERY MAN FOR HIMSELF!"
BLAM BLAM
PERSONALLY, I PREFER *ARISTOTLE* TO AESOP...

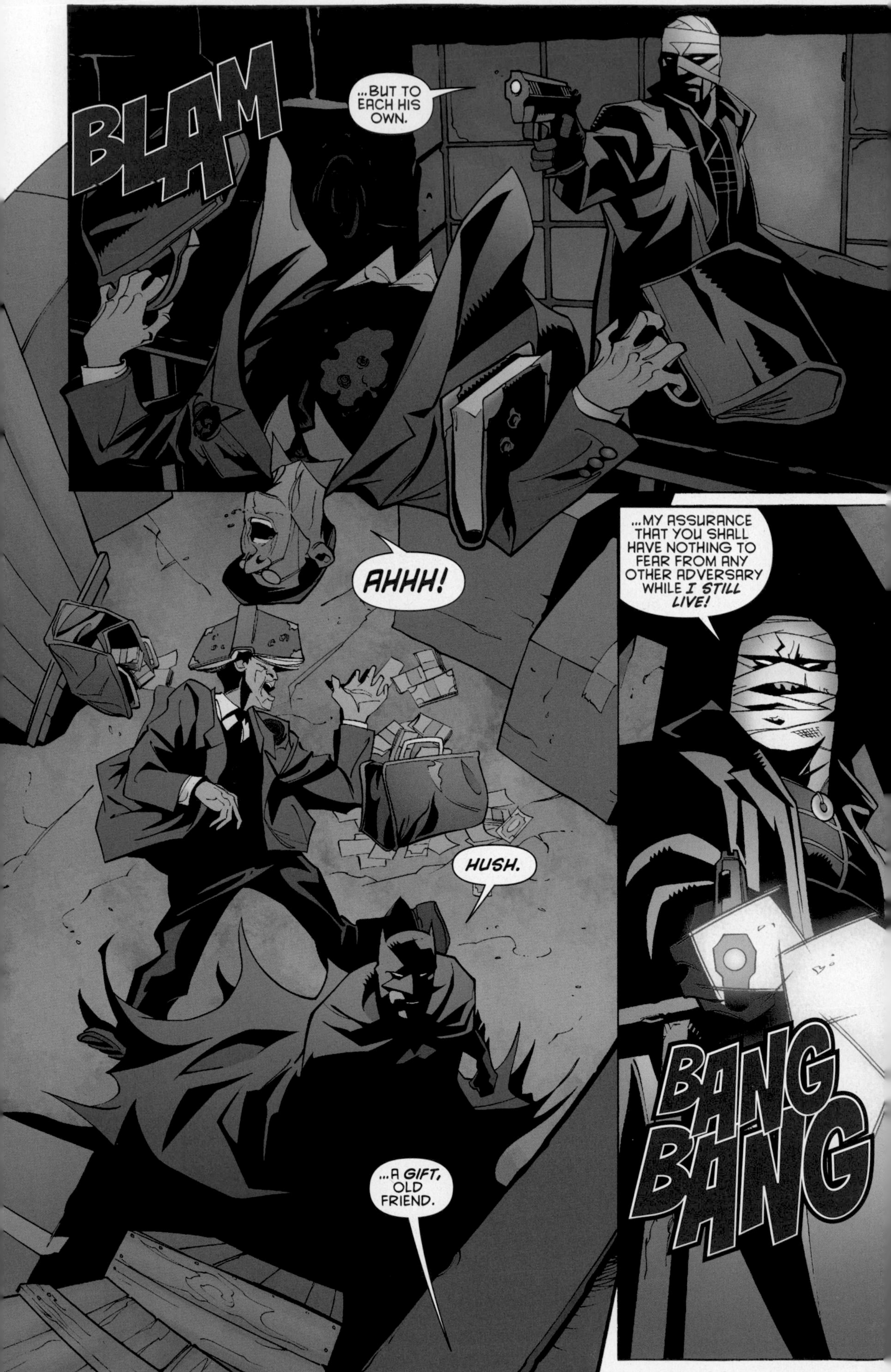
BLAM
...BUT TO EACH HIS OWN.
AHHH!
HUSH.
...A GIFT, OLD FRIEND.
...MY ASSURANCE THAT YOU SHALL HAVE NOTHING TO FEAR FROM ANY OTHER ADVERSARY WHILE I STILL LIVE!
BANG
BANG

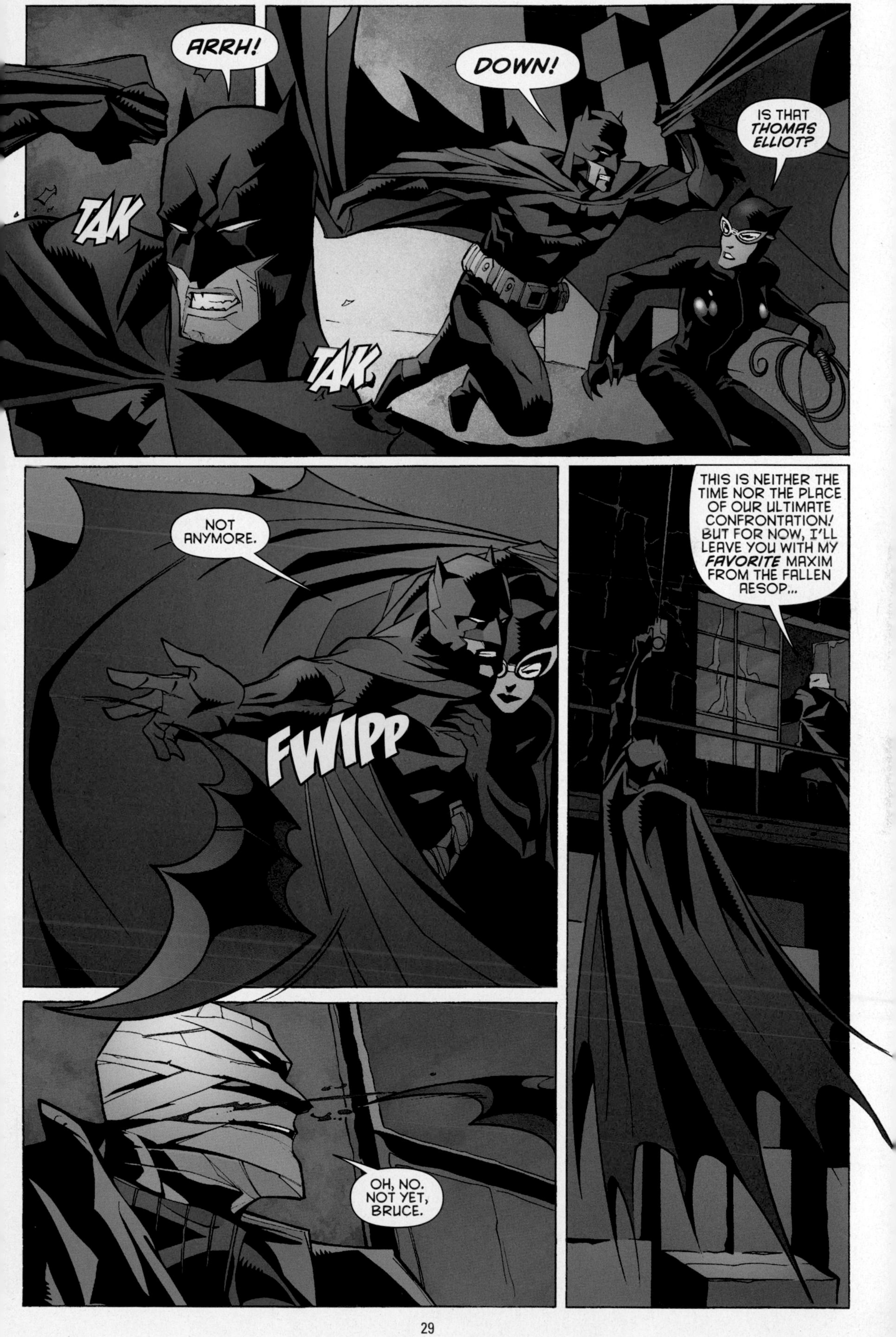

ARRH!
TAK
TAK
DOWN!
IS THAT THOMAS ELLIOT?
NOT ANYMORE.
FWIPP
THIS IS NEITHER THE TIME NOR THE PLACE OF OUR ULTIMATE CONFRONTATION! BUT FOR NOW, I'LL LEAVE YOU WITH MY FAVORITE MAXIM FROM THE FALLEN AESOP...
OH, NO. NOT YET, BRUCE.

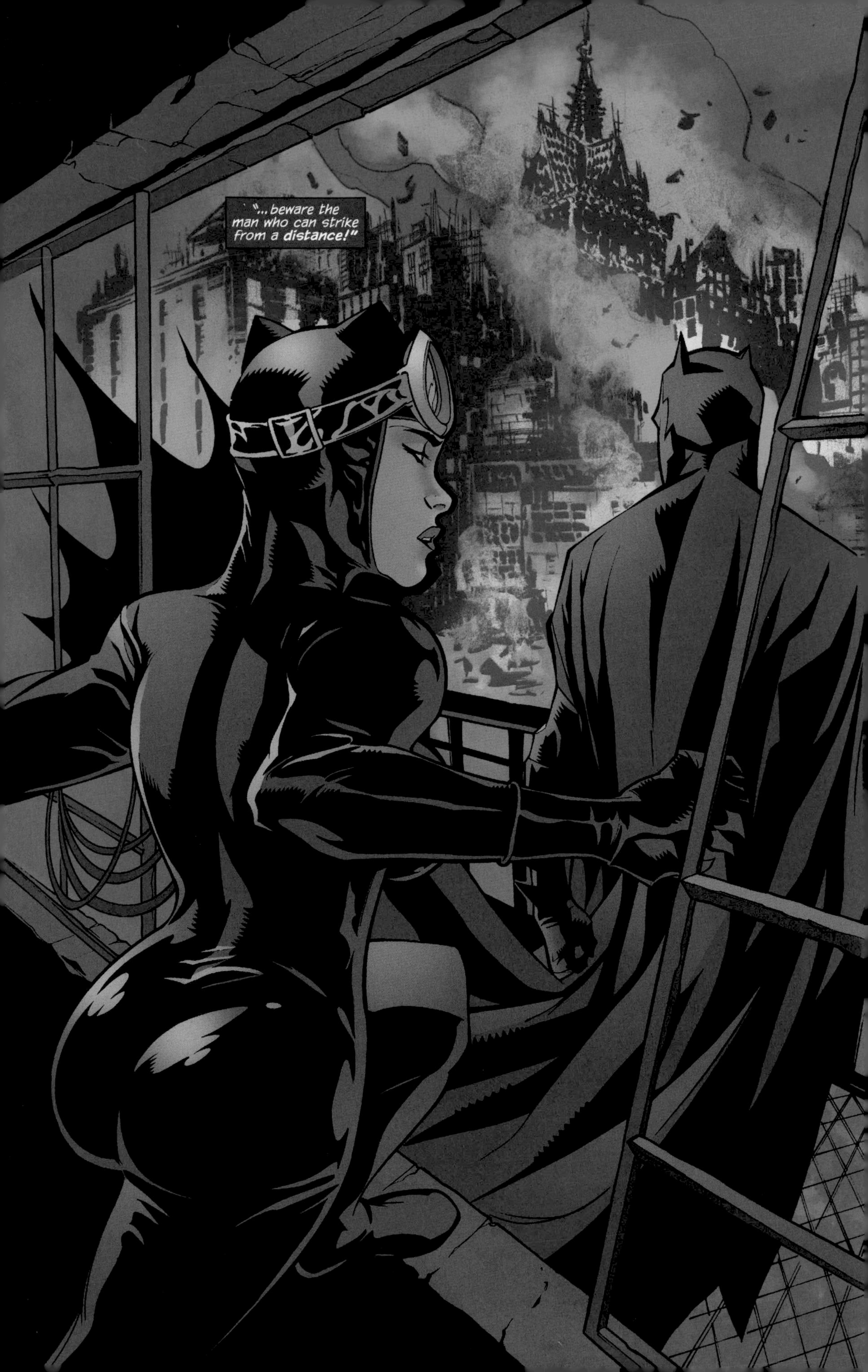
"...beware the man who can strike from a distance!"

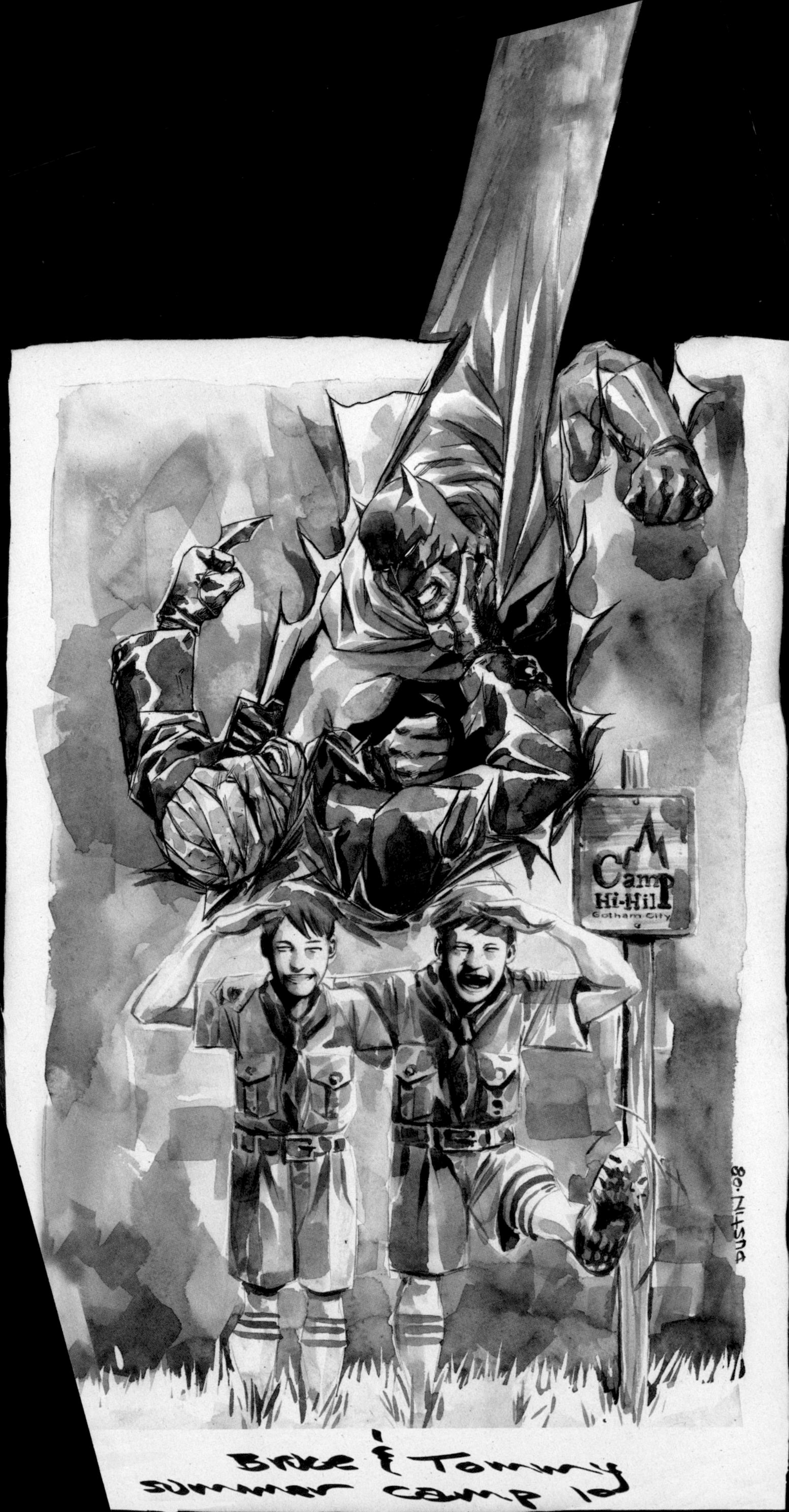
Camp
Hi-Hill
Gotham City
DUSTIN.08
Bruce & Tommy
summer camp

"How sharper than a serpent's tooth..."

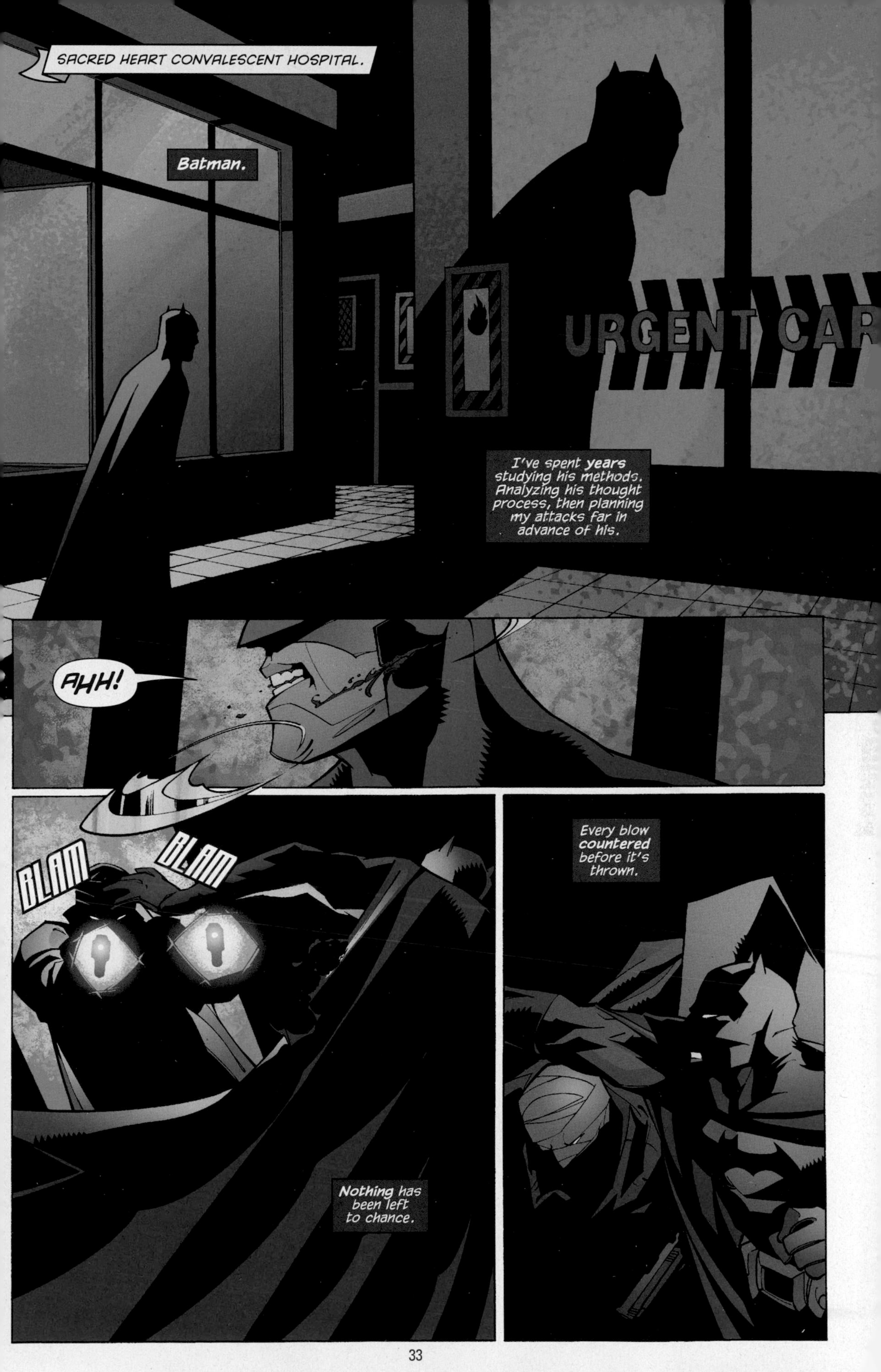

SACRED HEART CONVALESCENT HOSPITAL.
Batman.
URGENT CAR
I've spent years studying his methods. Analyzing his thought process, then planning my attacks far in advance of his.
AHH!
BLAM
BLAM
Nothing has been left to chance.
Every blow countered before it's thrown.

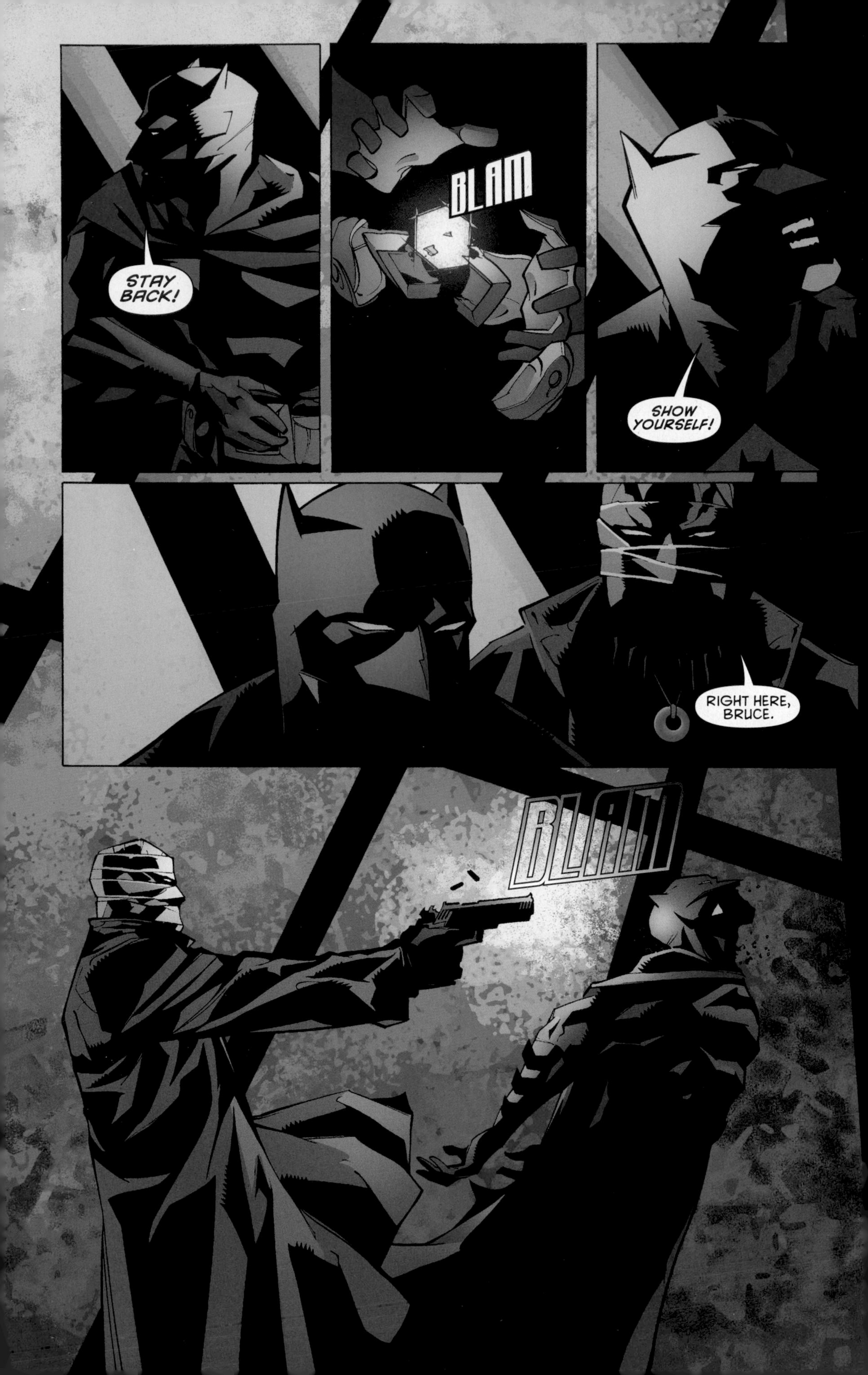
STAY BACK!
BLAM
SHOW YOURSELF!
RIGHT HERE, BRUCE.
BLAM

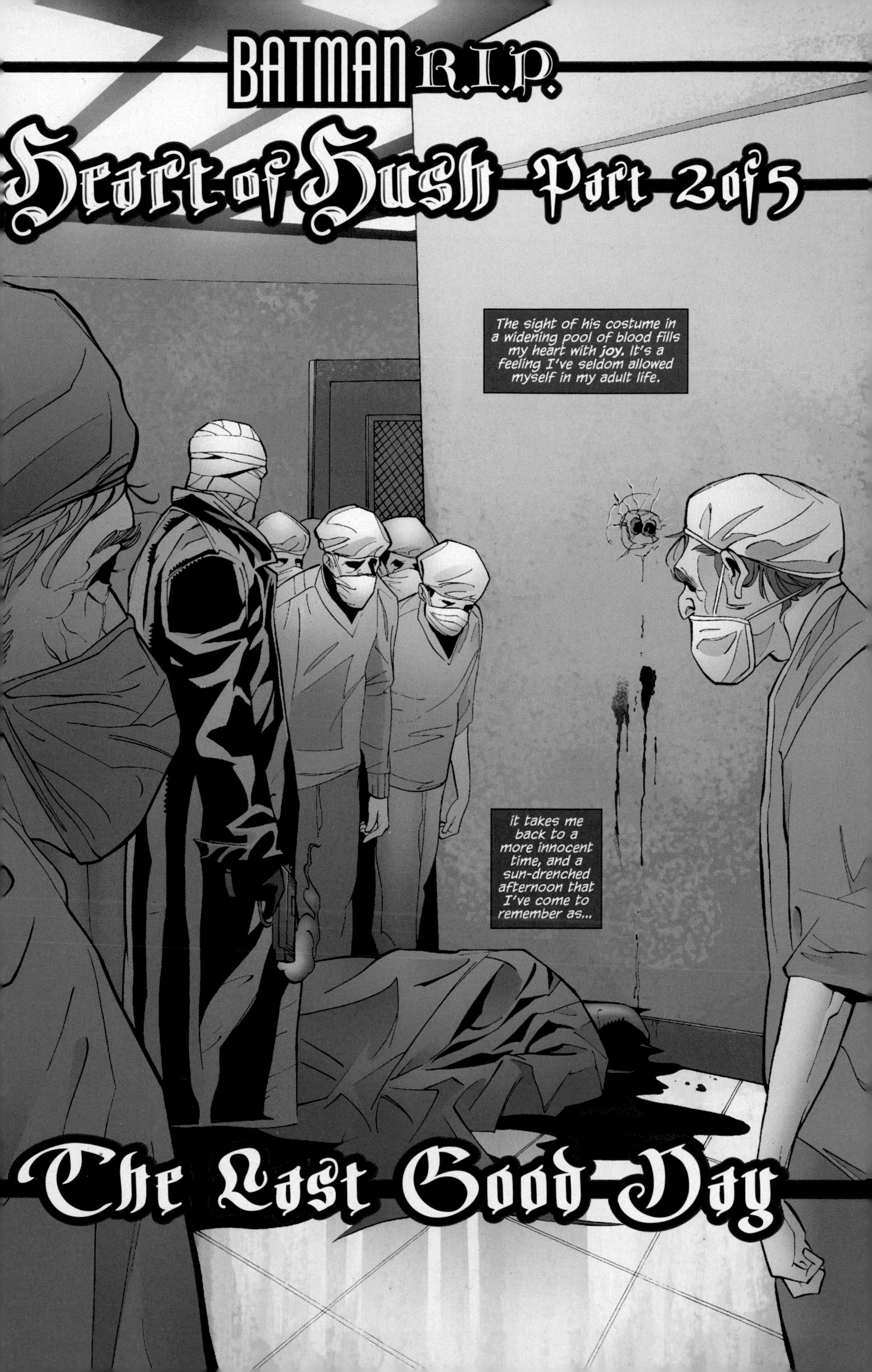

BATMAN R.I.P.
Heart of Hush Part 2 of 5
The sight of his costume in a widening pool of blood fills my heart with joy. It's a feeling I've seldom allowed myself in my adult life.
it takes me back to a more innocent time, and a sun-drenched afternoon that I've come to remember as...
The Last Good Day

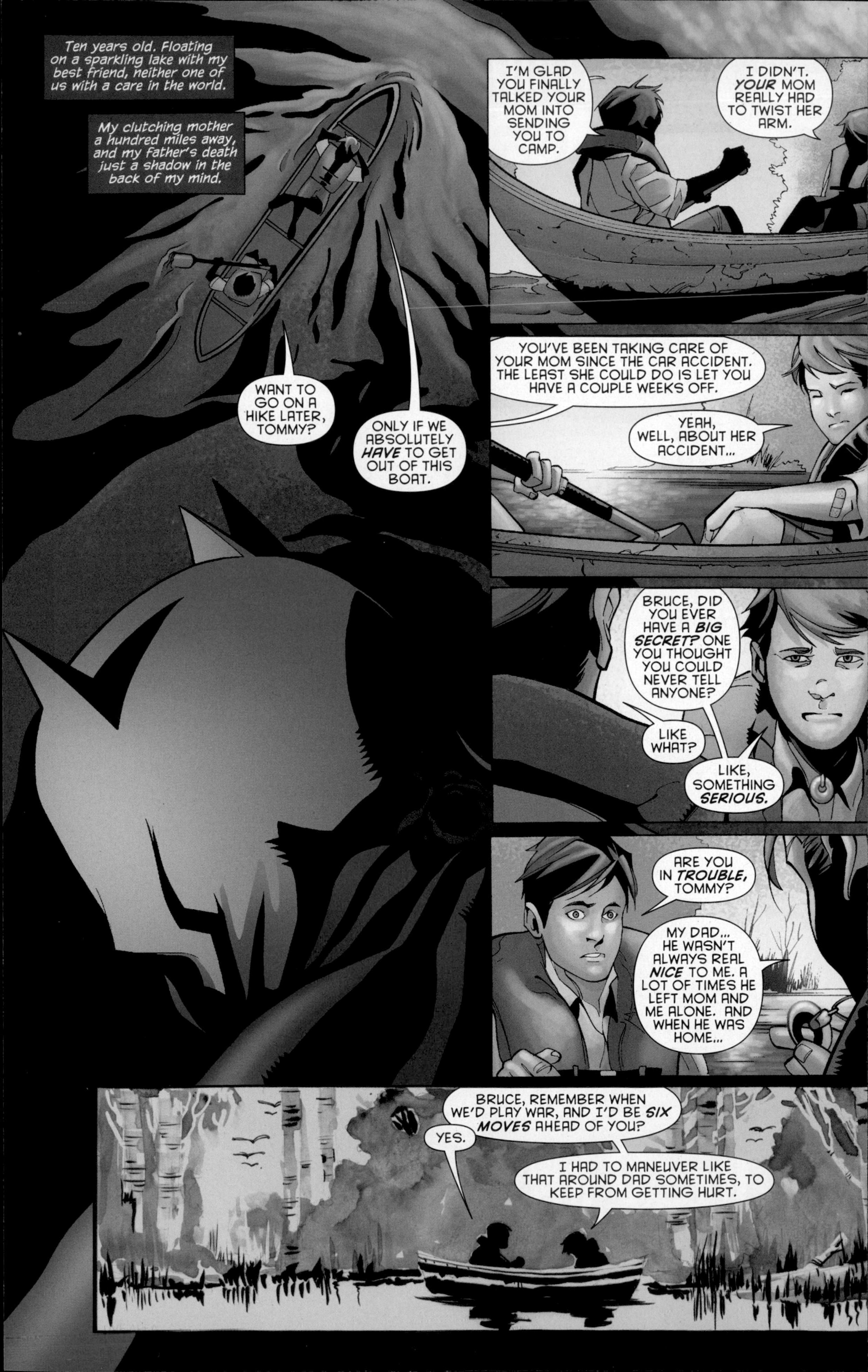
Ten years old. Floating on a sparkling lake with my best friend, neither one of us with a care in the world.
My clutching mother a hundred miles away, and my father's death just a shadow in the back of my mind.
WANT TO GO ON A HIKE LATER, TOMMY?
ONLY IF WE ABSOLUTELY HAVE TO GET OUT OF THIS BOAT.
I'M GLAD YOU FINALLY TALKED YOUR MOM INTO SENDING YOU TO CAMP.
I DIDN'T. YOUR MOM REALLY HAD TO TWIST HER ARM.
YOU'VE BEEN TAKING CARE OF YOUR MOM SINCE THE CAR ACCIDENT. THE LEAST SHE COULD DO IS LET YOU HAVE A COUPLE WEEKS OFF.
YEAH, WELL, ABOUT HER ACCIDENT...
BRUCE, DID YOU EVER HAVE A BIG SECRET? ONE YOU THOUGHT YOU COULD NEVER TELL ANYONE?
LIKE WHAT?
LIKE, SOMETHING SERIOUS.
ARE YOU IN TROUBLE, TOMMY?
MY DAD... HE WASN'T ALWAYS REAL NICE TO ME. A LOT OF TIMES HE LEFT MOM AND ME ALONE. AND WHEN HE WAS HOME...
BRUCE, REMEMBER WHEN WE'D PLAY WAR, AND I'D BE SIX MOVES AHEAD OF YOU?
YES.
I HAD TO MANEUVER LIKE THAT AROUND DAD SOMETIMES, TO KEEP FROM GETTING HURT.

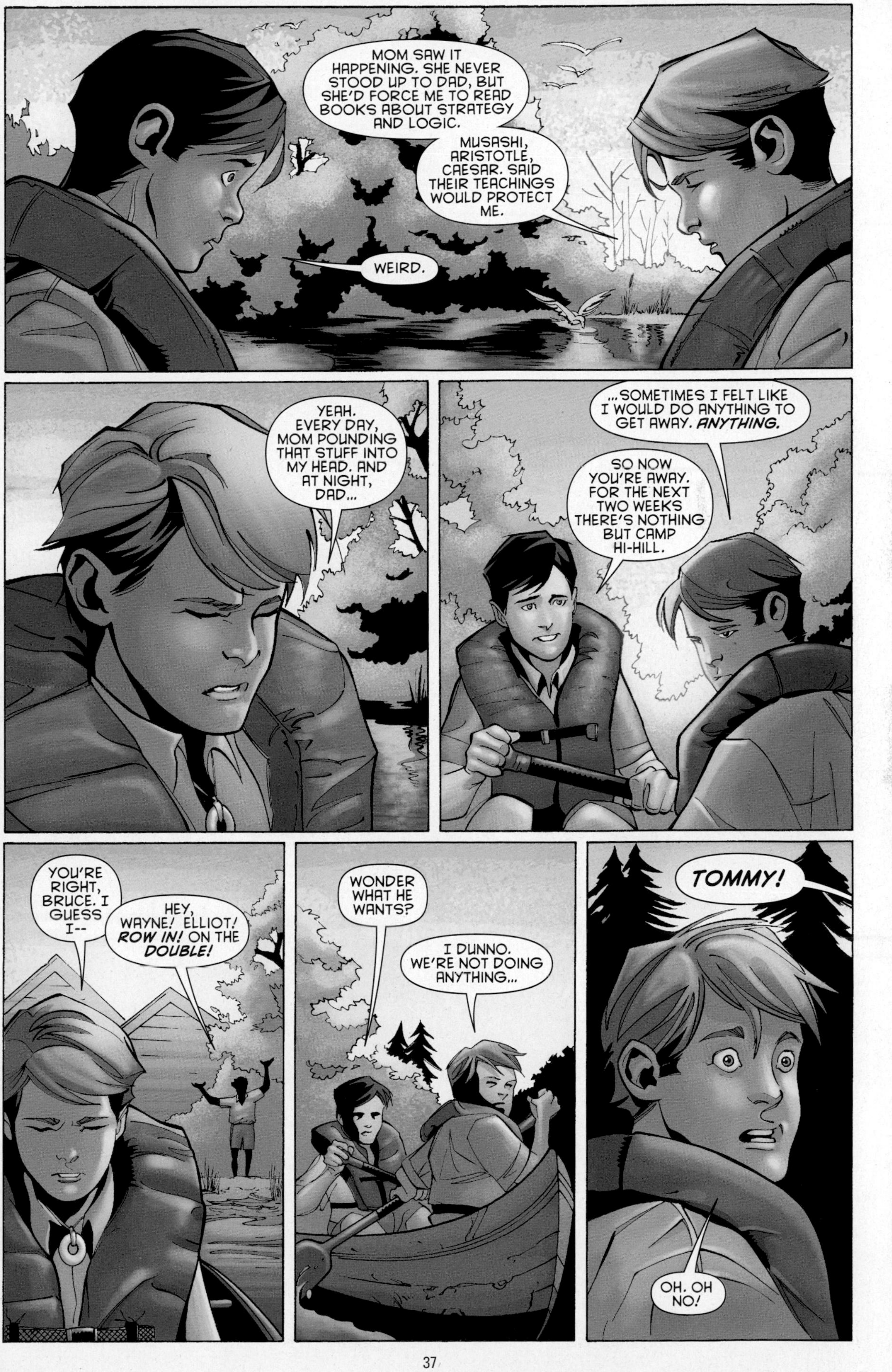
MOM SAW IT HAPPENING. SHE NEVER STOOD UP TO DAD, BUT SHE'D FORCE ME TO READ BOOKS ABOUT STRATEGY AND LOGIC.
MUSASHI, ARISTOTLE, CAESAR. SAID THEIR TEACHINGS WOULD PROTECT ME.
WEIRD.
YEAH. EVERY DAY, MOM POUNDING THAT STUFF INTO MY HEAD. AND AT NIGHT, DAD...
...SOMETIMES I FELT LIKE I WOULD DO ANYTHING TO GET AWAY. *ANYTHING.*
SO NOW YOU'RE AWAY. FOR THE NEXT TWO WEEKS THERE'S NOTHING BUT CAMP HI-HILL.
YOU'RE RIGHT, BRUCE. I GUESS I--
HEY, WAYNE! ELLIOT! **ROW IN!** ON THE **DOUBLE!**
WONDER WHAT HE WANTS?
I DUNNO. WE'RE NOT DOING ANYTHING...
TOMMY!
OH. OH NO!

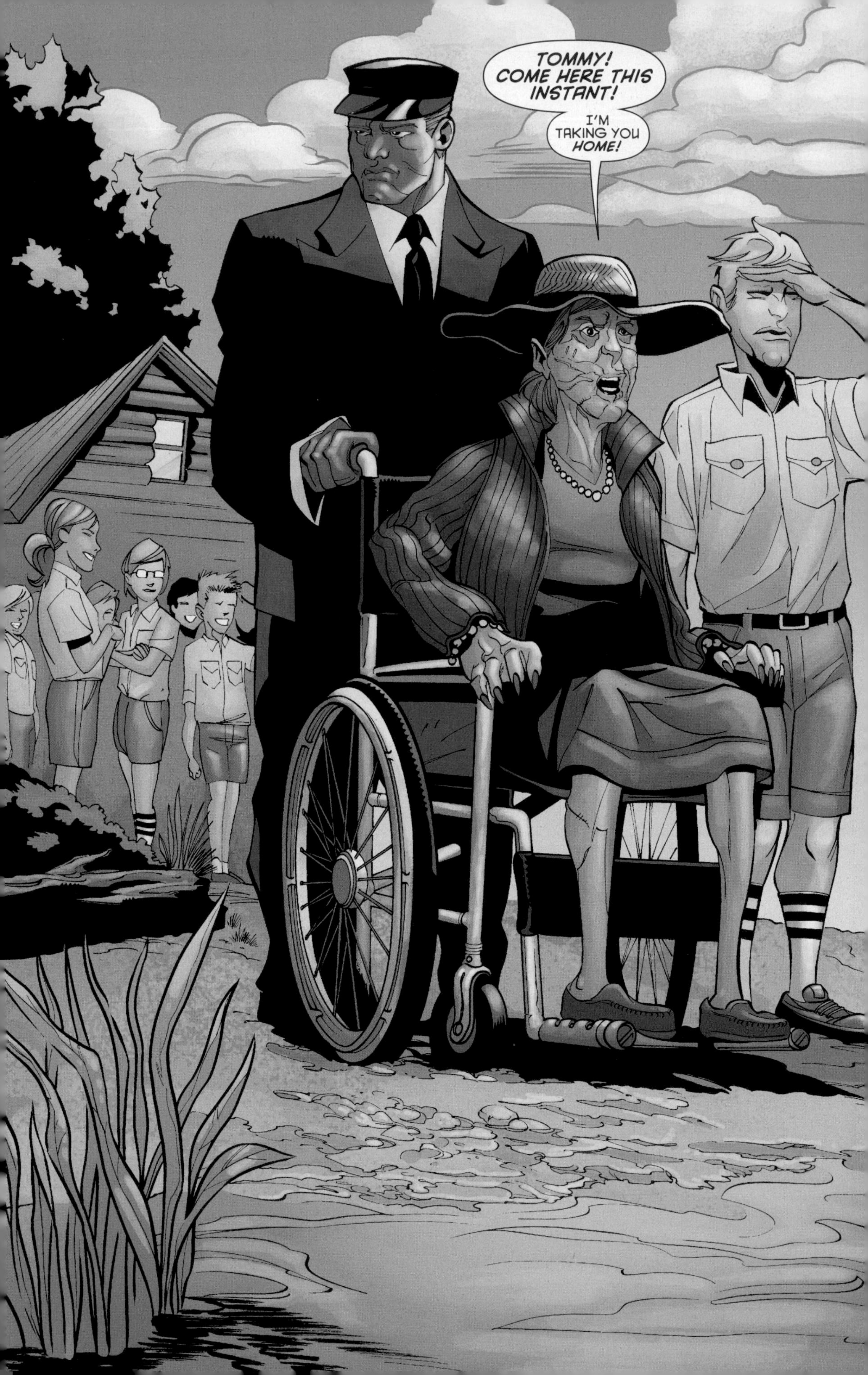
TOMMY! COME HERE THIS INSTANT!
I'M TAKING YOU HOME!

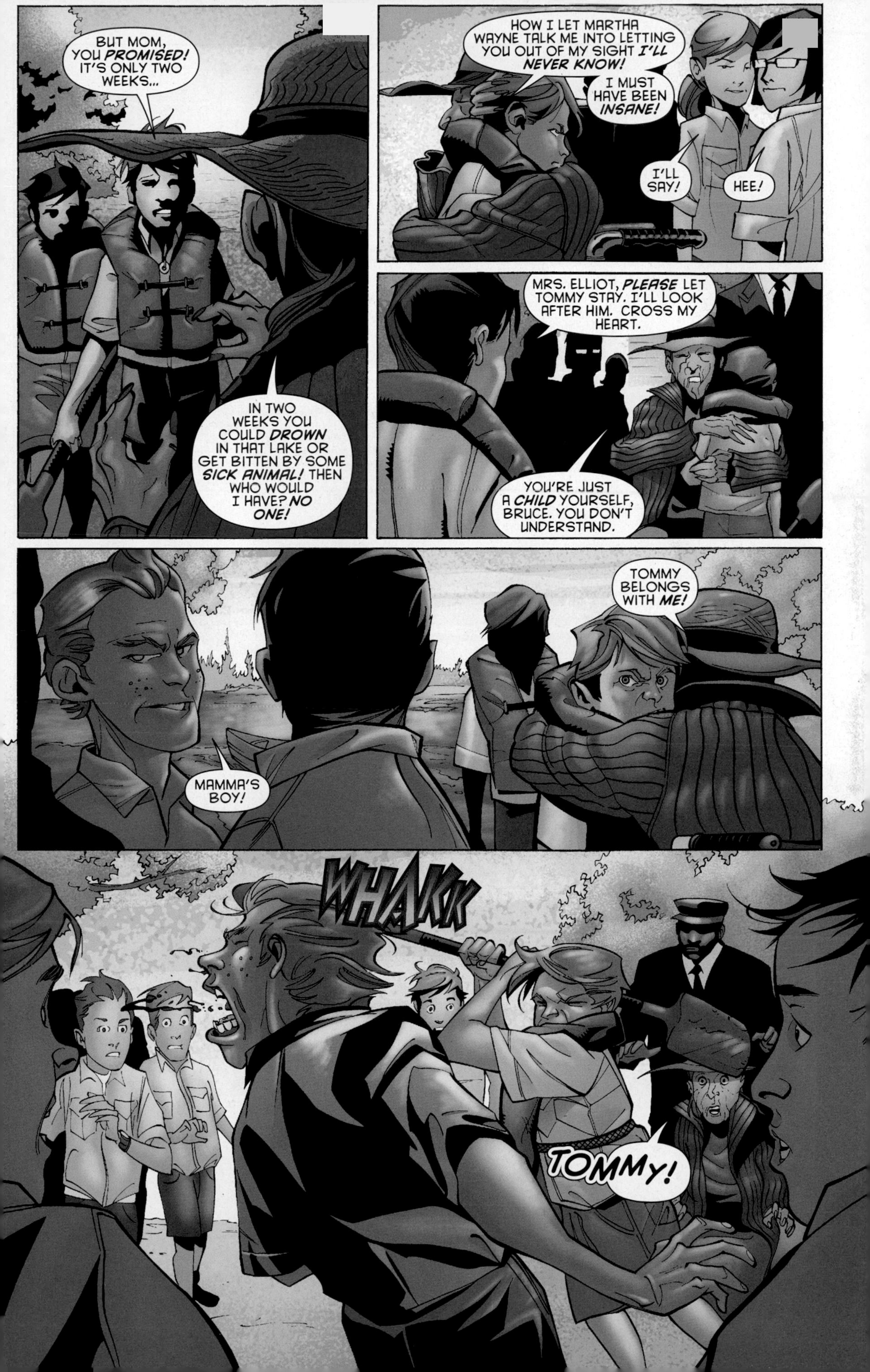

BUT MOM, YOU PROMISED! IT'S ONLY TWO WEEKS...
IN TWO WEEKS YOU COULD DROWN IN THAT LAKE OR GET BITTEN BY SOME SICK ANIMAL! THEN WHO WOULD I HAVE? NO ONE!
HOW I LET MARTHA WAYNE TALK ME INTO LETTING YOU OUT OF MY SIGHT I'LL NEVER KNOW!
I MUST HAVE BEEN INSANE!
I'LL SAY!
HEE!
MRS. ELLIOT, PLEASE LET TOMMY STAY. I'LL LOOK AFTER HIM. CROSS MY HEART.
YOU'RE JUST A CHILD YOURSELF, BRUCE. YOU DON'T UNDERSTAND.
TOMMY BELONGS WITH ME!
MAMMA'S BOY!
WHAKK
TOMMY!

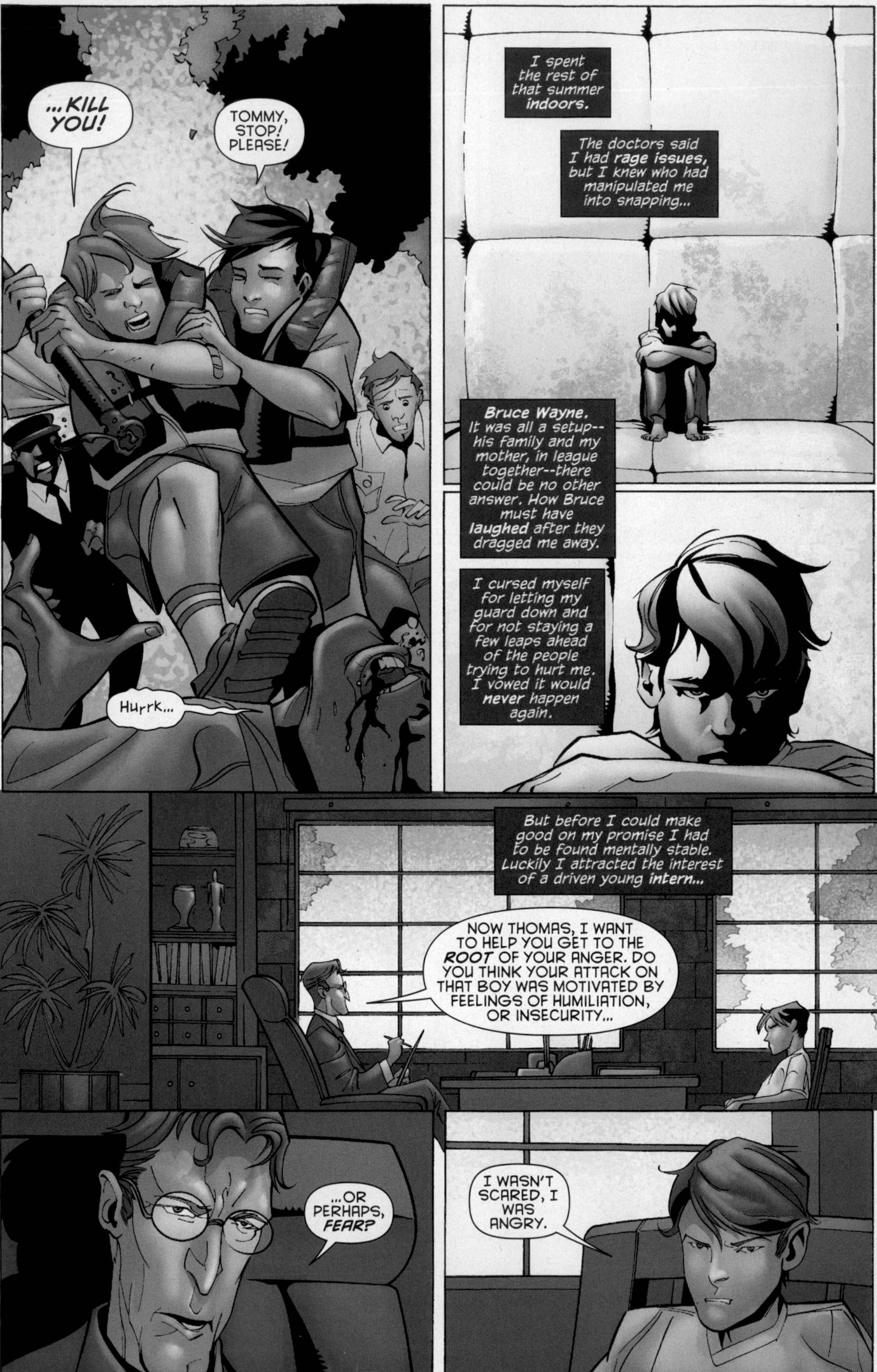

...KILL YOU!
TOMMY, STOP! PLEASE!
Hurrk...
I spent the rest of that summer indoors.
The doctors said I had rage issues, but I knew who had manipulated me into snapping...
Bruce Wayne. It was all a setup--his family and my mother, in league together--there could be no other answer. How Bruce must have laughed after they dragged me away.
I cursed myself for letting my guard down and for not staying a few leaps ahead of the people trying to hurt me. I vowed it would never happen again.
But before I could make good on my promise I had to be found mentally stable. Luckily I attracted the interest of a driven young intern...
NOW THOMAS, I WANT TO HELP YOU GET TO THE ROOT OF YOUR ANGER. DO YOU THINK YOUR ATTACK ON THAT BOY WAS MOTIVATED BY FEELINGS OF HUMILIATION, OR INSECURITY...
...OR PERHAPS, FEAR?
I WASN'T SCARED, I WAS ANGRY.

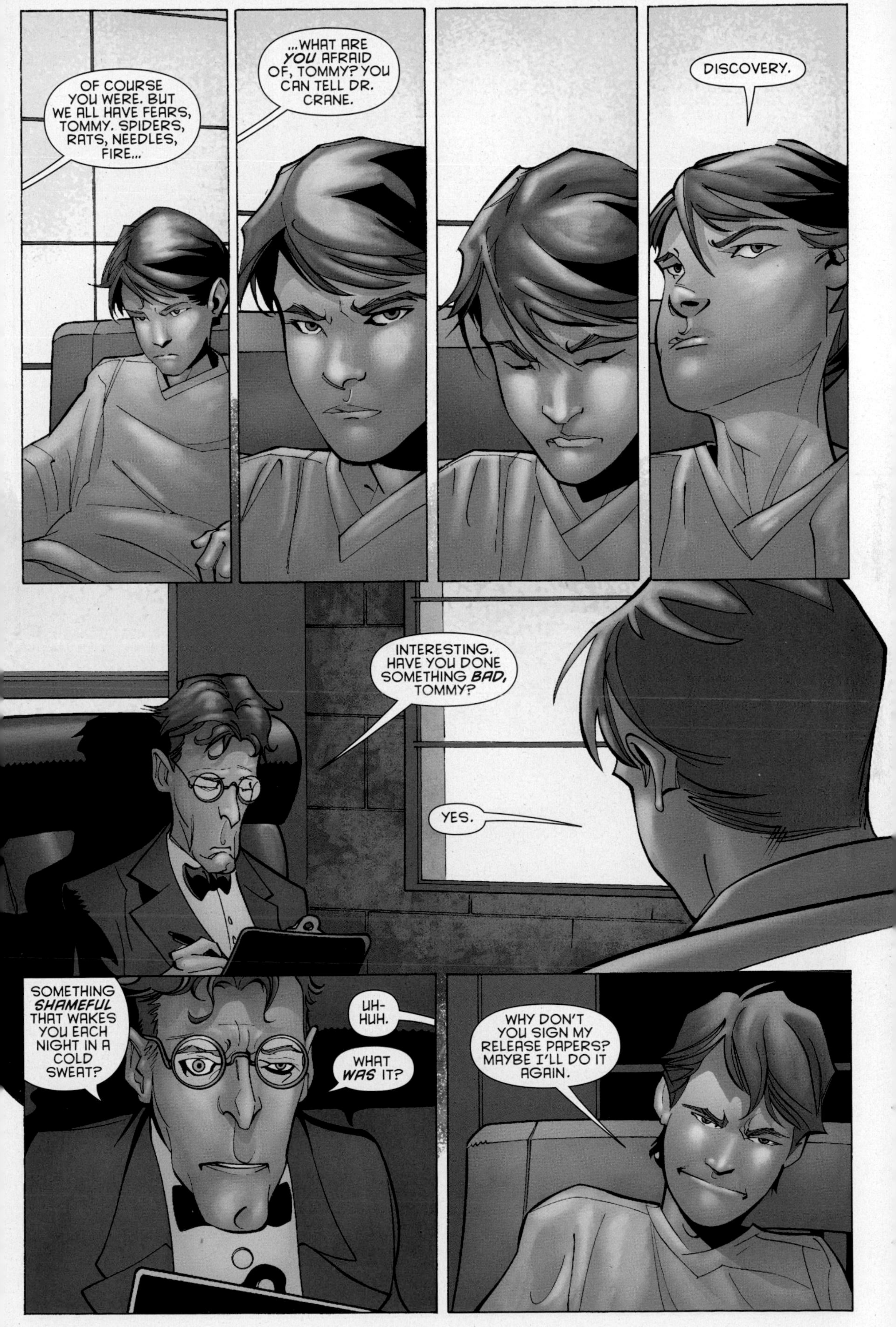

OF COURSE YOU WERE. BUT WE ALL HAVE FEARS, TOMMY. SPIDERS, RATS, NEEDLES, FIRE...
...WHAT ARE YOU AFRAID OF, TOMMY? YOU CAN TELL DR. CRANE.
DISCOVERY.
INTERESTING. HAVE YOU DONE SOMETHING BAD, TOMMY?
YES.
SOMETHING SHAMEFUL THAT WAKES YOU EACH NIGHT IN A COLD SWEAT?
UH-HUH.
WHAT WAS IT?
WHY DON'T YOU SIGN MY RELEASE PAPERS? MAYBE I'LL DO IT AGAIN.

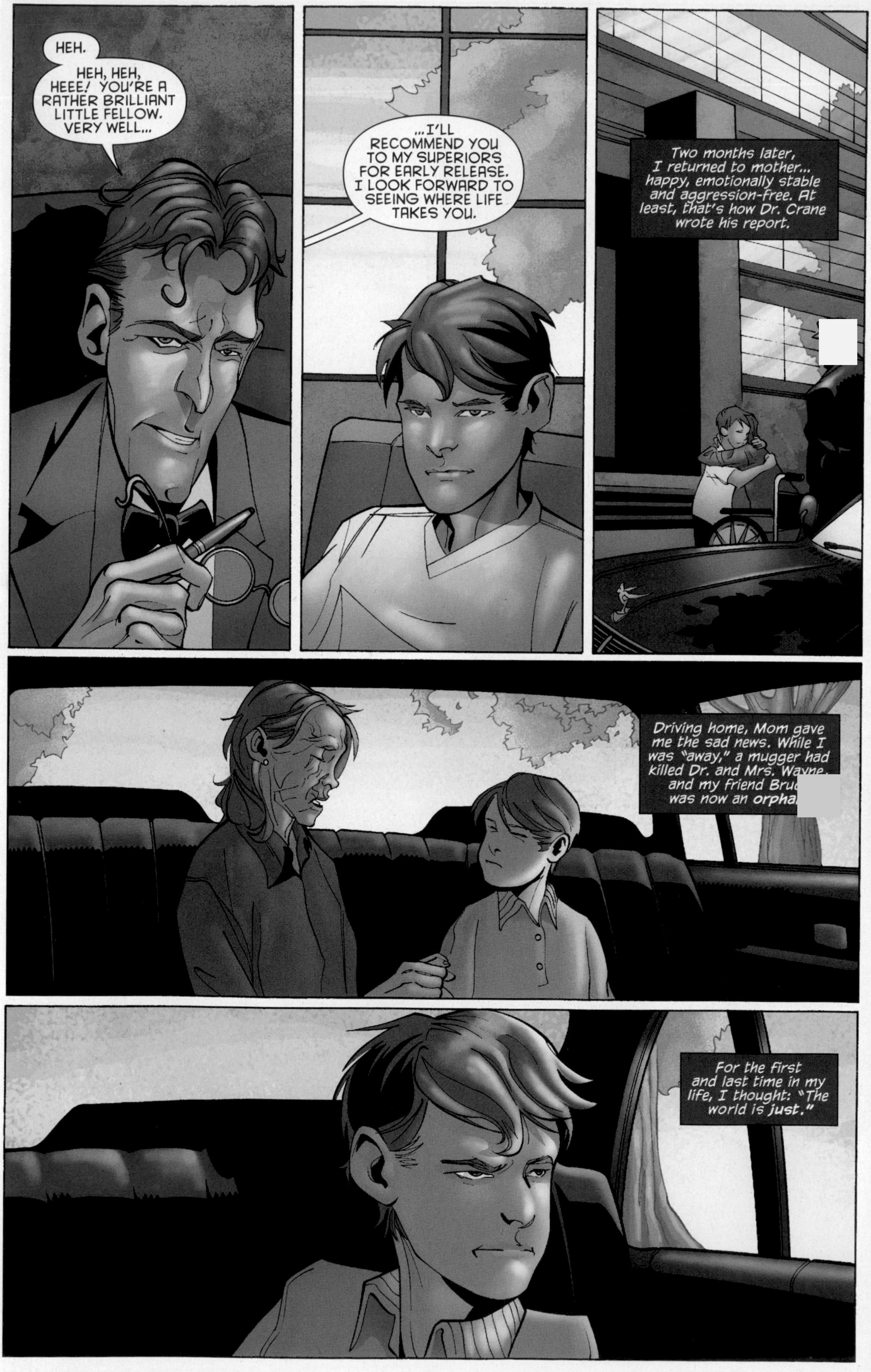
HEH.
HEH, HEH, HEEE! YOU'RE A RATHER BRILLIANT LITTLE FELLOW. VERY WELL...
...I'LL RECOMMEND YOU TO MY SUPERIORS FOR EARLY RELEASE. I LOOK FORWARD TO SEEING WHERE LIFE TAKES YOU.
Two months later, I returned to mother... happy, emotionally stable and aggression-free. At least, that's how Dr. Crane wrote his report.
Driving home, Mom gave me the sad news. While I was "away," a mugger had killed Dr. and Mrs. Wayn and my friend Bruc was now an orpha
For the first and last time in my life, I thought: "The world is just."

And yet, for all his sorrow, Bruce had been blessed with a freedom I could *only imagine.* While he spent the next decade traveling the world gaining knowledge and charting his heroic destiny, I wiped spittle from a jabbering madwoman's lips.

TURN HIM OVER.

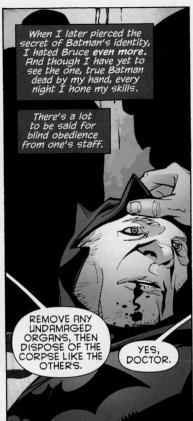

When I later pierced the secret of Batman's identity, I hated Bruce *even more.* And though I have yet to see the one, true Batman dead by my hand, every night I hone my skills.

There's a lot to be said for blind obedience from one's staff.

REMOVE ANY UNDAMAGED ORGANS, THEN DISPOSE OF THE CORPSE LIKE THE OTHERS.

YES, DOCTOR.

Soon, Bruce. Soon.

UNNH!

OKAY, SO YOU'RE *NOT* AS DUMB AS YOU LOOK!

WHUNK

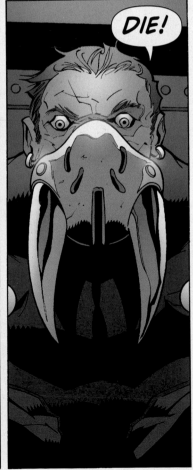

DIE!

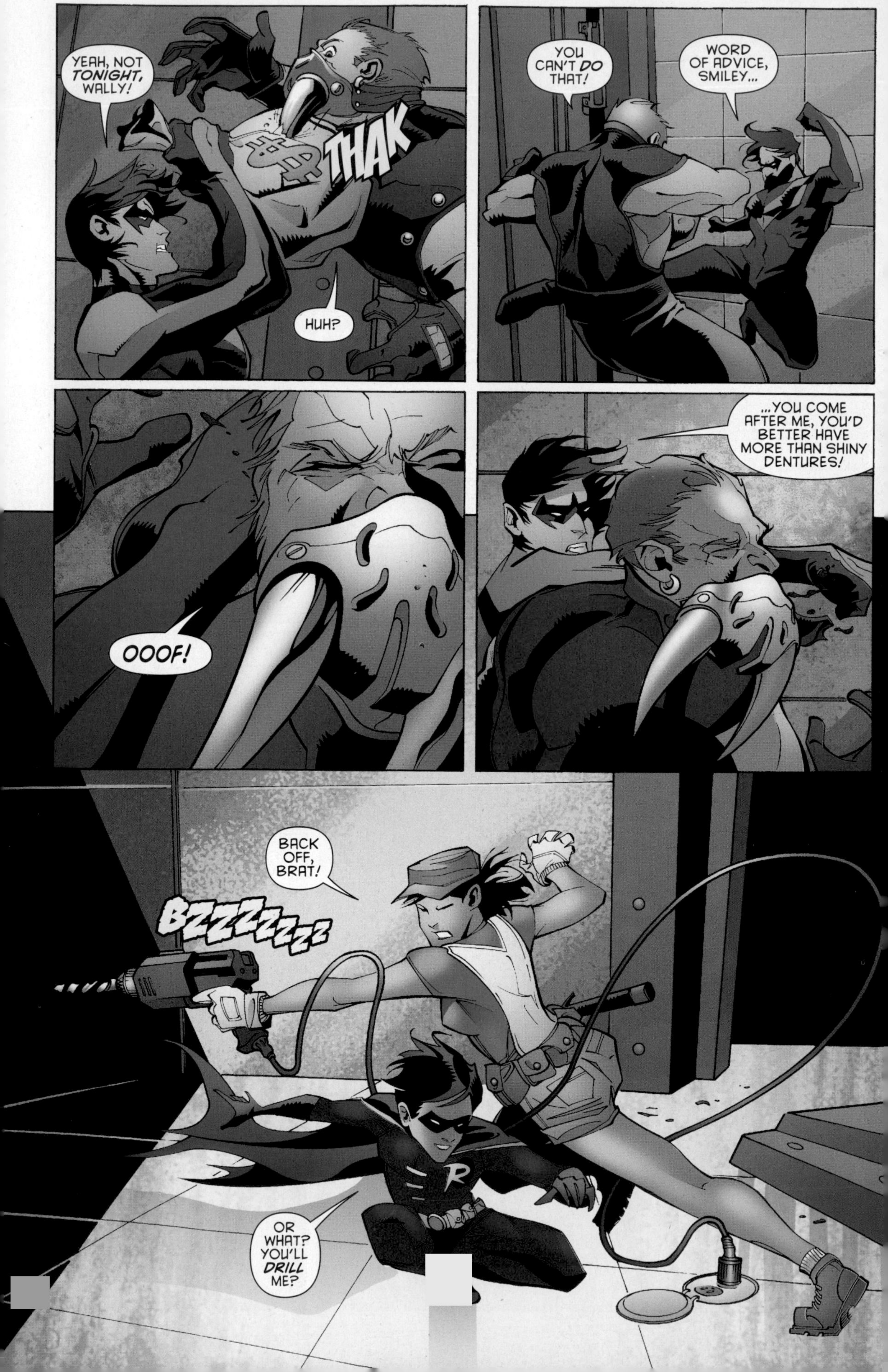
YEAH, NOT *TONIGHT,* WALLY!
THAK
HUH?
YOU CAN'T *DO* THAT!
WORD OF ADVICE, SMILEY...
OOOF!
...YOU COME AFTER ME, YOU'D BETTER HAVE MORE THAN SHINY DENTURES!
BACK OFF, BRAT!
BZZZZZZZZ
OR WHAT? YOU'LL *DRILL* ME?

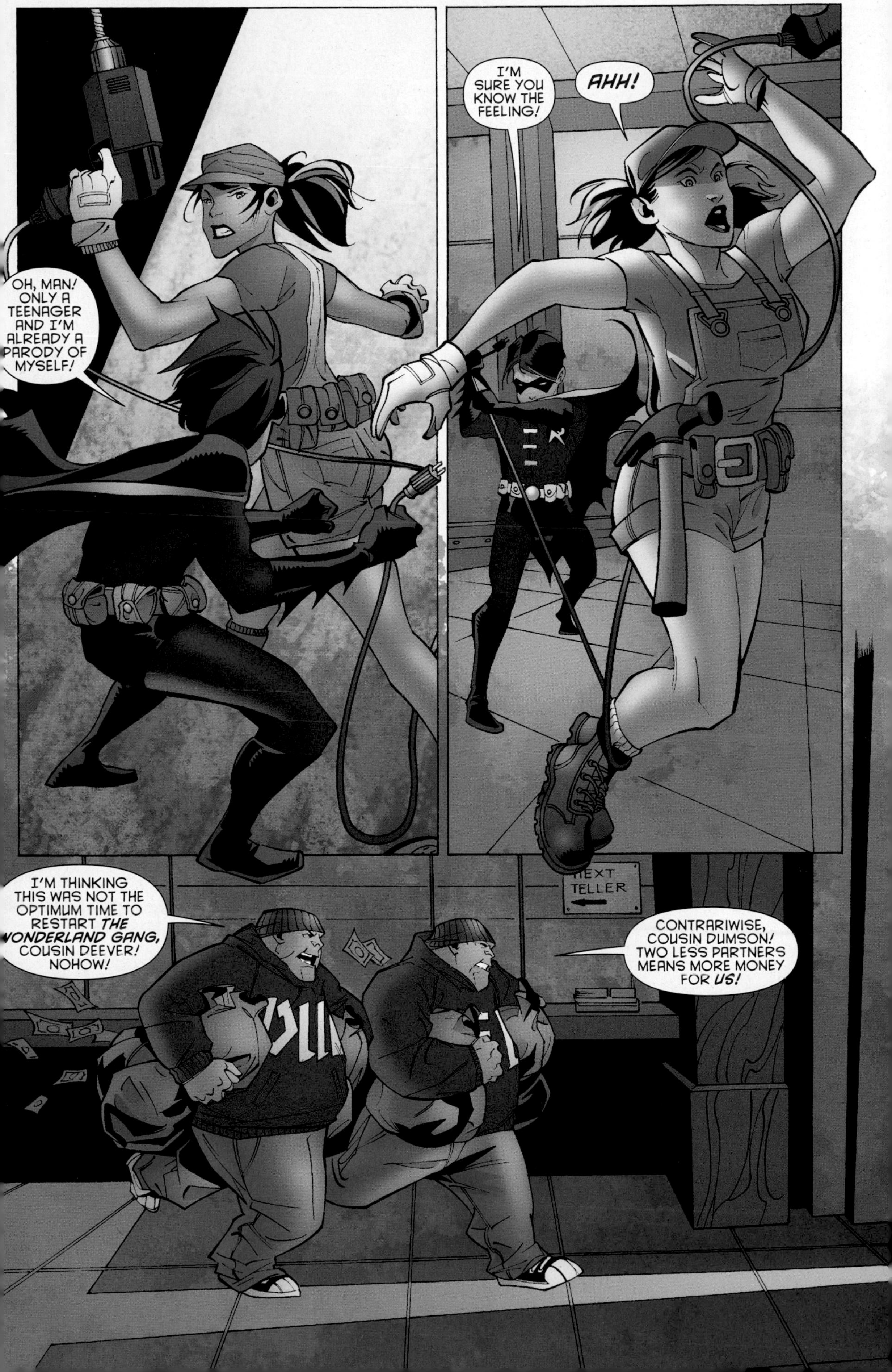
OH, MAN! ONLY A TEENAGER AND I'M ALREADY A PARODY OF MYSELF!
I'M SURE YOU KNOW THE FEELING!
AHH!
NEXT TELLER
I'M THINKING THIS WAS NOT THE OPTIMUM TIME TO RESTART THE WONDERLAND GANG, COUSIN DEEVER! NOHOW!
CONTRARIWISE, COUSIN DUMSON! TWO LESS PARTNERS MEANS MORE MONEY FOR US!

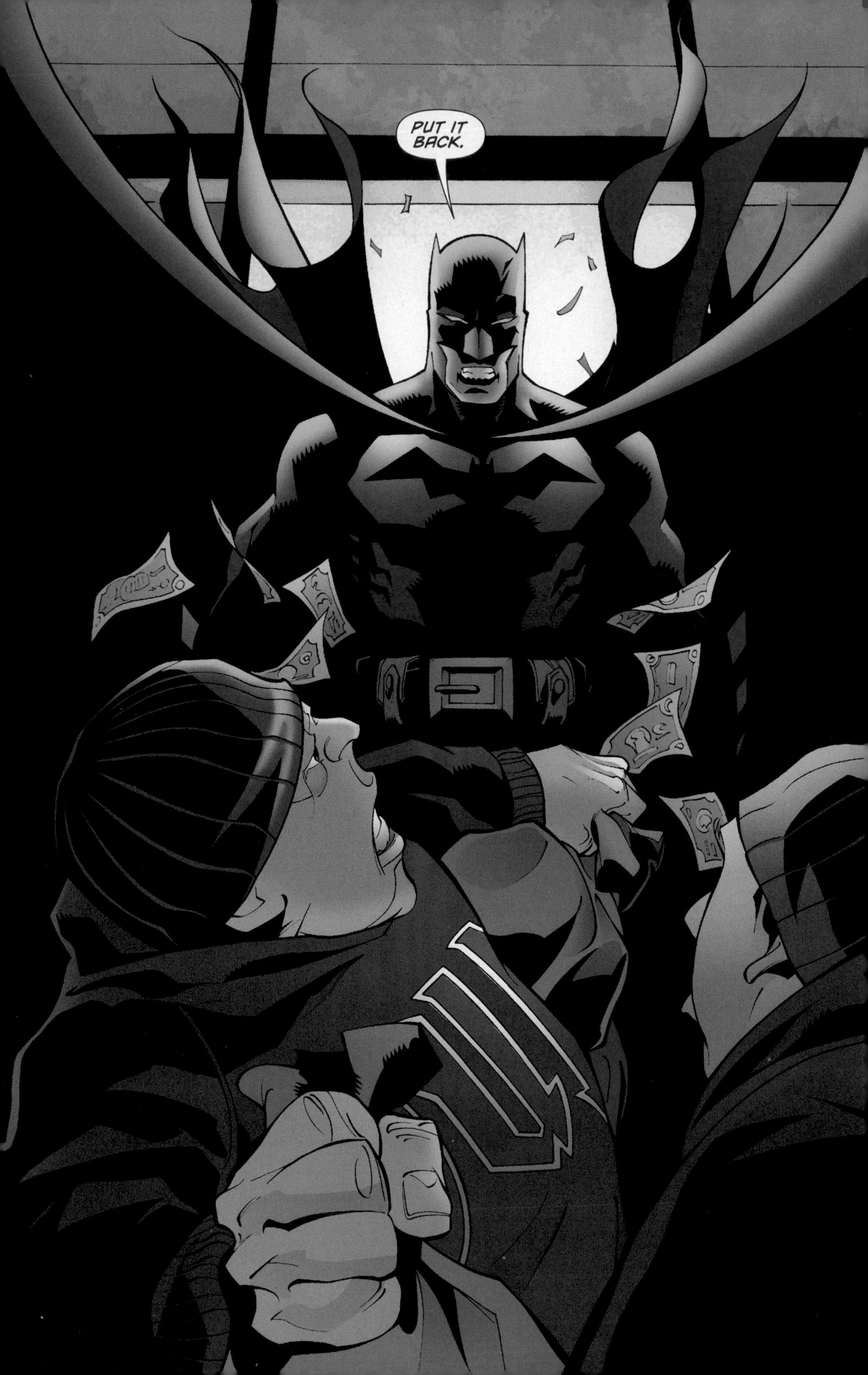
PUT IT BACK.

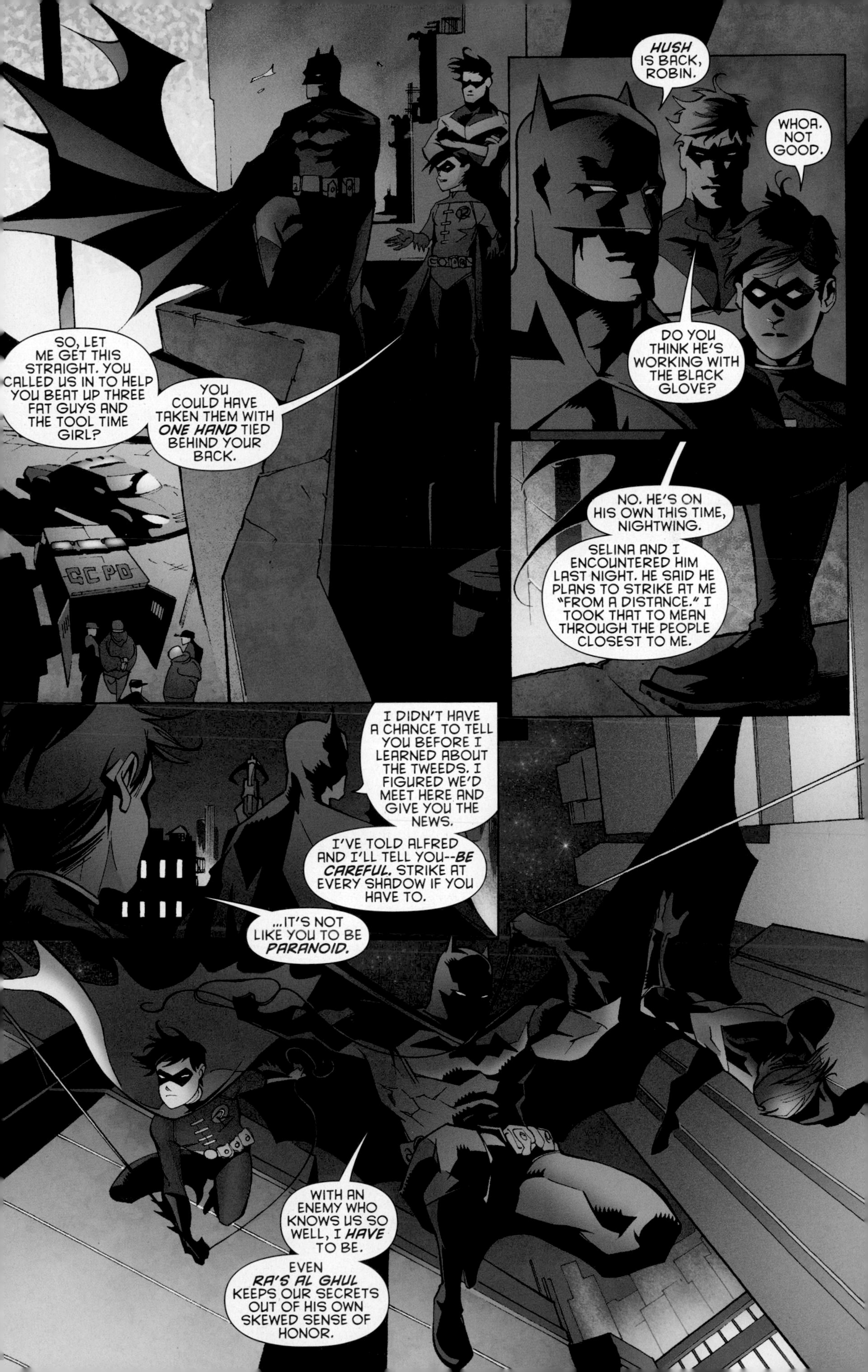
SO, LET ME GET THIS STRAIGHT. YOU CALLED US IN TO HELP YOU BEAT UP THREE FAT GUYS AND THE TOOL TIME GIRL?
YOU COULD HAVE TAKEN THEM WITH ONE HAND TIED BEHIND YOUR BACK.
HUSH IS BACK, ROBIN.
WHOA. NOT GOOD.
DO YOU THINK HE'S WORKING WITH THE BLACK GLOVE?
NO. HE'S ON HIS OWN THIS TIME, NIGHTWING.
SELINA AND I ENCOUNTERED HIM LAST NIGHT. HE SAID HE PLANS TO STRIKE AT ME "FROM A DISTANCE." I TOOK THAT TO MEAN THROUGH THE PEOPLE CLOSEST TO ME.
GCPD
I DIDN'T HAVE A CHANCE TO TELL YOU BEFORE I LEARNED ABOUT THE TWEEDS. I FIGURED WE'D MEET HERE AND GIVE YOU THE NEWS.
I'VE TOLD ALFRED AND I'LL TELL YOU--BE CAREFUL. STRIKE AT EVERY SHADOW IF YOU HAVE TO.
...IT'S NOT LIKE YOU TO BE PARANOID.
WITH AN ENEMY WHO KNOWS US SO WELL, I HAVE TO BE.
EVEN RA'S AL GHUL KEEPS OUR SECRETS OUT OF HIS OWN SKEWED SENSE OF HONOR.

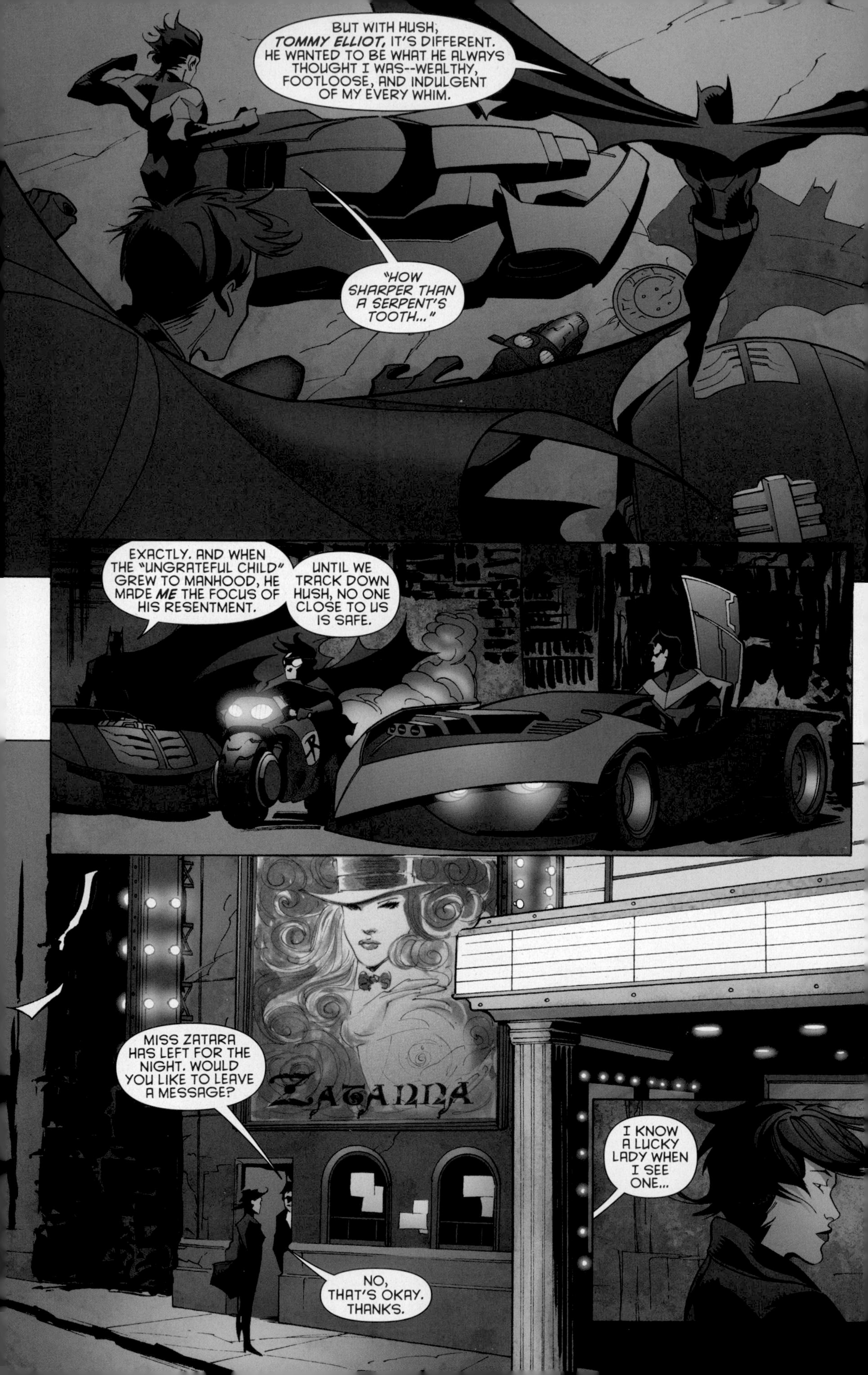
BUT WITH HUSH, *TOMMY ELLIOT,* IT'S DIFFERENT. HE WANTED TO BE WHAT HE ALWAYS THOUGHT I WAS--WEALTHY, FOOTLOOSE, AND INDULGENT OF MY EVERY WHIM.
"HOW SHARPER THAN A SERPENT'S TOOTH..."
EXACTLY. AND WHEN THE "UNGRATEFUL CHILD" GREW TO MANHOOD, HE MADE *ME* THE FOCUS OF HIS RESENTMENT.
UNTIL WE TRACK DOWN HUSH, NO ONE CLOSE TO US IS SAFE.
ZATANNA
MISS ZATARA HAS LEFT FOR THE NIGHT. WOULD YOU LIKE TO LEAVE A MESSAGE?
NO, THAT'S OKAY. THANKS.
I KNOW A LUCKY LADY WHEN I SEE ONE...

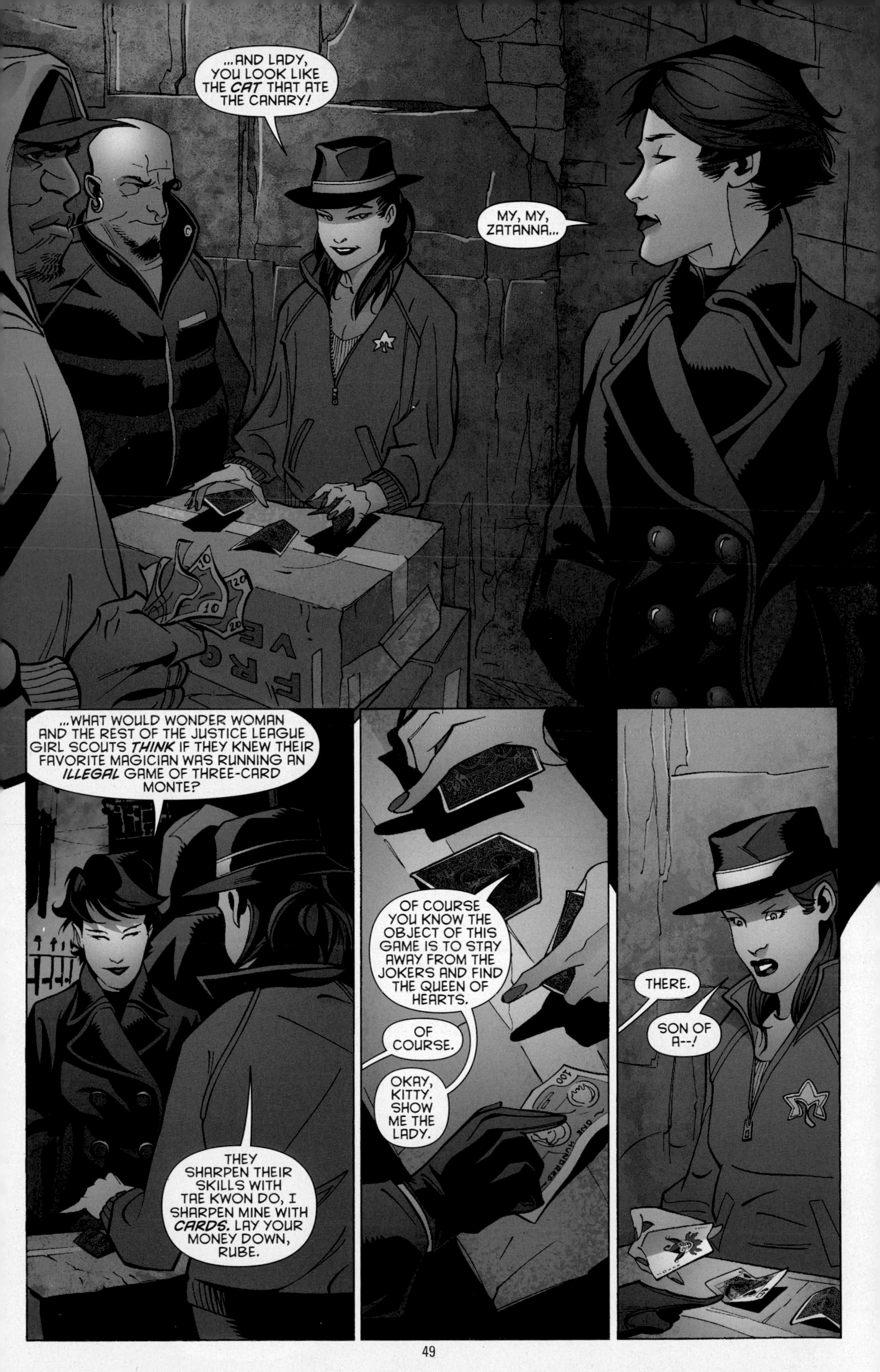
...AND LADY, YOU LOOK LIKE THE CAT THAT ATE THE CANARY!
MY, MY, ZATANNA...
...WHAT WOULD WONDER WOMAN AND THE REST OF THE JUSTICE LEAGUE GIRL SCOUTS THINK IF THEY KNEW THEIR FAVORITE MAGICIAN WAS RUNNING AN ILLEGAL GAME OF THREE-CARD MONTE?
THEY SHARPEN THEIR SKILLS WITH TAE KWON DO, I SHARPEN MINE WITH CARDS. LAY YOUR MONEY DOWN, RUBE.
OF COURSE YOU KNOW THE OBJECT OF THIS GAME IS TO STAY AWAY FROM THE JOKERS AND FIND THE QUEEN OF HEARTS.
OF COURSE.
OKAY, KITTY. SHOW ME THE LADY.
THERE.
SON OF A--!

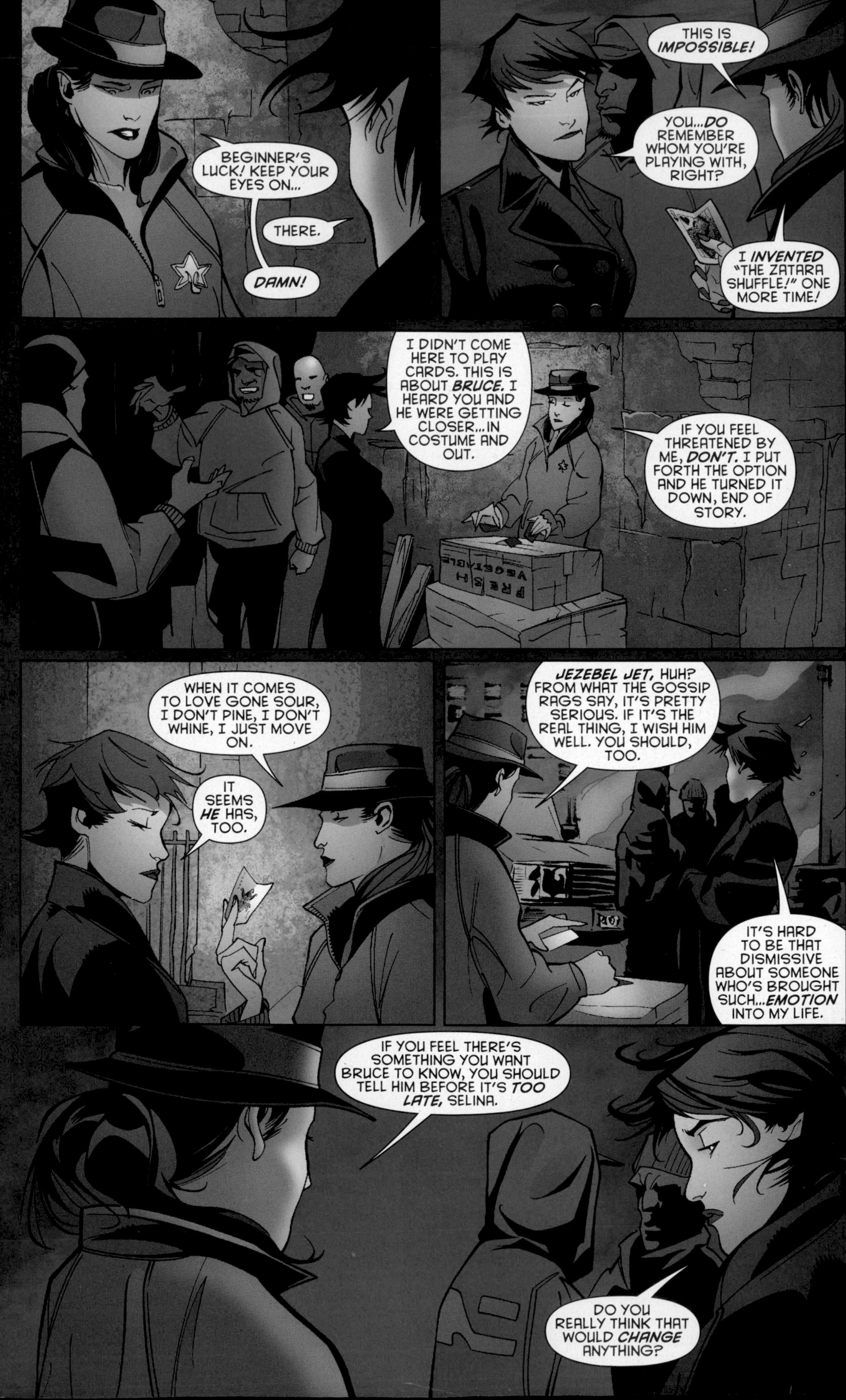
BEGINNER'S LUCK! KEEP YOUR EYES ON...
THERE.
DAMN!
THIS IS IMPOSSIBLE!
YOU...DO REMEMBER WHOM YOU'RE PLAYING WITH, RIGHT?
I INVENTED "THE ZATARA SHUFFLE!" ONE MORE TIME!
I DIDN'T COME HERE TO PLAY CARDS. THIS IS ABOUT BRUCE. I HEARD YOU AND HE WERE GETTING CLOSER...IN COSTUME AND OUT.
IF YOU FEEL THREATENED BY ME, DON'T. I PUT FORTH THE OPTION AND HE TURNED IT DOWN, END OF STORY.
FRESH VEGETABLE
WHEN IT COMES TO LOVE GONE SOUR, I DON'T PINE, I DON'T WHINE, I JUST MOVE ON.
IT SEEMS HE HAS, TOO.
JEZEBEL JET, HUH? FROM WHAT THE GOSSIP RAGS SAY, IT'S PRETTY SERIOUS. IF IT'S THE REAL THING, I WISH HIM WELL. YOU SHOULD, TOO.
IT'S HARD TO BE THAT DISMISSIVE ABOUT SOMEONE WHO'S BROUGHT SUCH...EMOTION INTO MY LIFE.
IF YOU FEEL THERE'S SOMETHING YOU WANT BRUCE TO KNOW, YOU SHOULD TELL HIM BEFORE IT'S TOO LATE, SELINA.
DO YOU REALLY THINK THAT WOULD CHANGE ANYTHING?

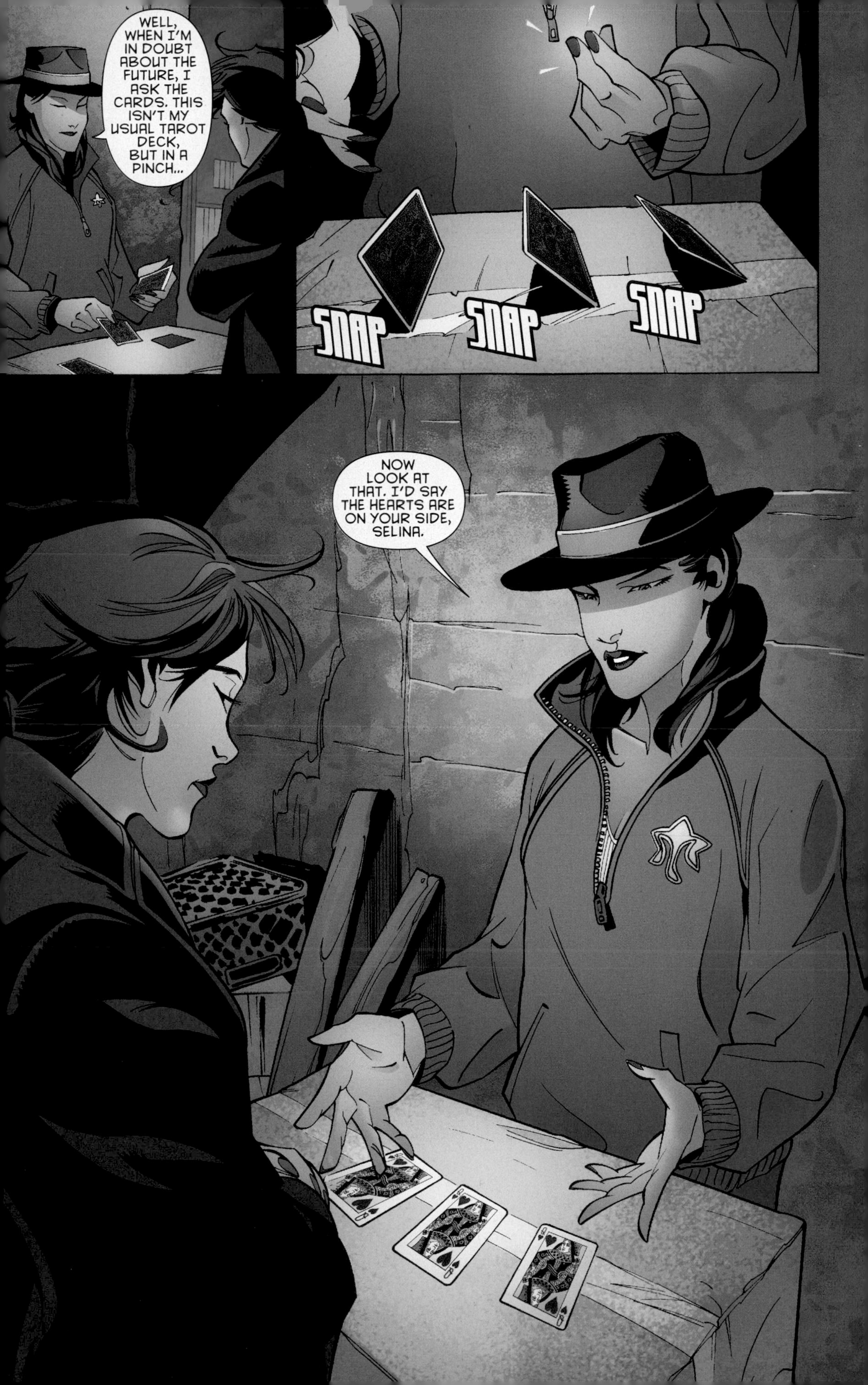
WELL, WHEN I'M IN DOUBT ABOUT THE FUTURE, I ASK THE CARDS. THIS ISN'T MY USUAL TAROT DECK, BUT IN A PINCH...
SNAP
SNAP
SNAP
NOW LOOK AT THAT. I'D SAY THE HEARTS ARE ON YOUR SIDE, SELINA.

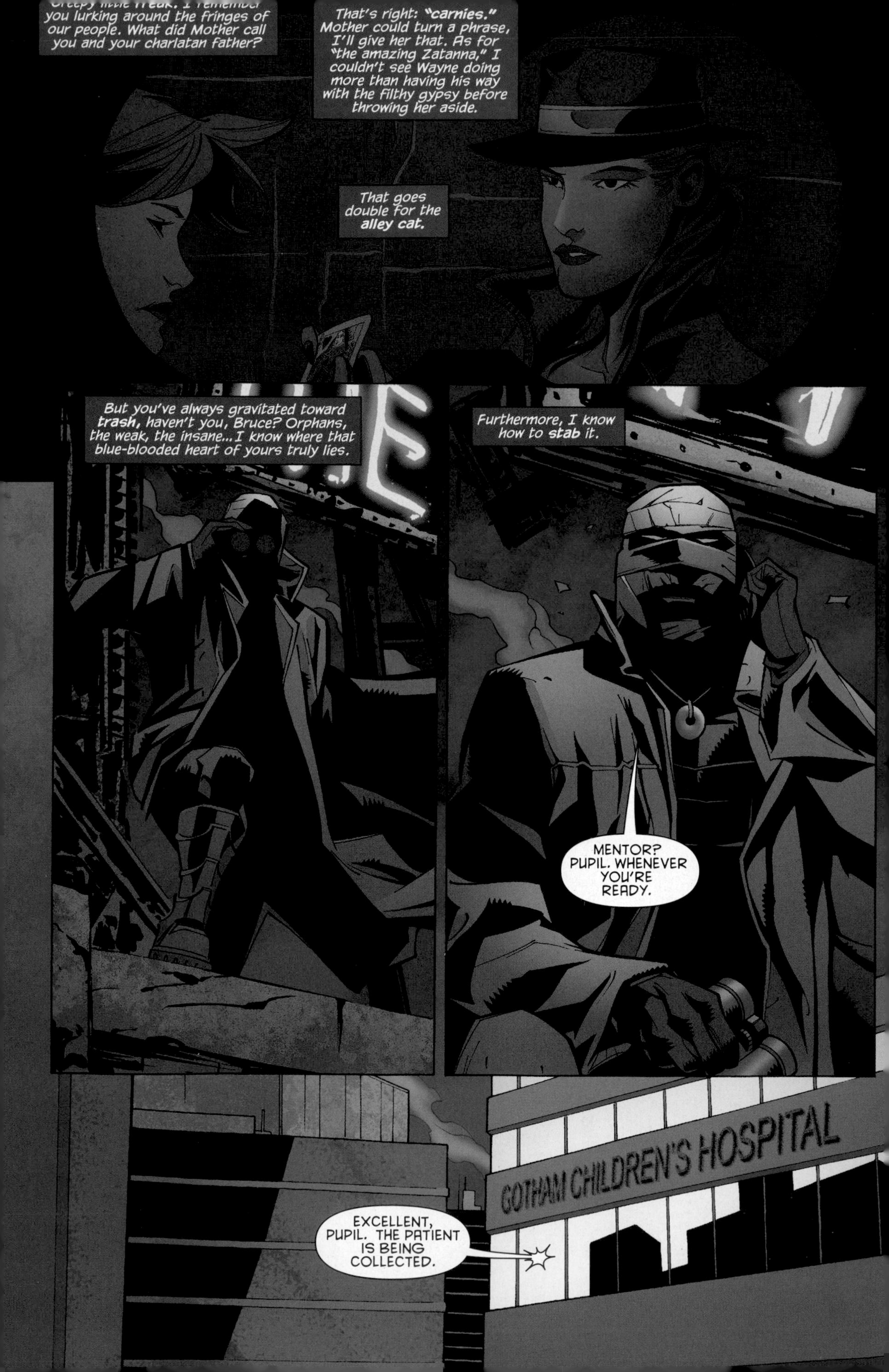

Creepy little freak. I remember you lurking around the fringes of our people. What did Mother call you and your charlatan father?
That's right: **"carnies."** Mother could turn a phrase, I'll give her that. As for "the amazing Zatanna," I couldn't see Wayne doing more than having his way with the filthy gypsy before throwing her aside.
That goes double for the **alley cat.**
But you've always gravitated toward **trash,** haven't you, Bruce? Orphans, the weak, the insane...I know where that blue-blooded heart of yours truly lies.
Furthermore, I know how to **stab** it.
MENTOR? PUPIL. WHENEVER YOU'RE READY.
GOTHAM CHILDREN'S HOSPITAL
EXCELLENT, PUPIL. THE PATIENT IS BEING COLLECTED.

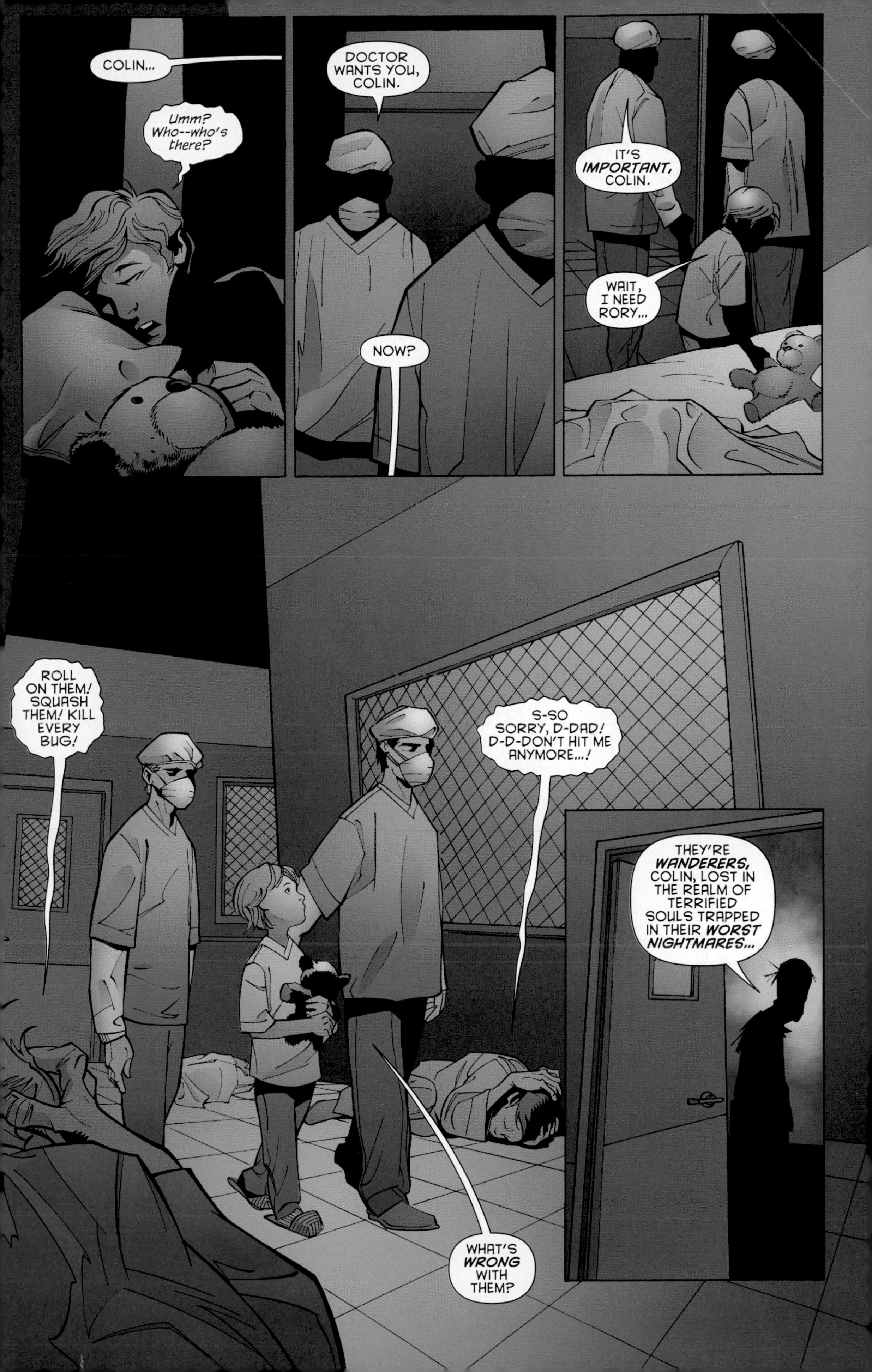

COLIN...
Umm? Who--who's there?
DOCTOR WANTS YOU, COLIN.
NOW?
IT'S IMPORTANT, COLIN.
WAIT, I NEED RORY...
ROLL ON THEM! SQUASH THEM! KILL EVERY BUG!
S-SO SORRY, D-DAD! D-D-DON'T HIT ME ANYMORE...!
WHAT'S WRONG WITH THEM?
THEY'RE WANDERERS, COLIN, LOST IN THE REALM OF TERRIFIED SOULS TRAPPED IN THEIR WORST NIGHTMARES...

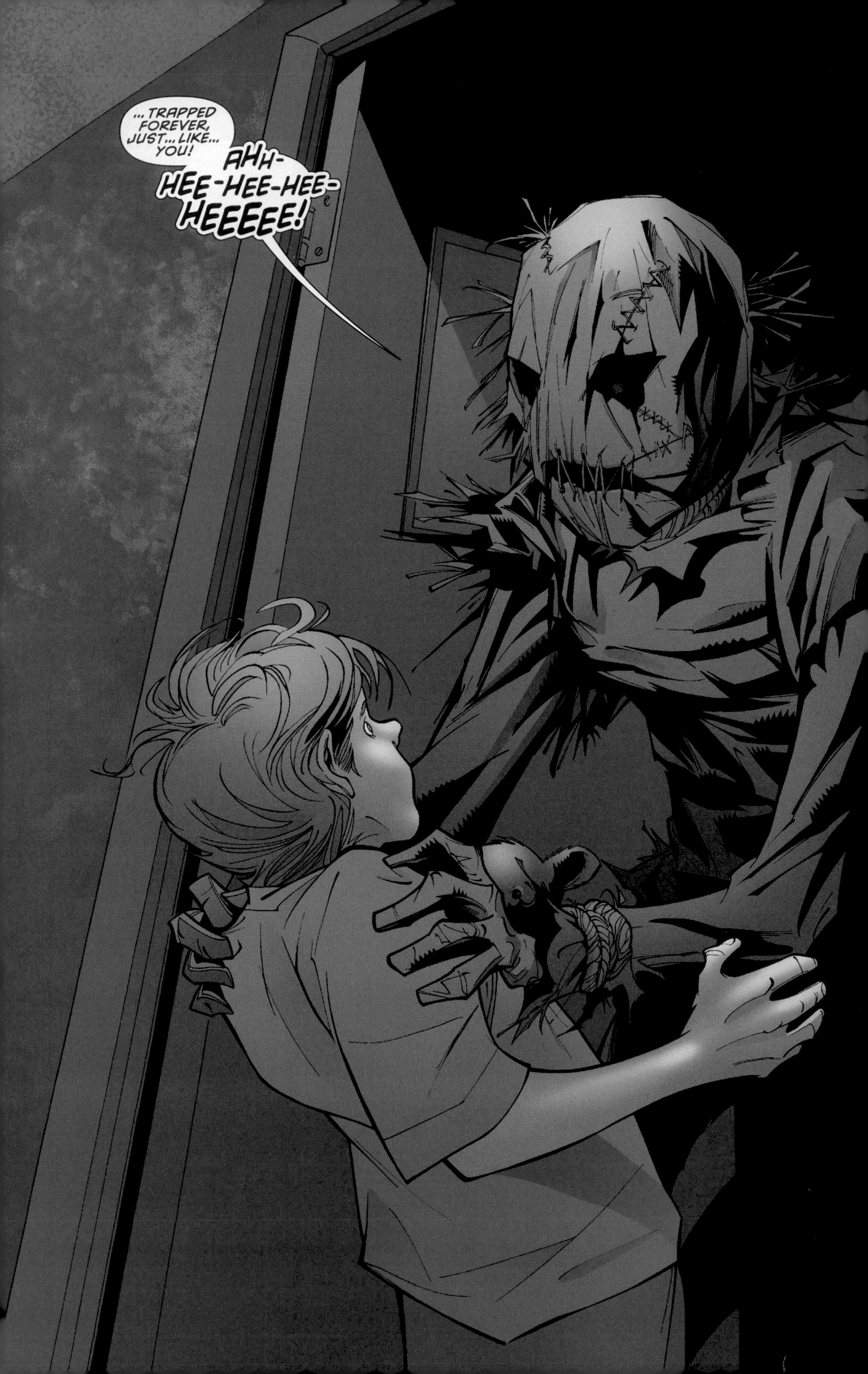
...TRAPPED FOREVER, JUST...LIKE... YOU!
AHH-HEE-HEE-HEE-HEEEEEE!

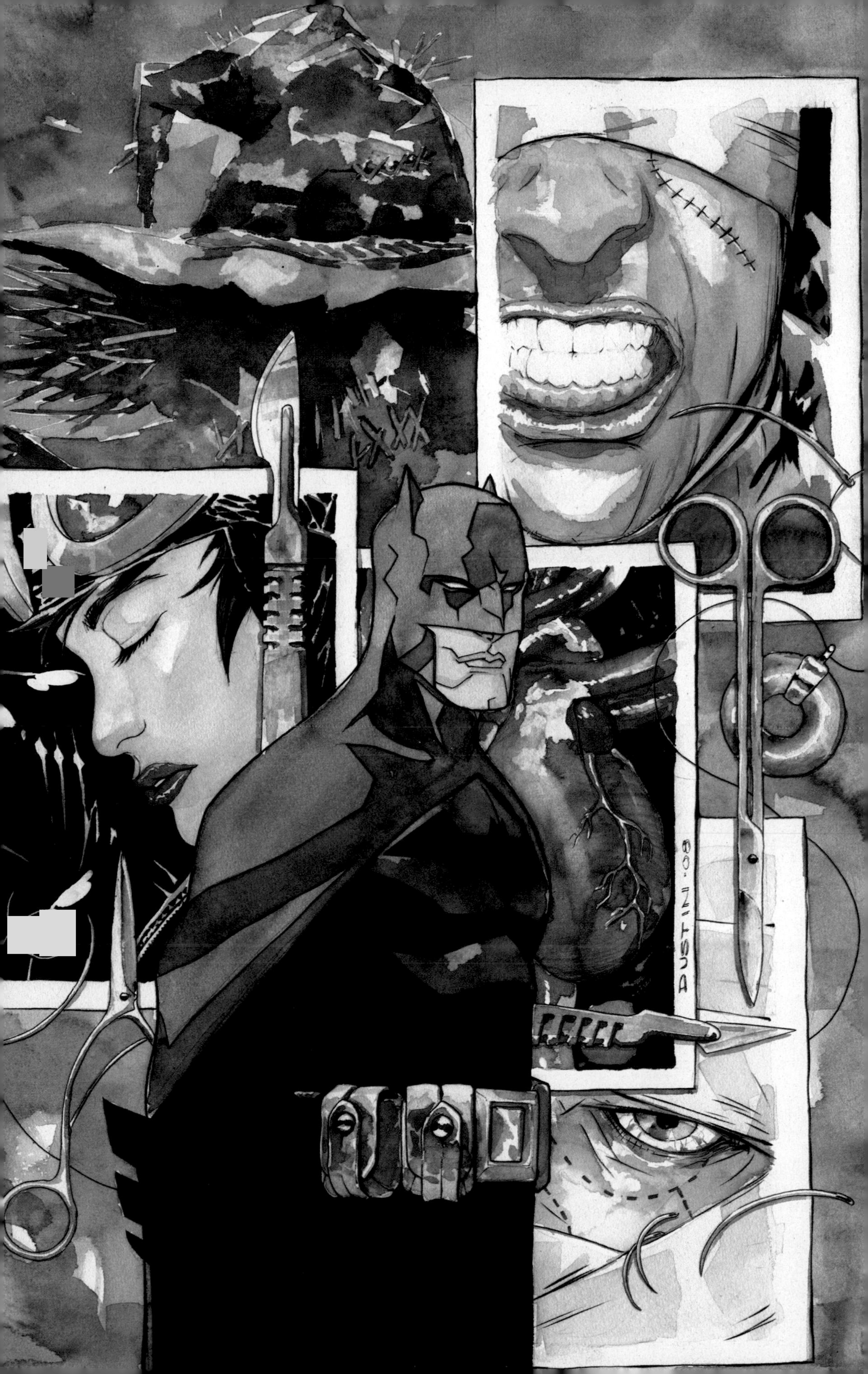
DUSTIN '08

"Another madman's round of hide and seek."

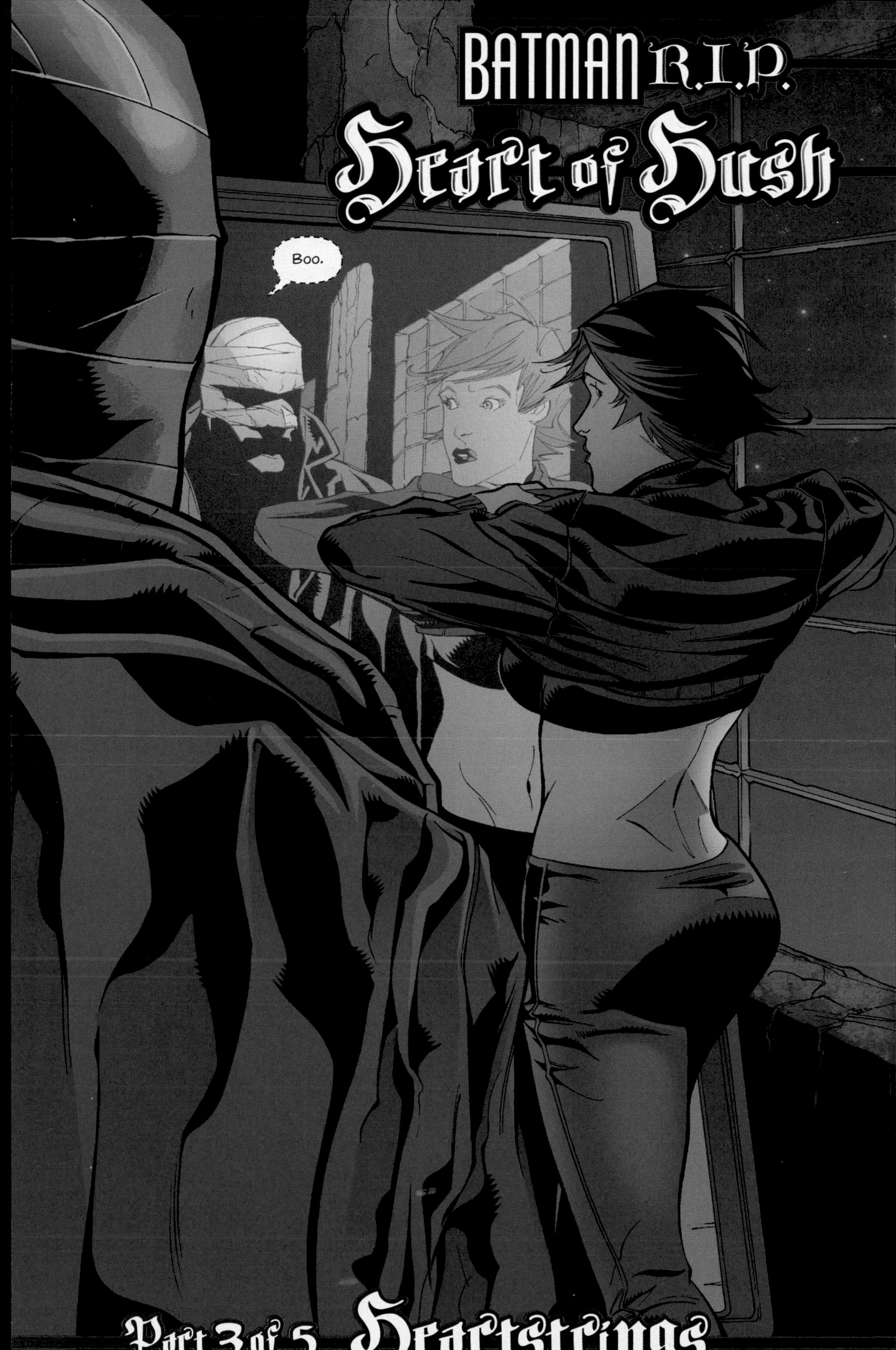
BATMAN R.I.P.
Heart of Hush
Boo.
Part 3 of 5 Heartstrings

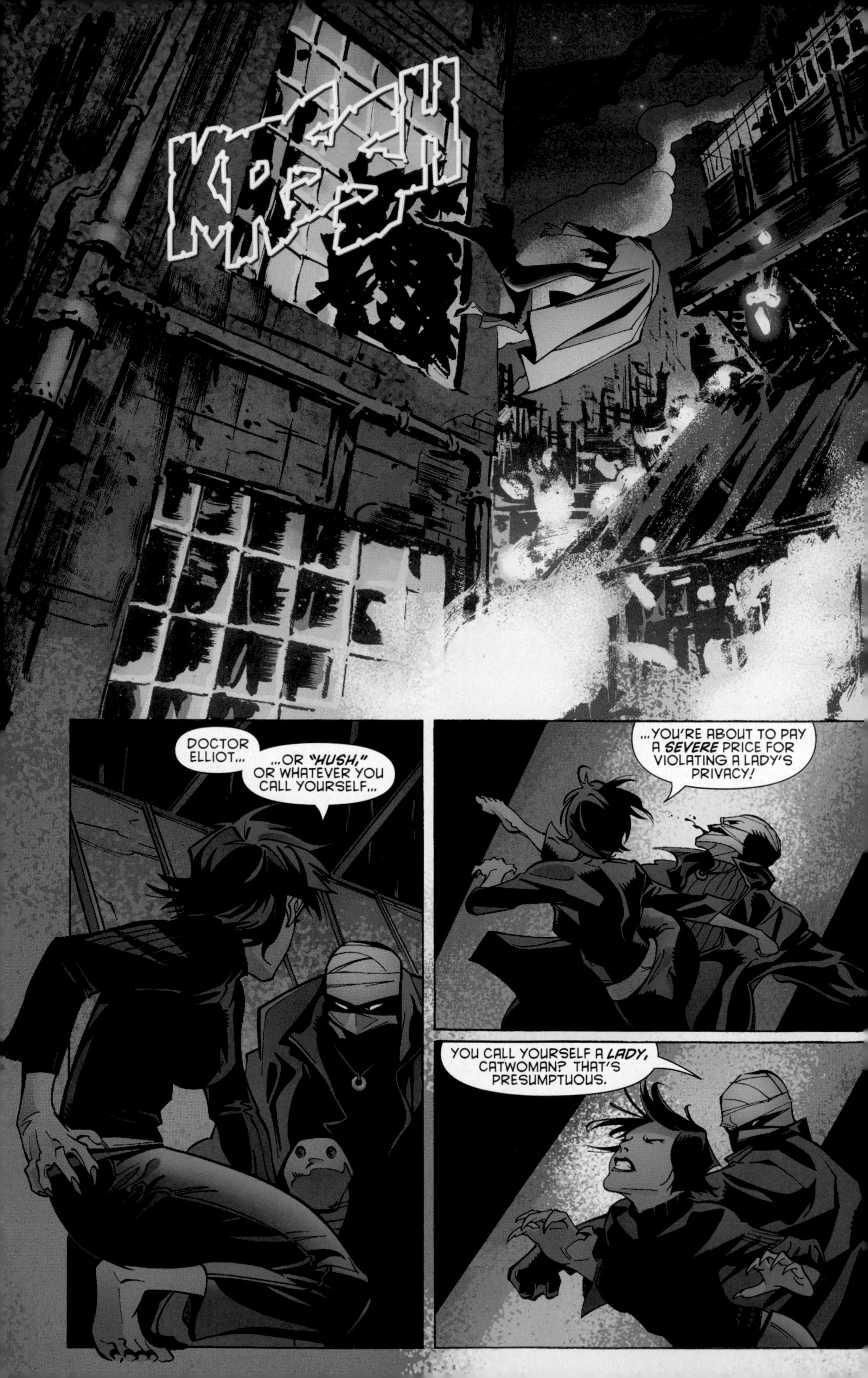
KRASH
DOCTOR ELLIOT...
...OR "HUSH," OR WHATEVER YOU CALL YOURSELF...
...YOU'RE ABOUT TO PAY A SEVERE PRICE FOR VIOLATING A LADY'S PRIVACY!
YOU CALL YOURSELF A LADY, CATWOMAN? THAT'S PRESUMPTUOUS.

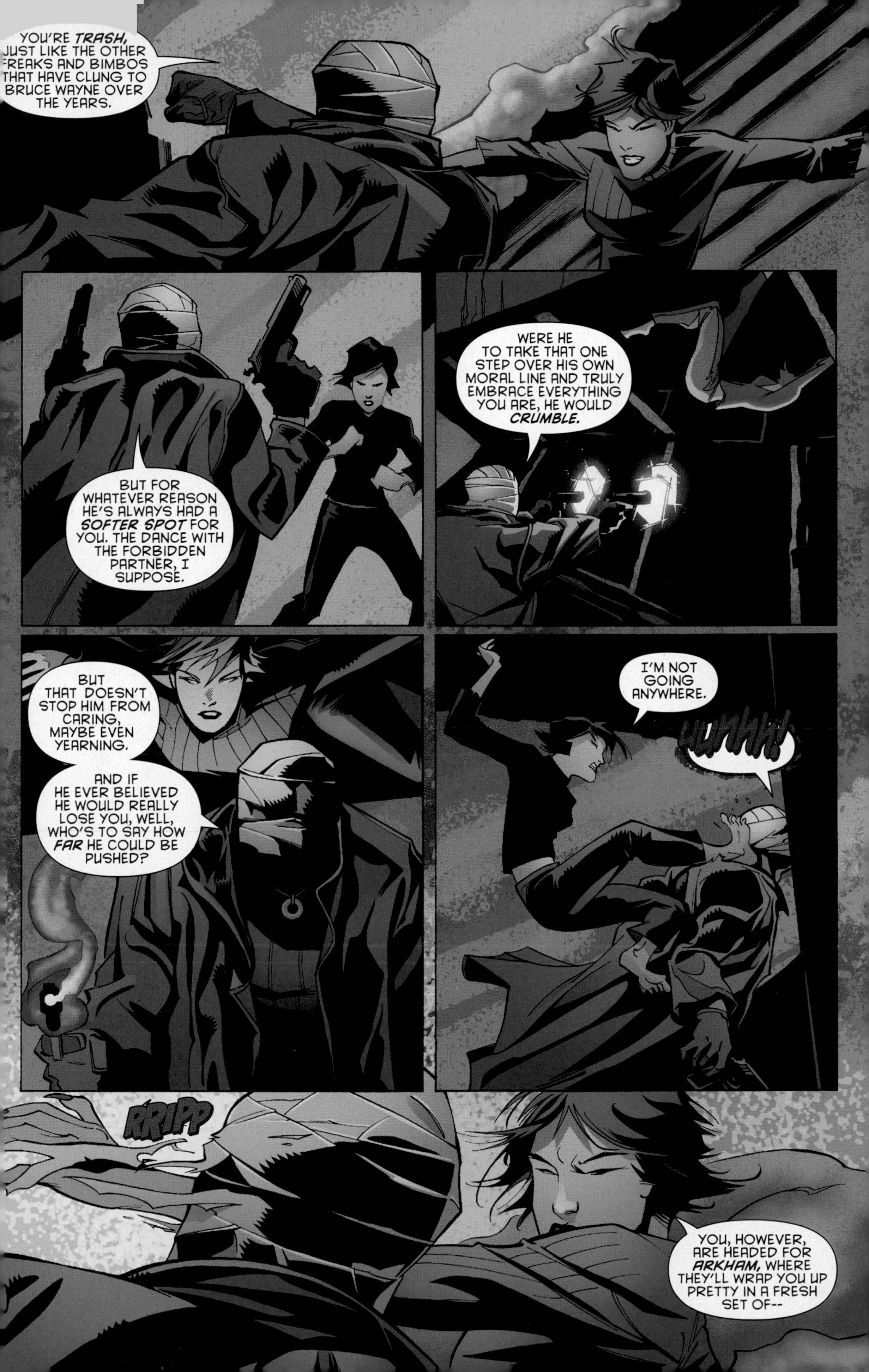
YOU'RE TRASH, JUST LIKE THE OTHER FREAKS AND BIMBOS THAT HAVE CLUNG TO BRUCE WAYNE OVER THE YEARS.
BUT FOR WHATEVER REASON HE'S ALWAYS HAD A SOFTER SPOT FOR YOU. THE DANCE WITH THE FORBIDDEN PARTNER, I SUPPOSE.
WERE HE TO TAKE THAT ONE STEP OVER HIS OWN MORAL LINE AND TRULY EMBRACE EVERYTHING YOU ARE, HE WOULD CRUMBLE.
BUT THAT DOESN'T STOP HIM FROM CARING, MAYBE EVEN YEARNING.
AND IF HE EVER BELIEVED HE WOULD REALLY LOSE YOU, WELL, WHO'S TO SAY HOW FAR HE COULD BE PUSHED?
I'M NOT GOING ANYWHERE.
UUNHH!
RRIPP
YOU, HOWEVER, ARE HEADED FOR ARKHAM, WHERE THEY'LL WRAP YOU UP PRETTY IN A FRESH SET OF--

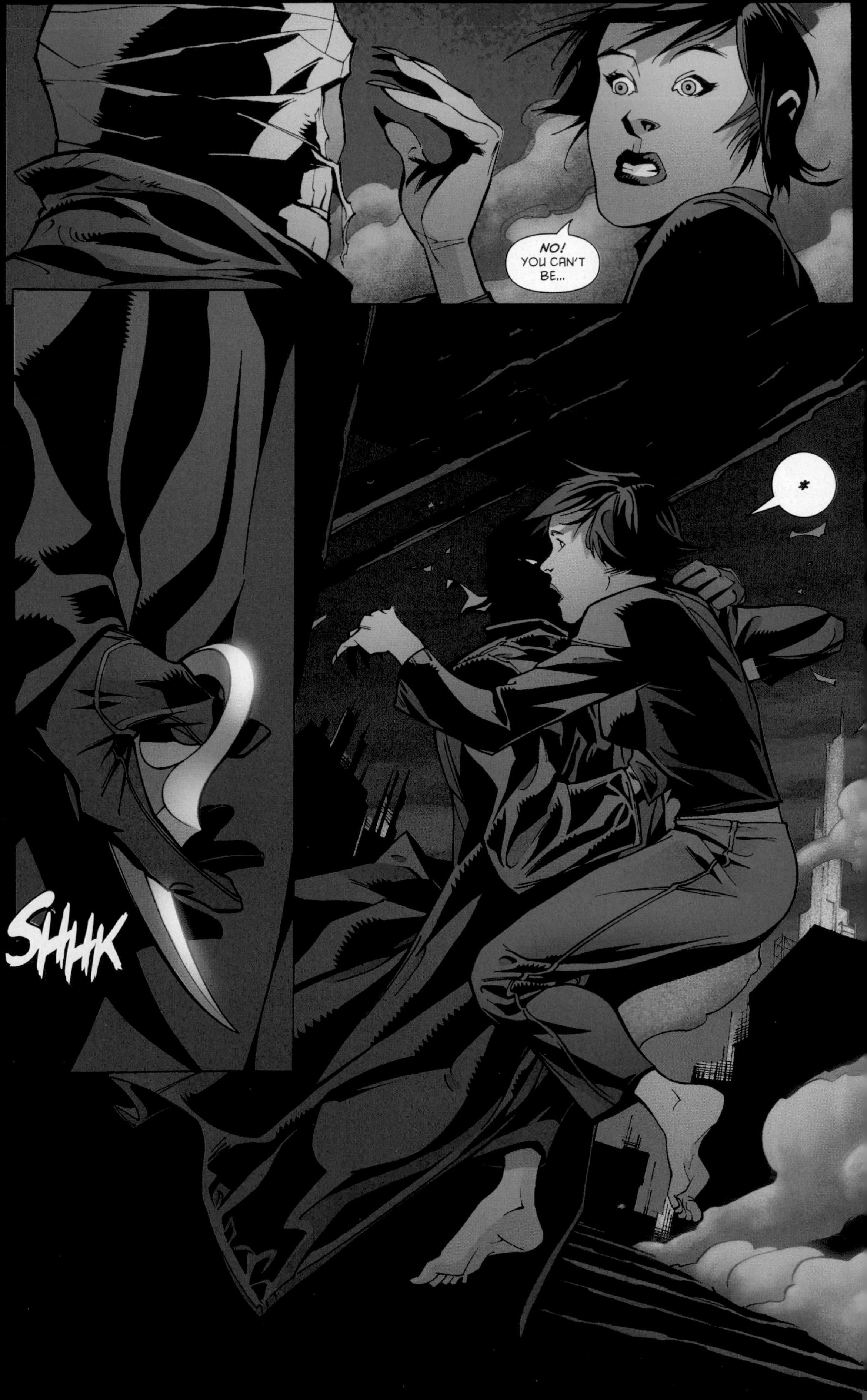
NO! YOU CAN'T BE...
*
SHHK

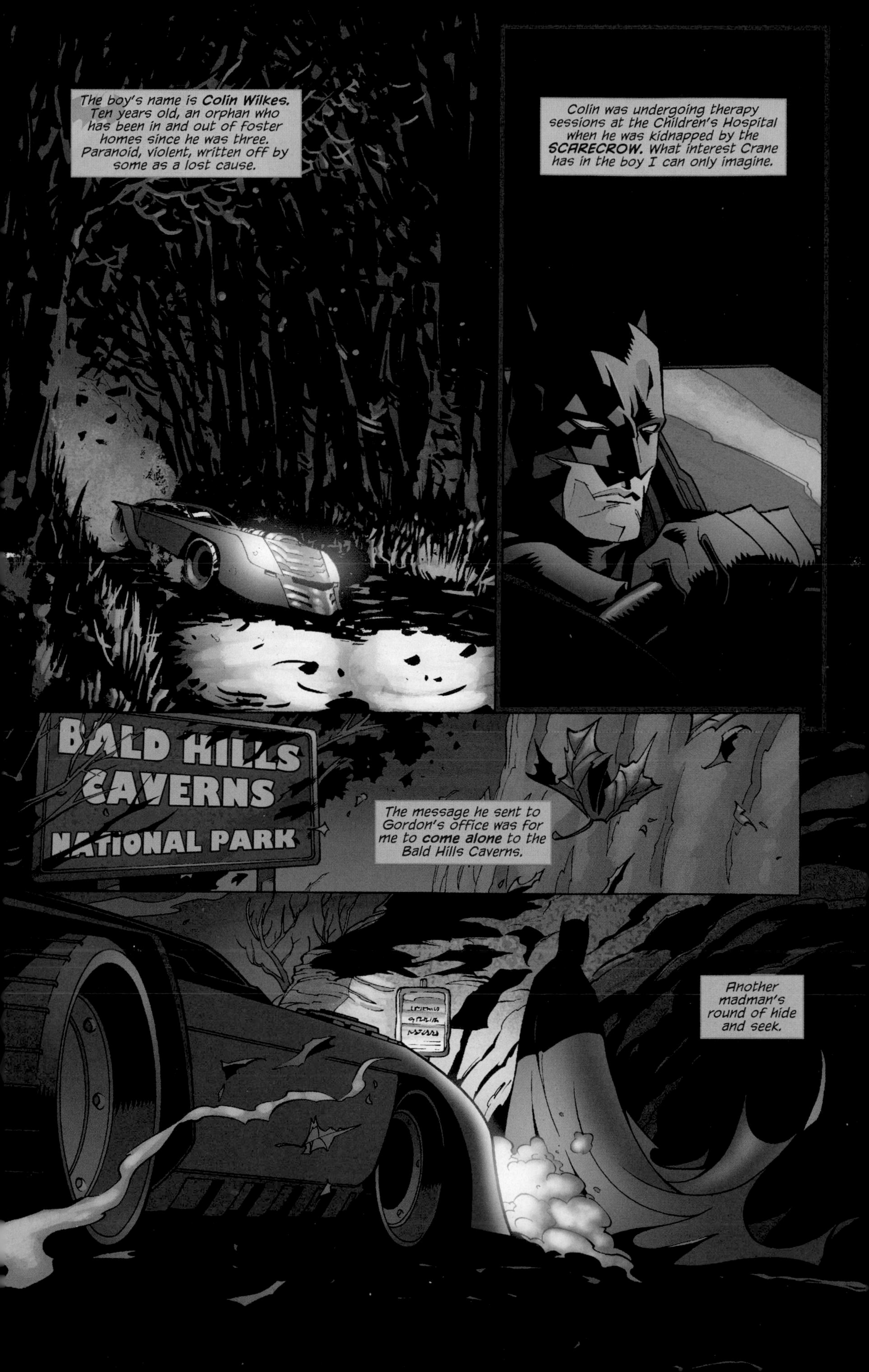
The boy's name is **Colin Wilkes.** Ten years old, an orphan who has been in and out of foster homes since he was three. Paranoid, violent, written off by some as a lost cause.
Colin was undergoing therapy sessions at the Children's Hospital when he was kidnapped by the **SCARECROW.** What interest Crane has in the boy I can only imagine.
BALD HILLS CAVERNS NATIONAL PARK
The message he sent to Gordon's office was for me to **come alone** to the Bald Hills Caverns.
Another madman's round of hide and seek.

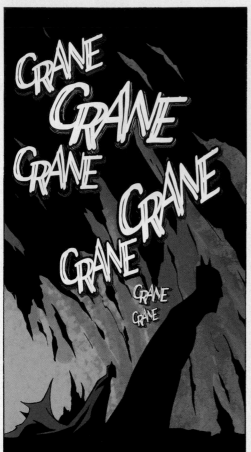

CRANE CRANE
CRANE CRANE
CRANE CRANE
CRANE CRANE
CRANE
CRANE

NO NEED TO *SHOUT,* BATMAN. YOU KNOW I'M HERE.

WHERE'S THE *BOY?*

TUCKED AWAY SAFELY IN A NEARBY CRAWLSPACE. THE POOR FELLOW--HE'S QUITE *CLAUSTROPHOBIC.*

HE'S A BALL OF NEUROSES, REALLY. FEAR OF STRANGERS, ABANDONMENT ISSUES, PRONE TO LASH OUT *VIOLENTLY* WHEN SCARED...

...THE POOR DEAR REALLY SHOULD BE *LOBOTOMIZED.*

ONLY ONE HAVING HIS HEAD RIPPED OPEN TONIGHT WILL BE *YOU.*

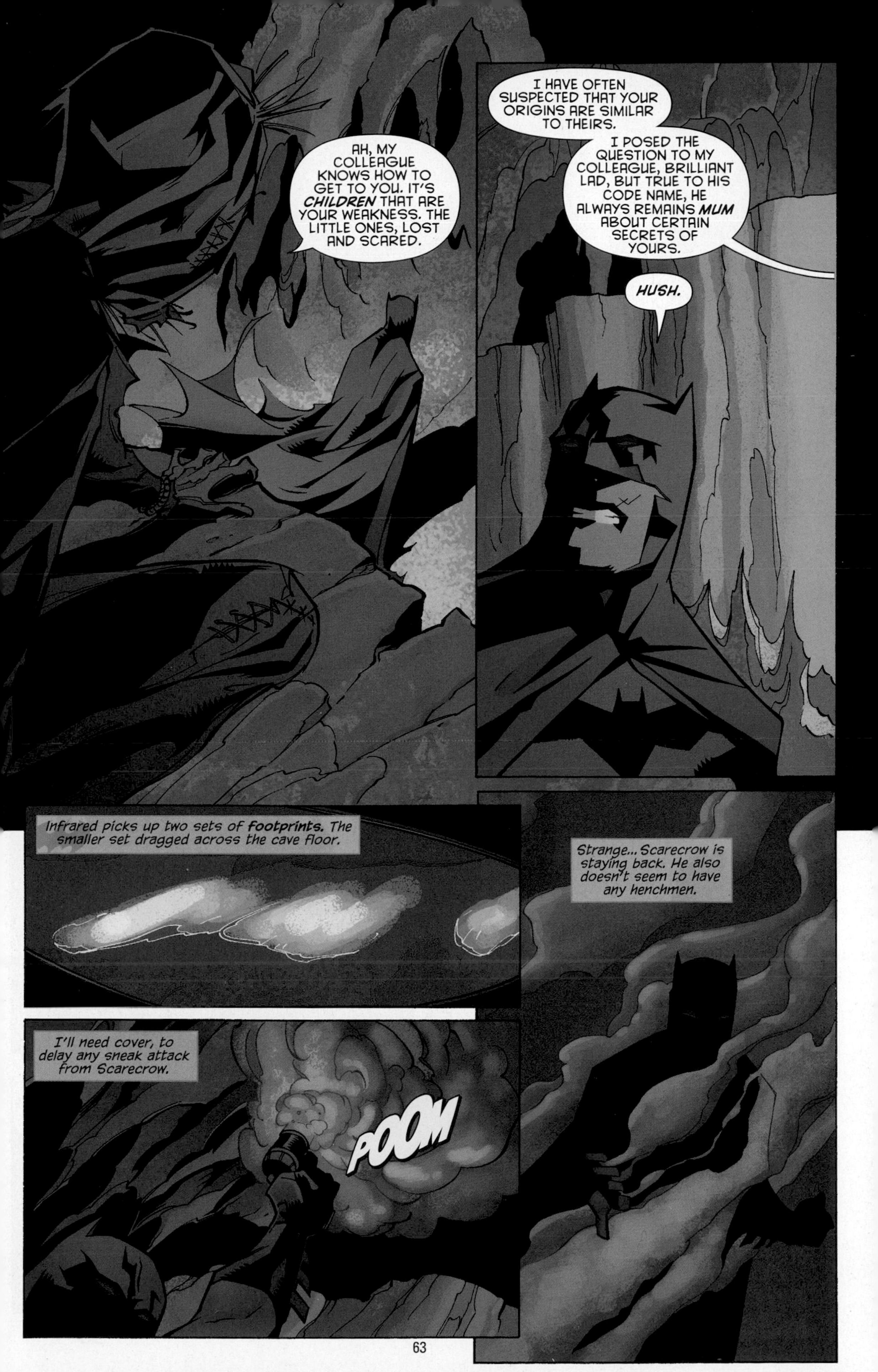
AH, MY COLLEAGUE KNOWS HOW TO GET TO YOU. IT'S **CHILDREN** THAT ARE YOUR WEAKNESS. THE LITTLE ONES, LOST AND SCARED.
I HAVE OFTEN SUSPECTED THAT YOUR ORIGINS ARE SIMILAR TO THEIRS.
I POSED THE QUESTION TO MY COLLEAGUE, BRILLIANT LAD, BUT TRUE TO HIS CODE NAME, HE ALWAYS REMAINS **MUM** ABOUT CERTAIN SECRETS OF YOURS.
HUSH.
*Infrared picks up two sets of **footprints.** The smaller set dragged across the cave floor.*
Strange... Scarecrow is staying back. He also doesn't seem to have any henchmen.
I'll need cover, to delay any sneak attack from Scarecrow.
POOM

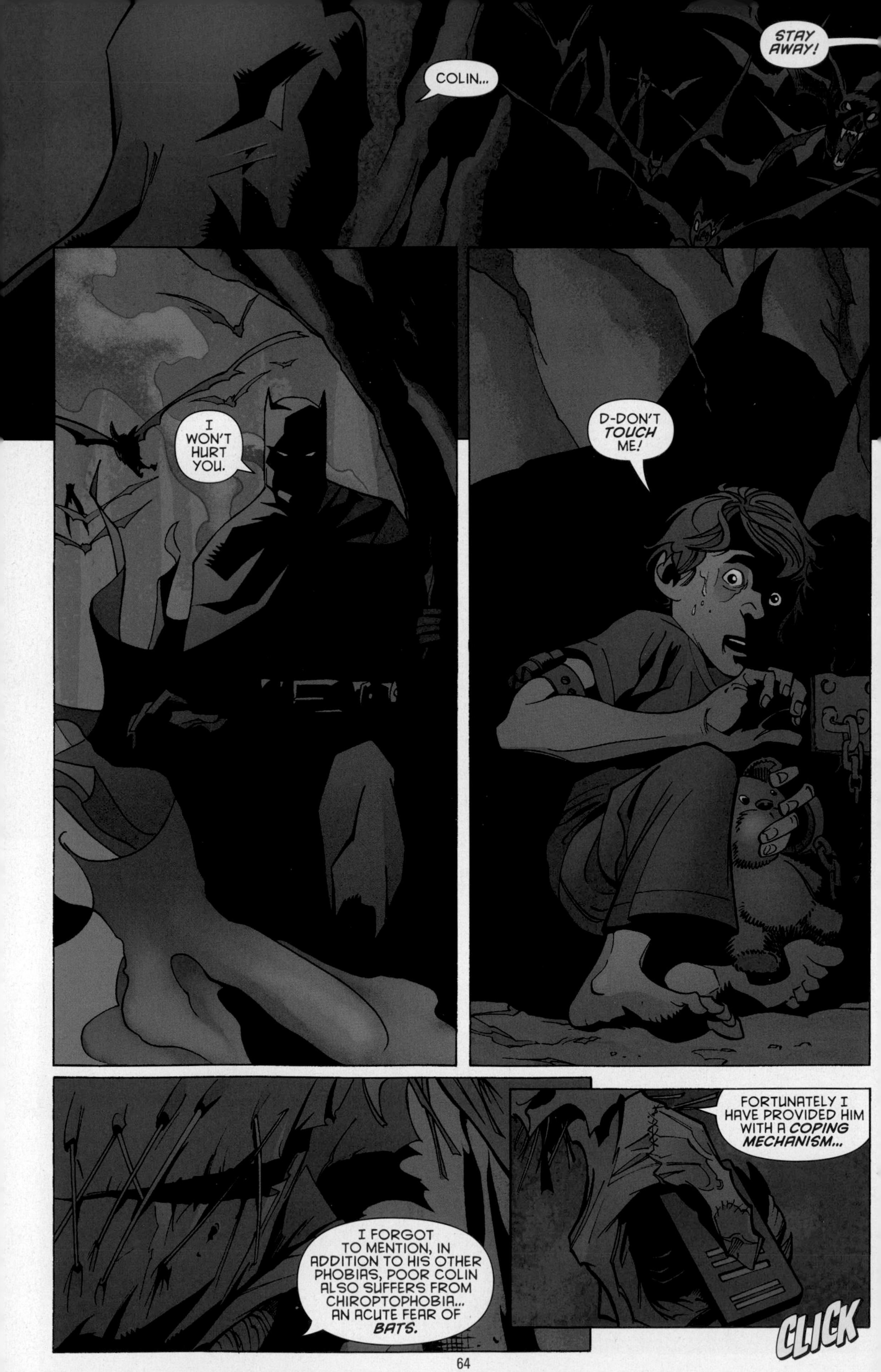
COLIN...
STAY AWAY!
I WON'T HURT YOU.
D-DON'T TOUCH ME!
I FORGOT TO MENTION, IN ADDITION TO HIS OTHER PHOBIAS, POOR COLIN ALSO SUFFERS FROM CHIROPTOPHOBIA... AN ACUTE FEAR OF BATS.
FORTUNATELY I HAVE PROVIDED HIM WITH A COPING MECHANISM...
CLICK

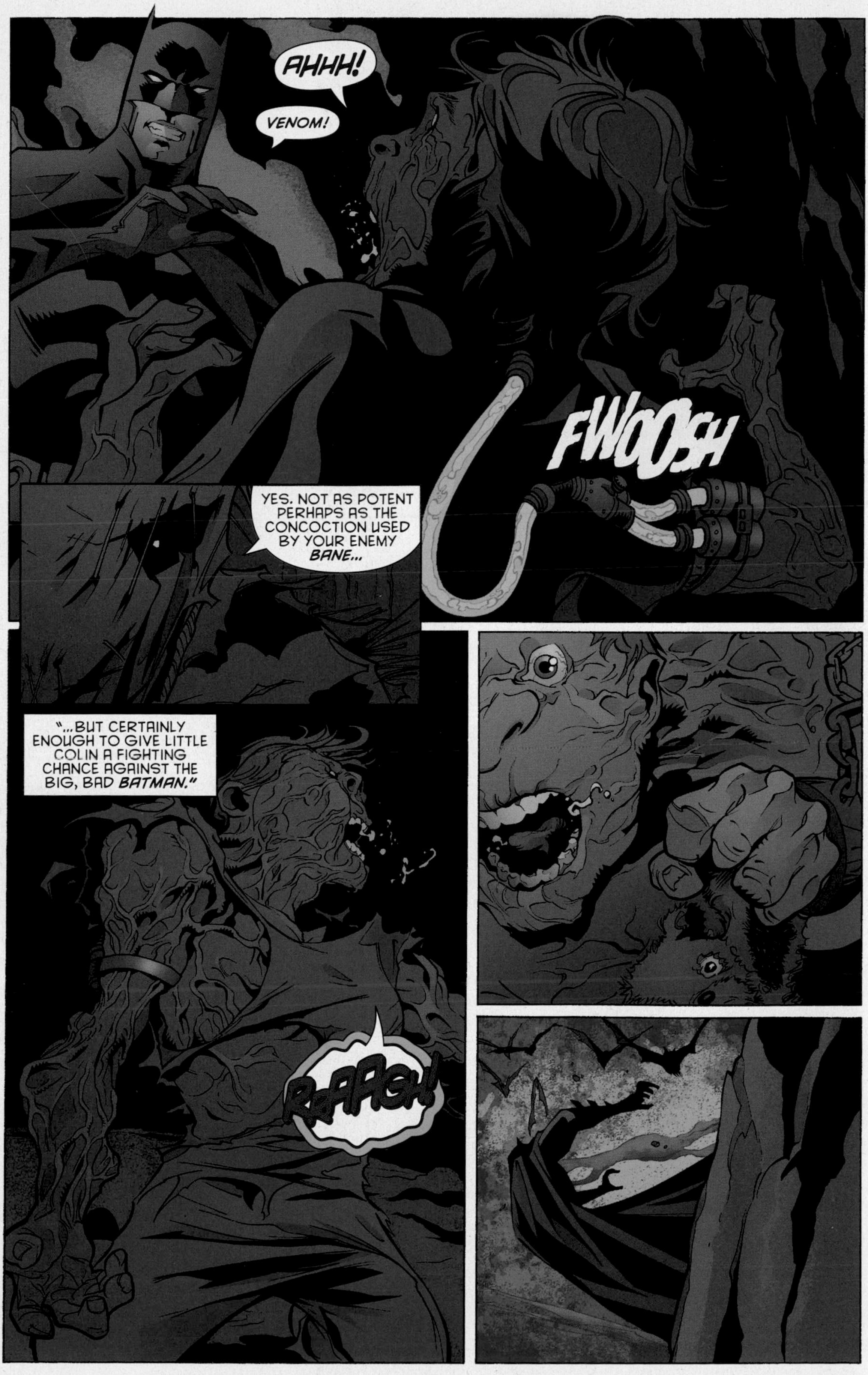
AHHH!
VENOM!
FWOOSH
YES. NOT AS POTENT PERHAPS AS THE CONCOCTION USED BY YOUR ENEMY BANE...
"...BUT CERTAINLY ENOUGH TO GIVE LITTLE COLIN A FIGHTING CHANCE AGAINST THE BIG, BAD BATMAN."
RAAGH!

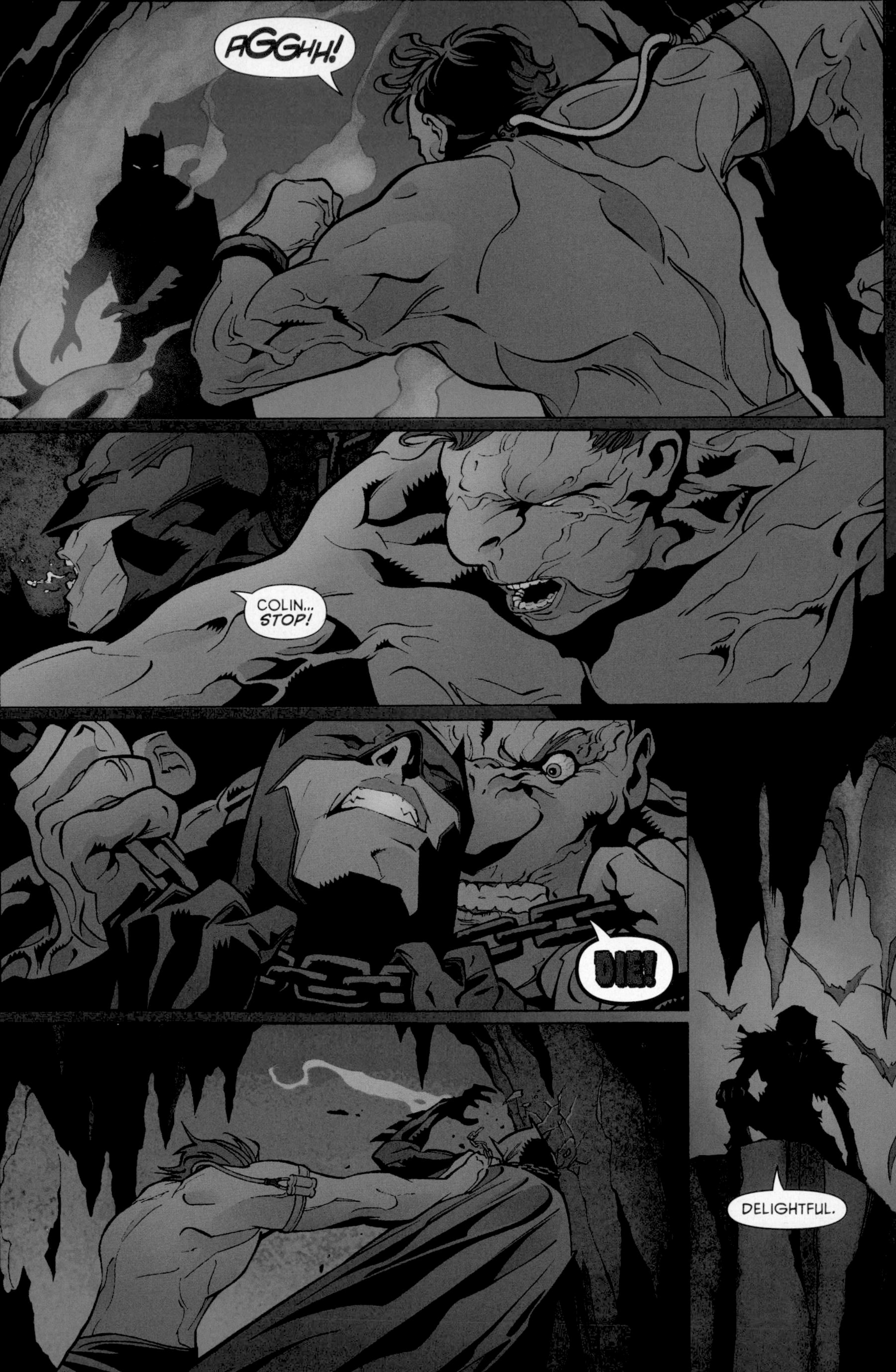
AGGHH!
COLIN... STOP!
DIE!
DELIGHTFUL.

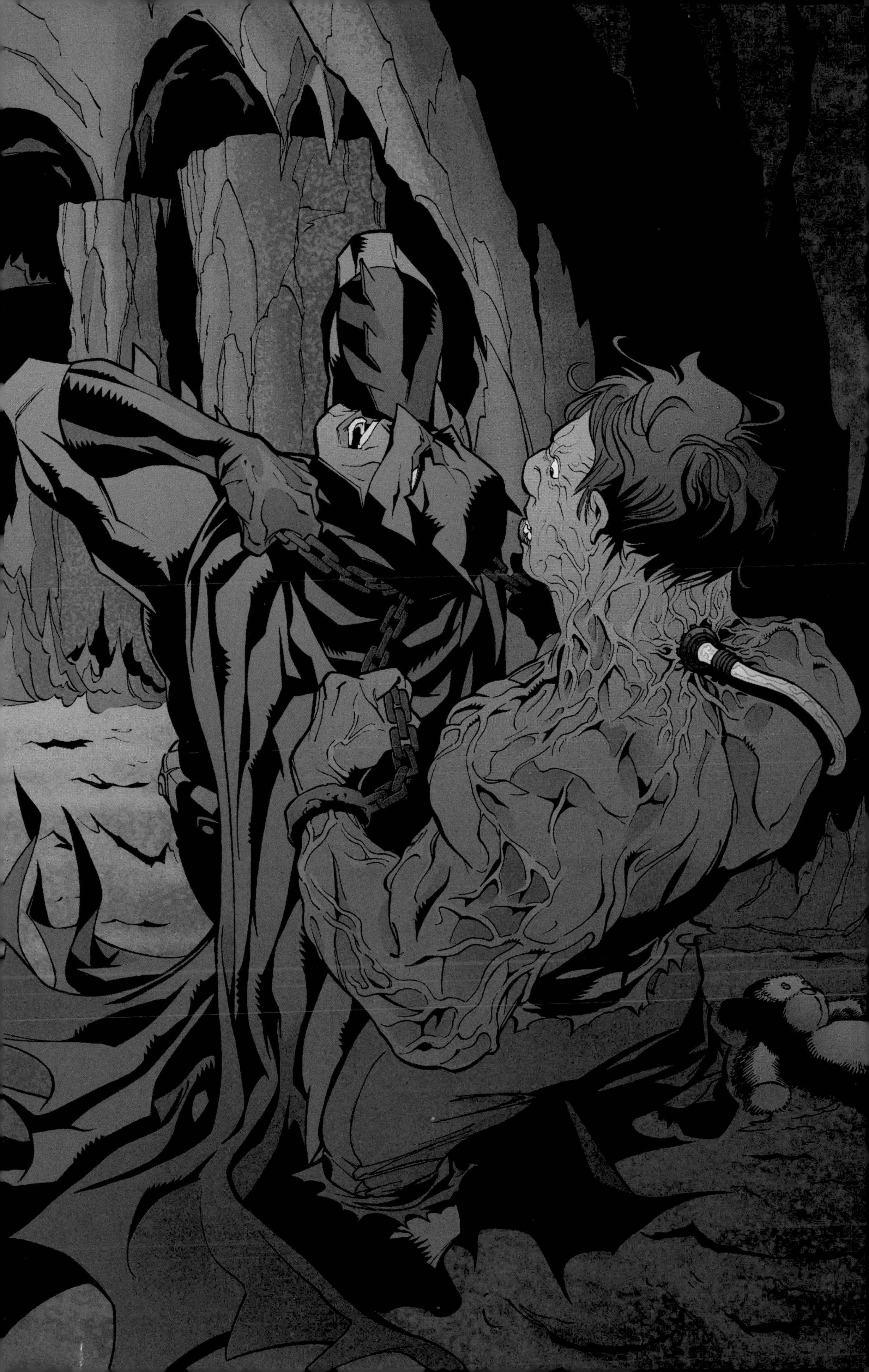

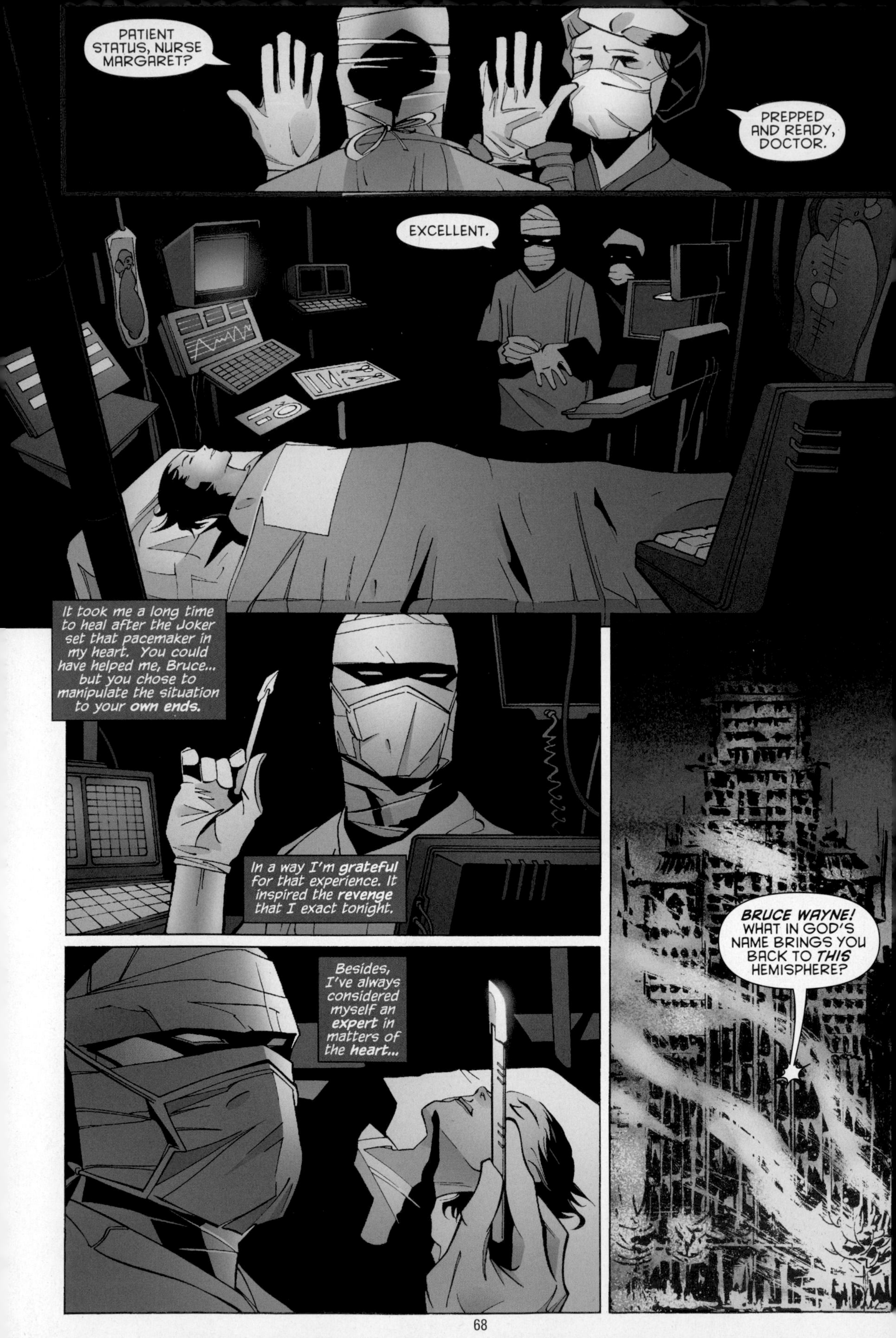
PATIENT STATUS, NURSE MARGARET?
PREPPED AND READY, DOCTOR.
EXCELLENT.
It took me a long time to heal after the Joker set that pacemaker in my heart. You could have helped me, Bruce... but you chose to manipulate the situation to your own ends.
In a way I'm grateful for that experience. It inspired the revenge that I exact tonight.
Besides, I've always considered myself an expert in matters of the heart...
BRUCE WAYNE! WHAT IN GOD'S NAME BRINGS YOU BACK TO THIS HEMISPHERE?

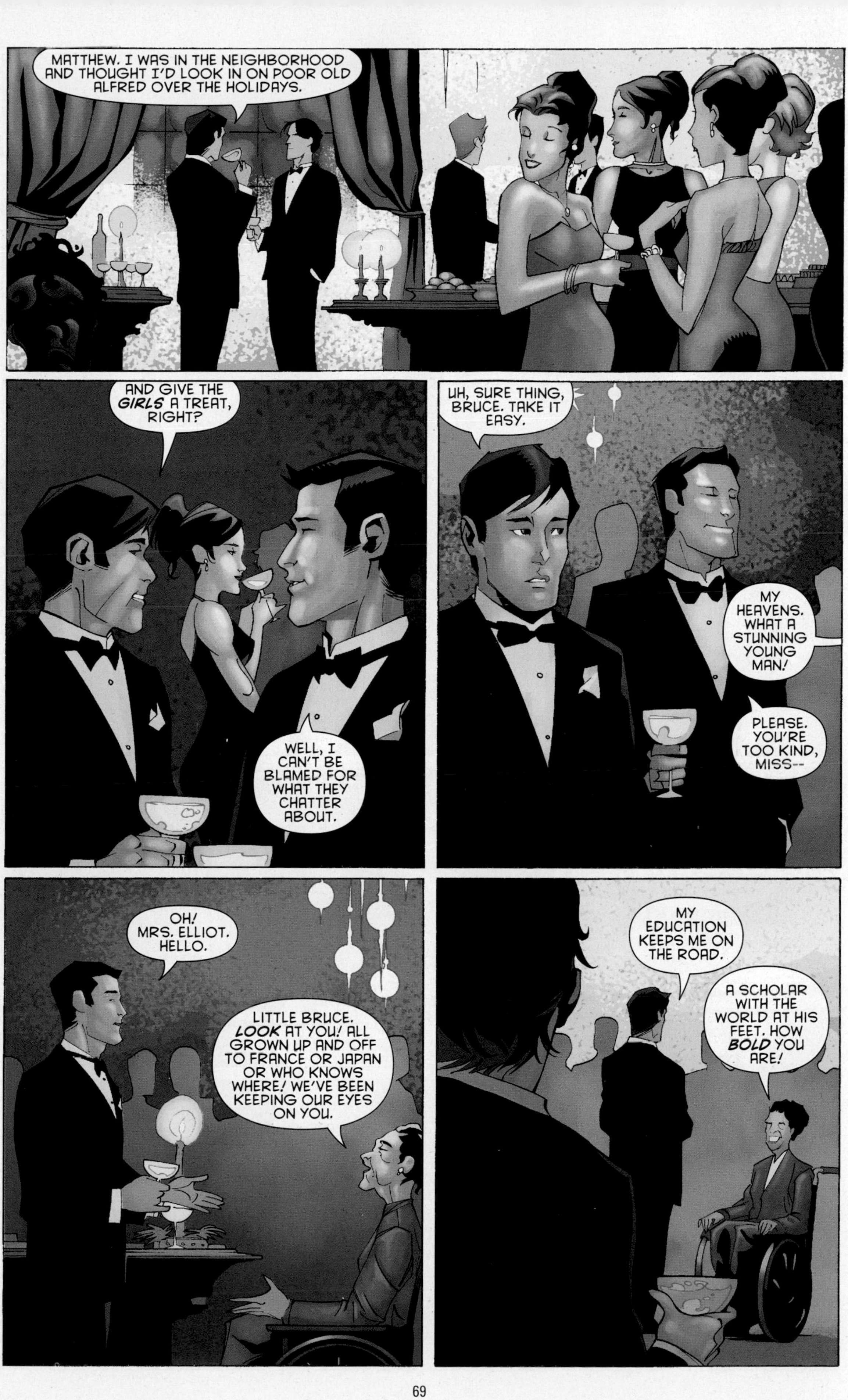
MATTHEW. I WAS IN THE NEIGHBORHOOD AND THOUGHT I'D LOOK IN ON POOR OLD ALFRED OVER THE HOLIDAYS.
AND GIVE THE GIRLS A TREAT, RIGHT?
WELL, I CAN'T BE BLAMED FOR WHAT THEY CHATTER ABOUT.
UH, SURE THING, BRUCE. TAKE IT EASY.
MY HEAVENS. WHAT A STUNNING YOUNG MAN!
PLEASE. YOU'RE TOO KIND, MISS--
OH! MRS. ELLIOT. HELLO.
LITTLE BRUCE. LOOK AT YOU! ALL GROWN UP AND OFF TO FRANCE OR JAPAN OR WHO KNOWS WHERE! WE'VE BEEN KEEPING OUR EYES ON YOU.
MY EDUCATION KEEPS ME ON THE ROAD.
A SCHOLAR WITH THE WORLD AT HIS FEET. HOW BOLD YOU ARE!

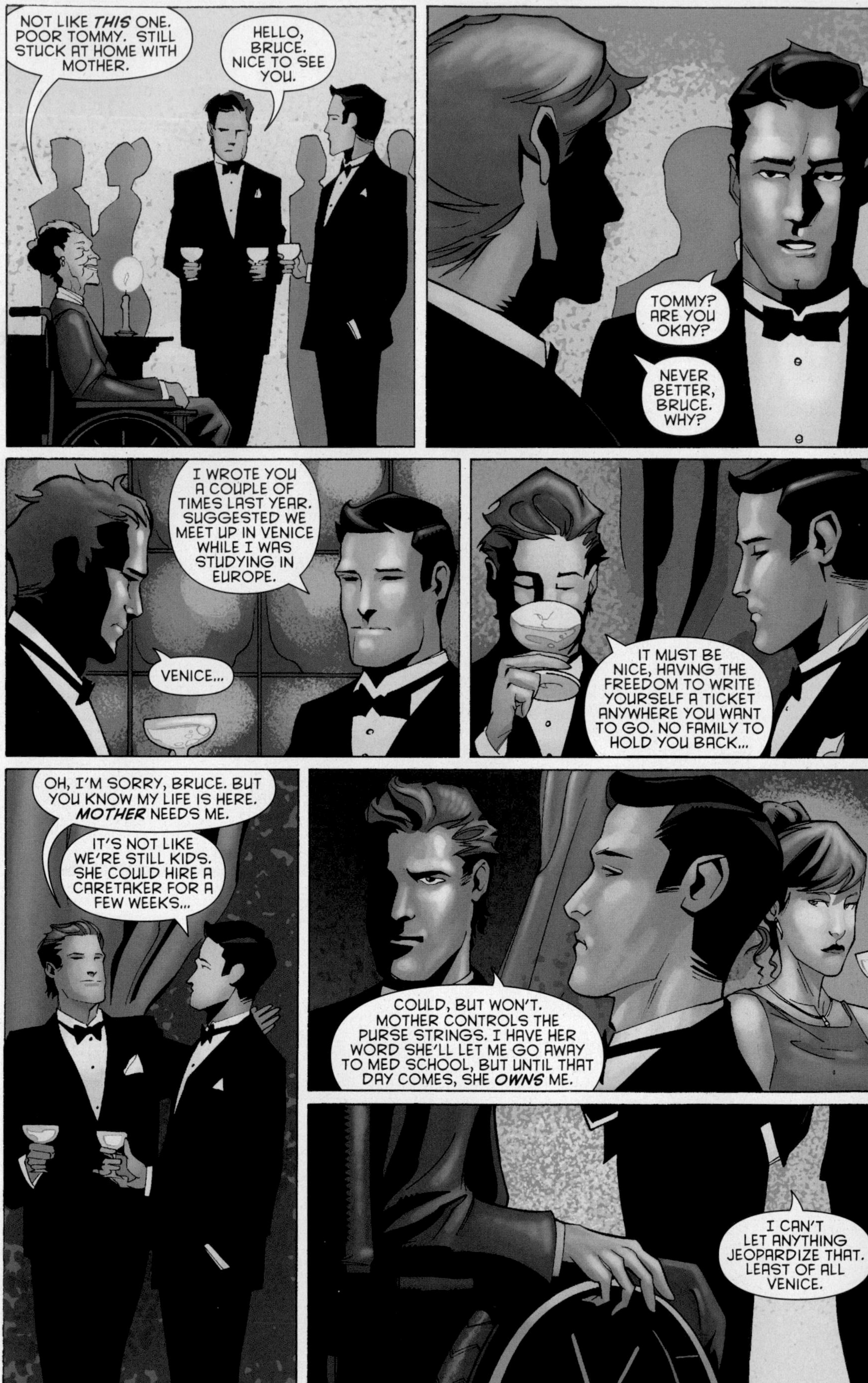

NOT LIKE *THIS* ONE. POOR TOMMY. STILL STUCK AT HOME WITH MOTHER.
HELLO, BRUCE. NICE TO SEE YOU.
TOMMY? ARE YOU OKAY?
NEVER BETTER, BRUCE. WHY?
I WROTE YOU A COUPLE OF TIMES LAST YEAR. SUGGESTED WE MEET UP IN VENICE WHILE I WAS STUDYING IN EUROPE.
VENICE...
IT MUST BE NICE, HAVING THE FREEDOM TO WRITE YOURSELF A TICKET ANYWHERE YOU WANT TO GO. NO FAMILY TO HOLD YOU BACK...
OH, I'M SORRY, BRUCE. BUT YOU KNOW MY LIFE IS HERE. *MOTHER* NEEDS ME.
IT'S NOT LIKE WE'RE STILL KIDS. SHE COULD HIRE A CARETAKER FOR A FEW WEEKS...
COULD, BUT WON'T. MOTHER CONTROLS THE PURSE STRINGS. I HAVE HER WORD SHE'LL LET ME GO AWAY TO MED SCHOOL, BUT UNTIL THAT DAY COMES, SHE *OWNS* ME.
I CAN'T LET ANYTHING JEOPARDIZE THAT. LEAST OF ALL VENICE.

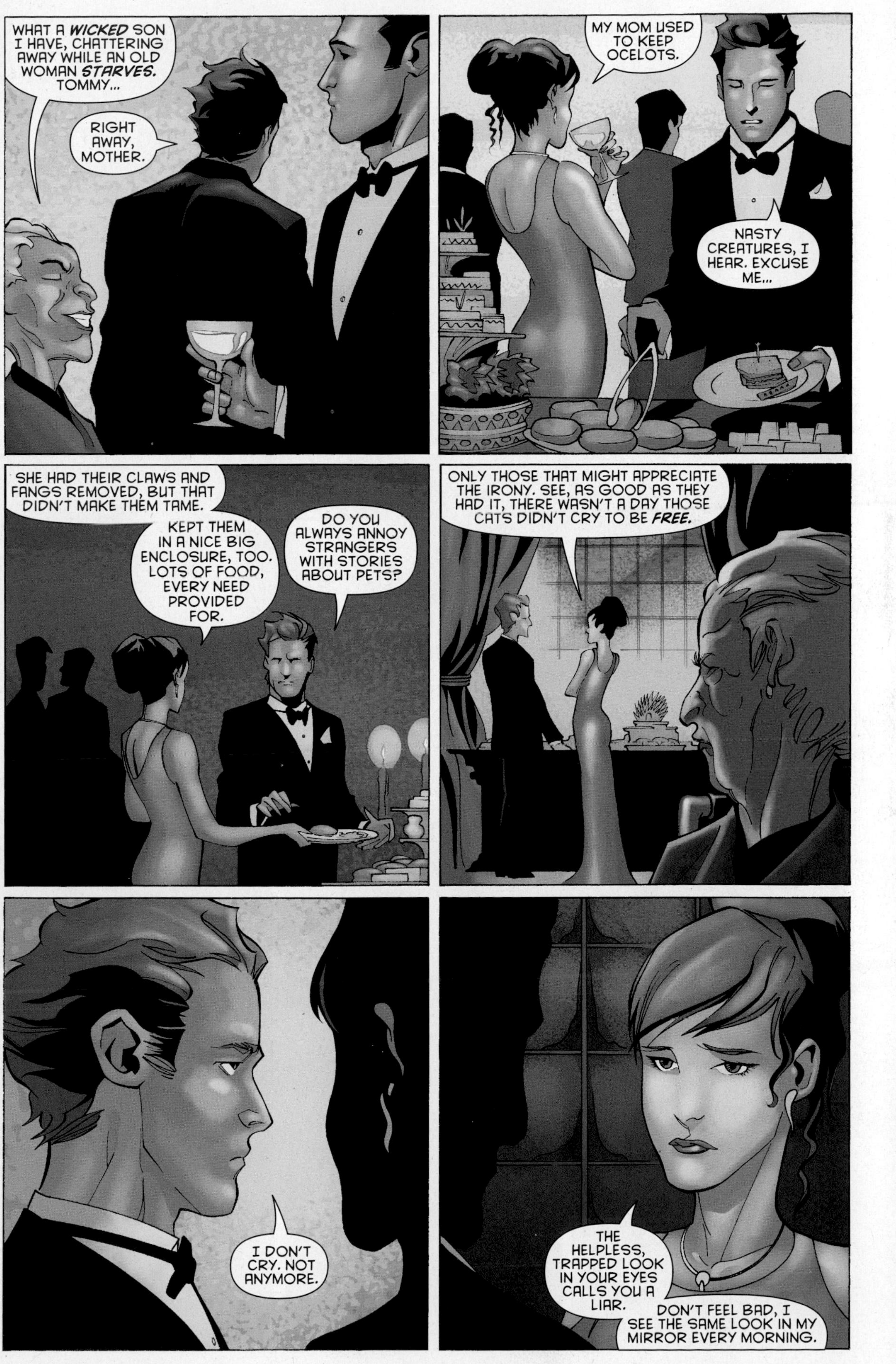

WHAT A *WICKED* SON I HAVE, CHATTERING AWAY WHILE AN OLD WOMAN *STARVES.* TOMMY...
RIGHT AWAY, MOTHER.
MY MOM USED TO KEEP OCELOTS.
NASTY CREATURES, I HEAR. EXCUSE ME...
SHE HAD THEIR CLAWS AND FANGS REMOVED, BUT THAT DIDN'T MAKE THEM TAME.
KEPT THEM IN A NICE BIG ENCLOSURE, TOO. LOTS OF FOOD, EVERY NEED PROVIDED FOR.
DO YOU ALWAYS ANNOY STRANGERS WITH STORIES ABOUT PETS?
ONLY THOSE THAT MIGHT APPRECIATE THE IRONY. SEE, AS GOOD AS THEY HAD IT, THERE WASN'T A DAY THOSE CATS DIDN'T CRY TO BE *FREE.*
I DON'T CRY. NOT ANYMORE.
THE HELPLESS, TRAPPED LOOK IN YOUR EYES CALLS YOU A LIAR.
DON'T FEEL BAD, I SEE THE SAME LOOK IN MY MIRROR EVERY MORNING.

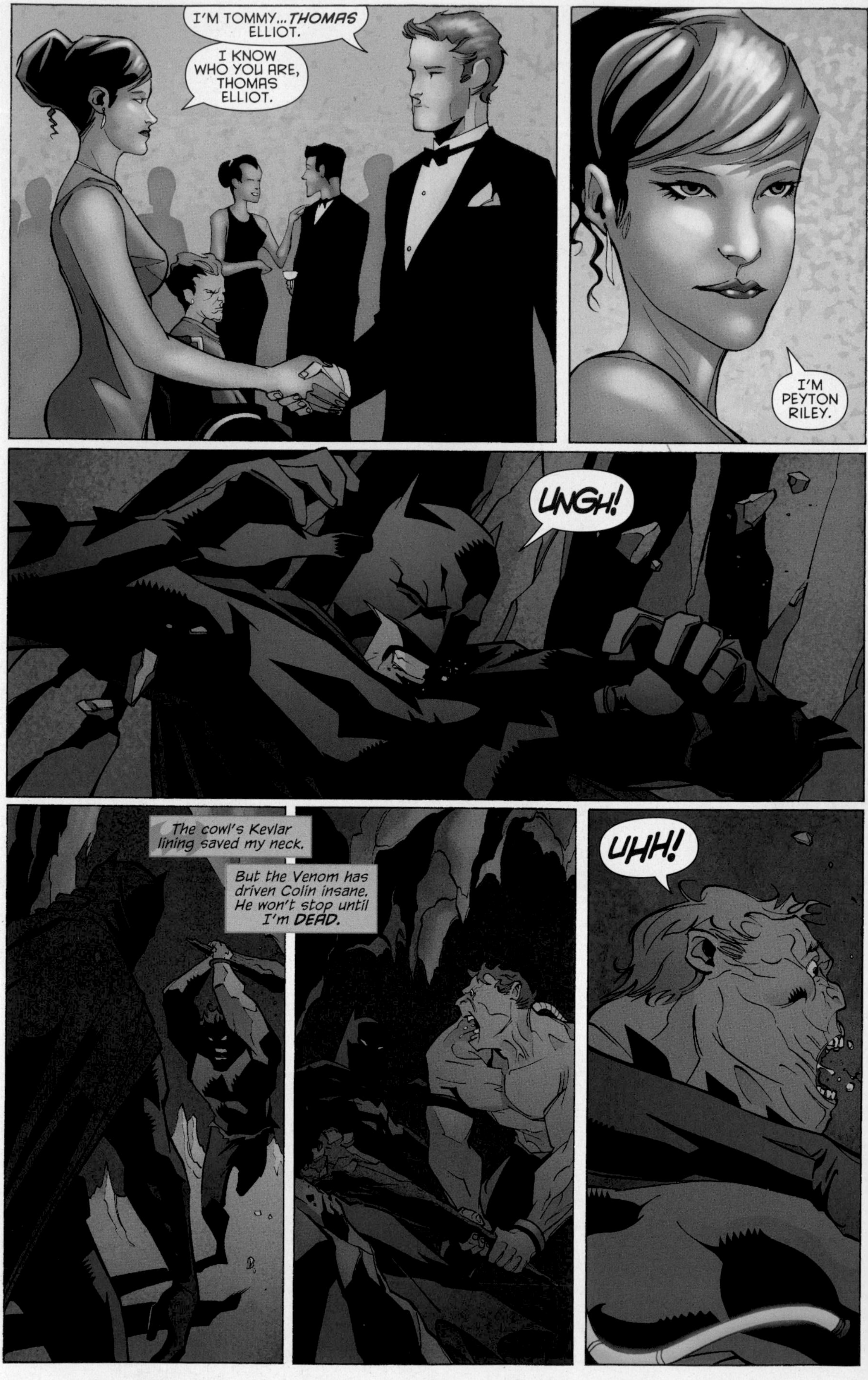
I'M TOMMY... *THOMAS* ELLIOT.
I KNOW WHO YOU ARE, THOMAS ELLIOT.
I'M PEYTON RILEY.
UNGH!
The cowl's Kevlar lining saved my neck.
But the Venom has driven Colin insane. He won't stop until I'm **DEAD.**
UHH!

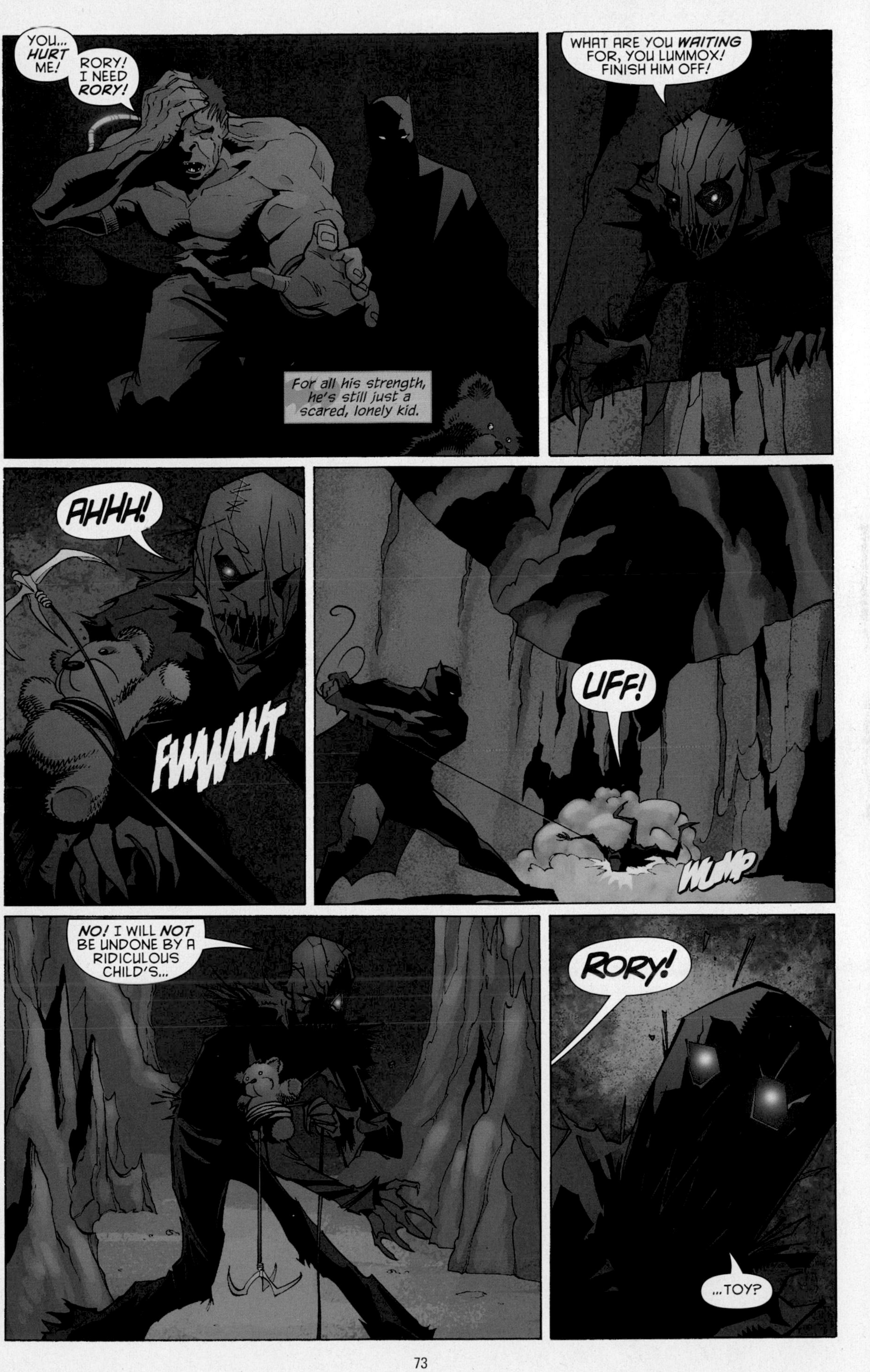
YOU... HURT ME!
RORY! I NEED RORY!
For all his strength, he's still just a scared, lonely kid.
WHAT ARE YOU WAITING FOR, YOU LUMMOX! FINISH HIM OFF!
AHHH!
FWWWT
UFF!
WUMP
NO! I WILL NOT BE UNDONE BY A RIDICULOUS CHILD'S...
RORY!
...TOY?

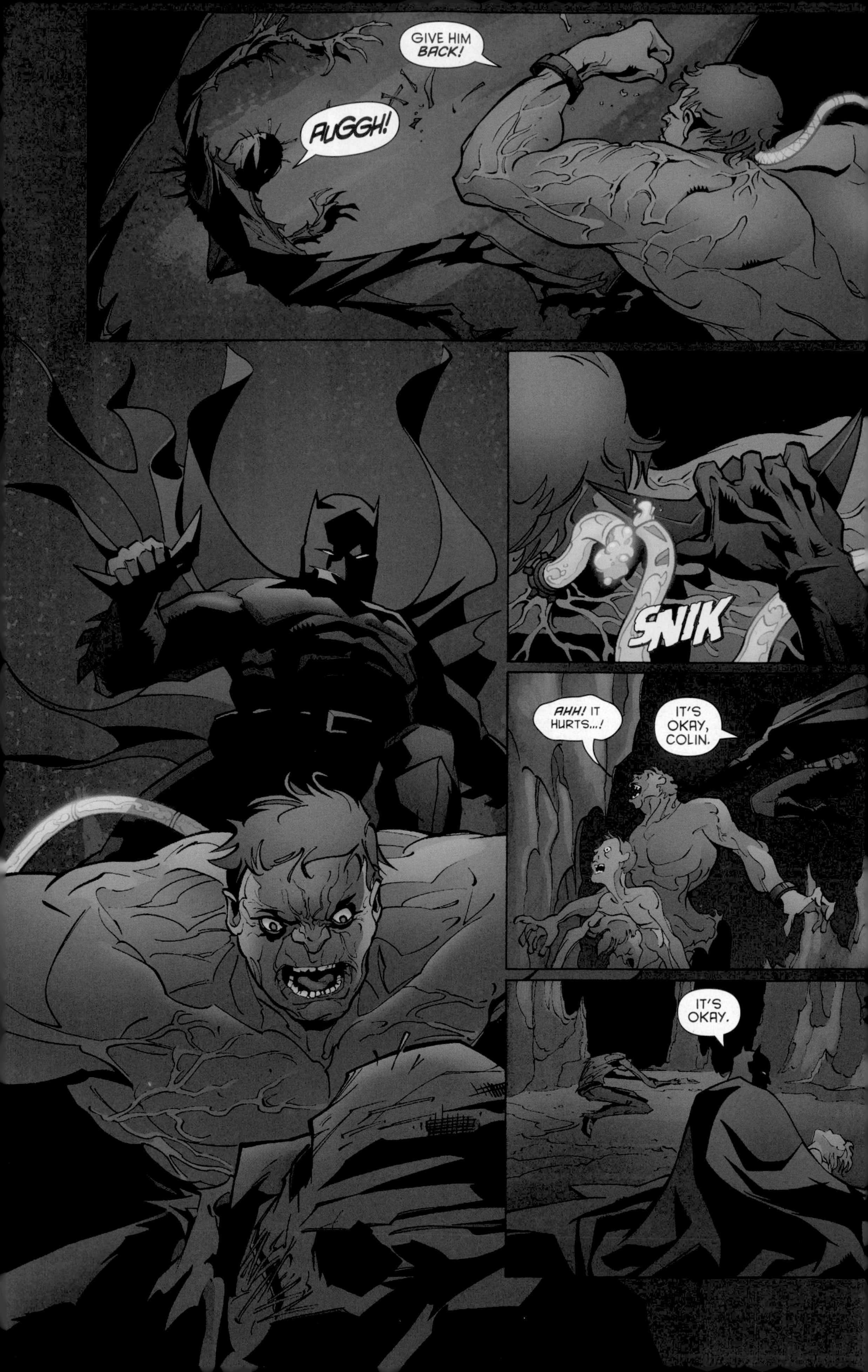
GIVE HIM BACK!
RUGGH!
SNIK
AHH! IT HURTS...!
IT'S OKAY, COLIN.
IT'S OKAY.

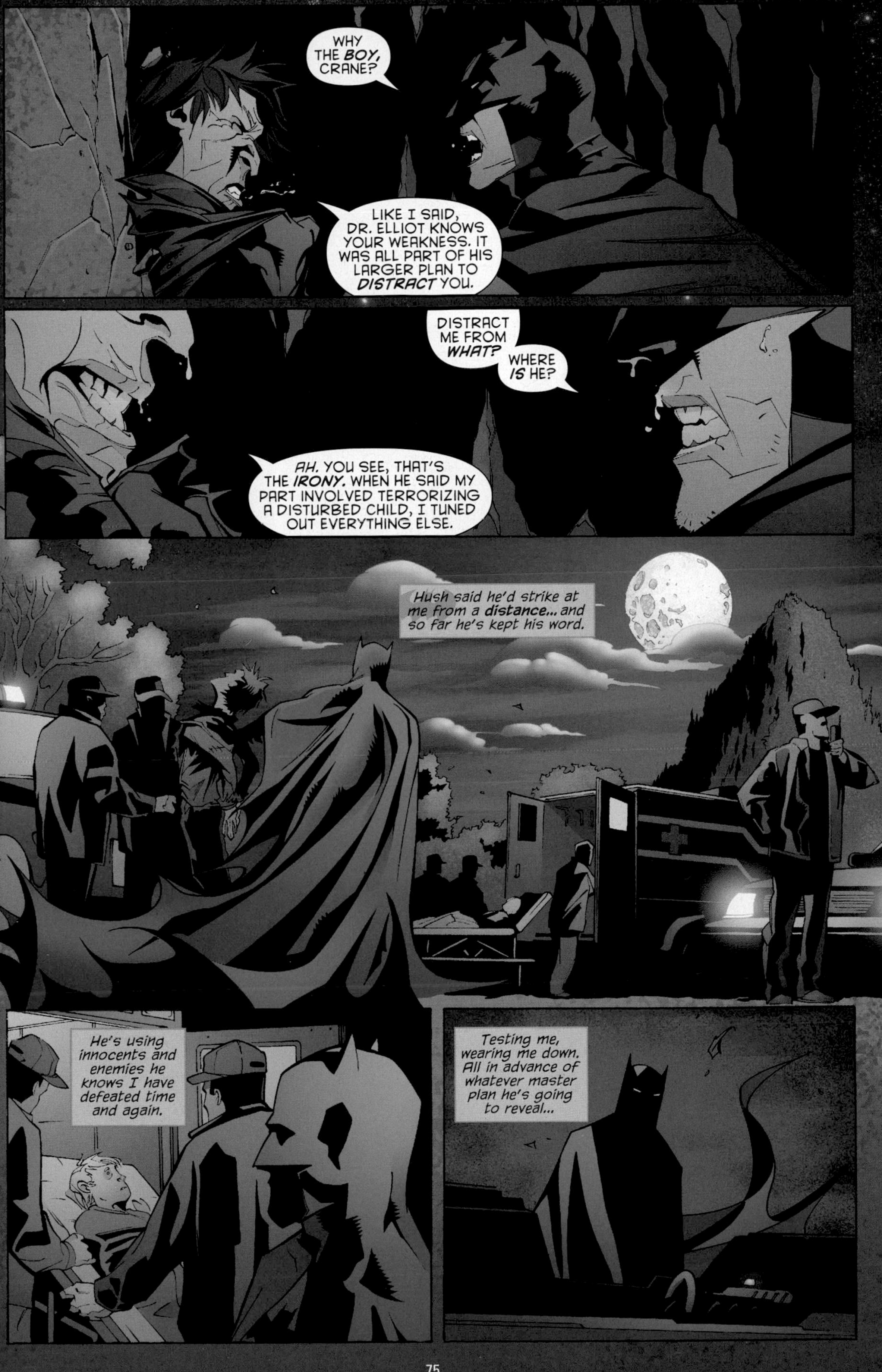
WHY THE BOY, CRANE?
LIKE I SAID, DR. ELLIOT KNOWS YOUR WEAKNESS. IT WAS ALL PART OF HIS LARGER PLAN TO DISTRACT YOU.
DISTRACT ME FROM WHAT?
WHERE IS HE?
AH. YOU SEE, THAT'S THE IRONY. WHEN HE SAID MY PART INVOLVED TERRORIZING A DISTURBED CHILD, I TUNED OUT EVERYTHING ELSE.
Hush said he'd strike at me from a distance... and so far he's kept his word.
He's using innocents and enemies he knows I have defeated time and again.
Testing me, wearing me down. All in advance of whatever master plan he's going to reveal...

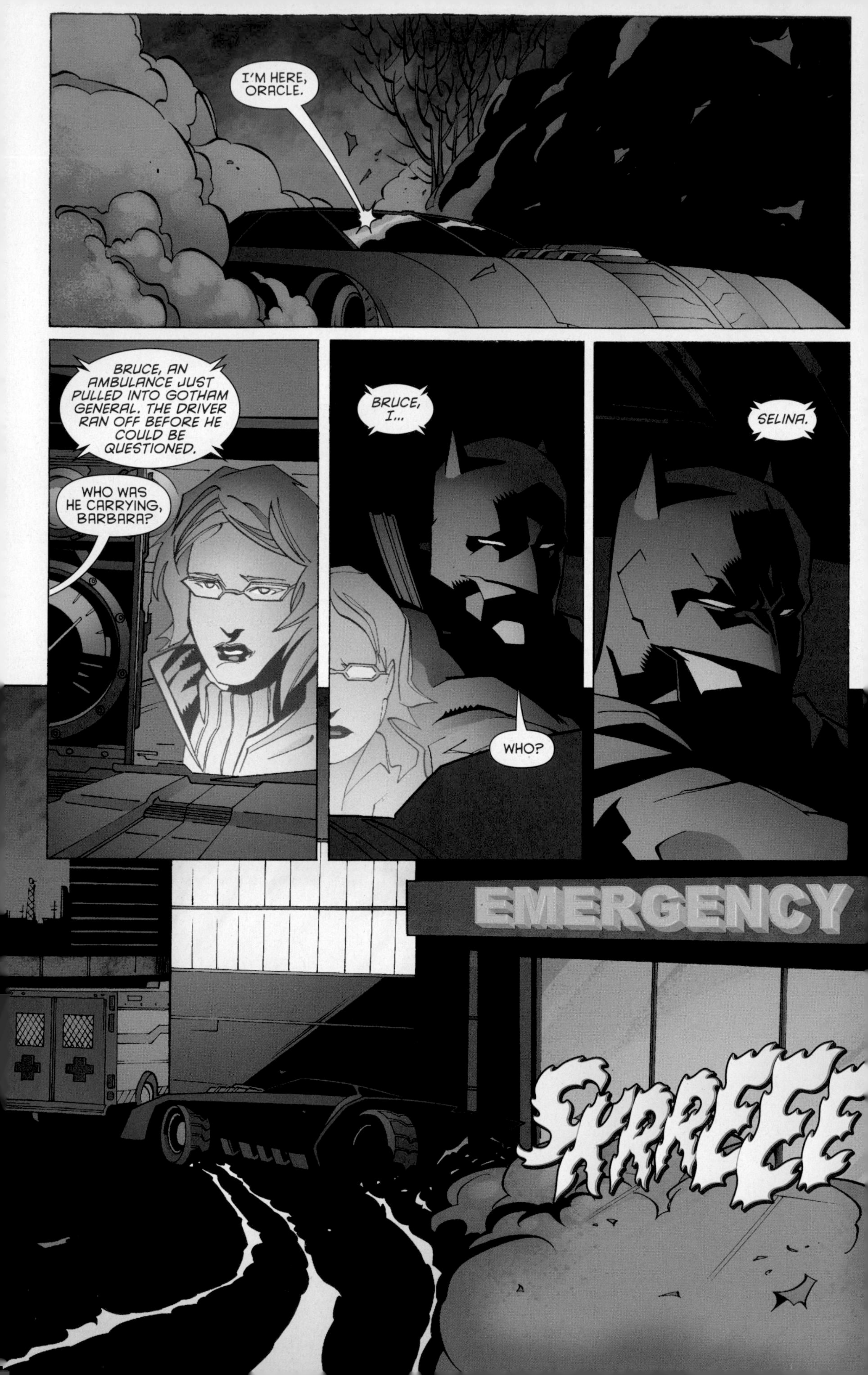
I'M HERE, ORACLE.
BRUCE, AN AMBULANCE JUST PULLED INTO GOTHAM GENERAL. THE DRIVER RAN OFF BEFORE HE COULD BE QUESTIONED.
WHO WAS HE CARRYING, BARBARA?
BRUCE, I...
WHO?
SELINA.
EMERGENCY
SKREEE

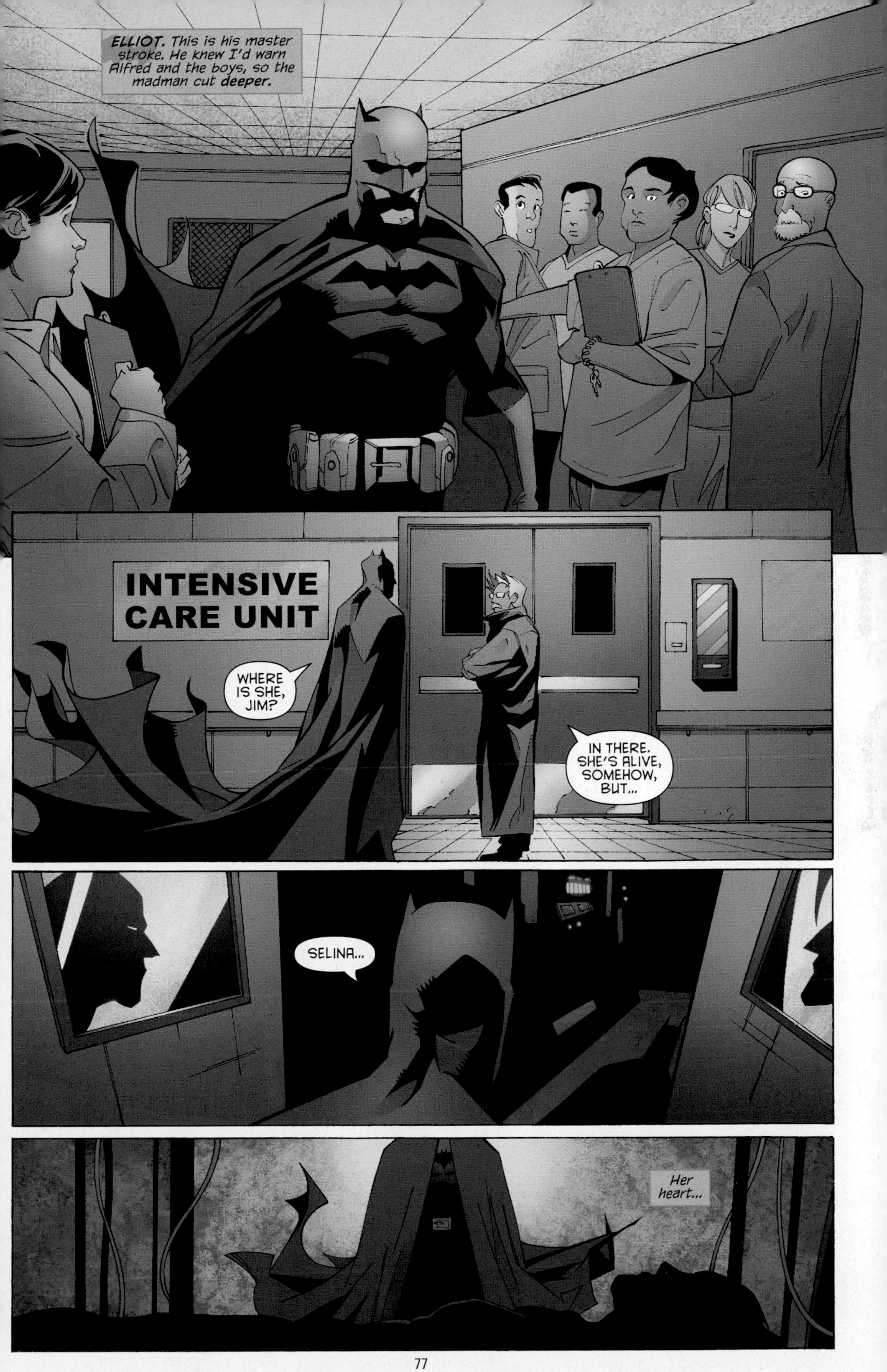
ELLIOT. This is his master stroke. He knew I'd warn Alfred and the boys, so the madman cut deeper.
INTENSIVE CARE UNIT
WHERE IS SHE, JIM?
IN THERE. SHE'S ALIVE, SOMEHOW, BUT...
SELINA...
Her heart...

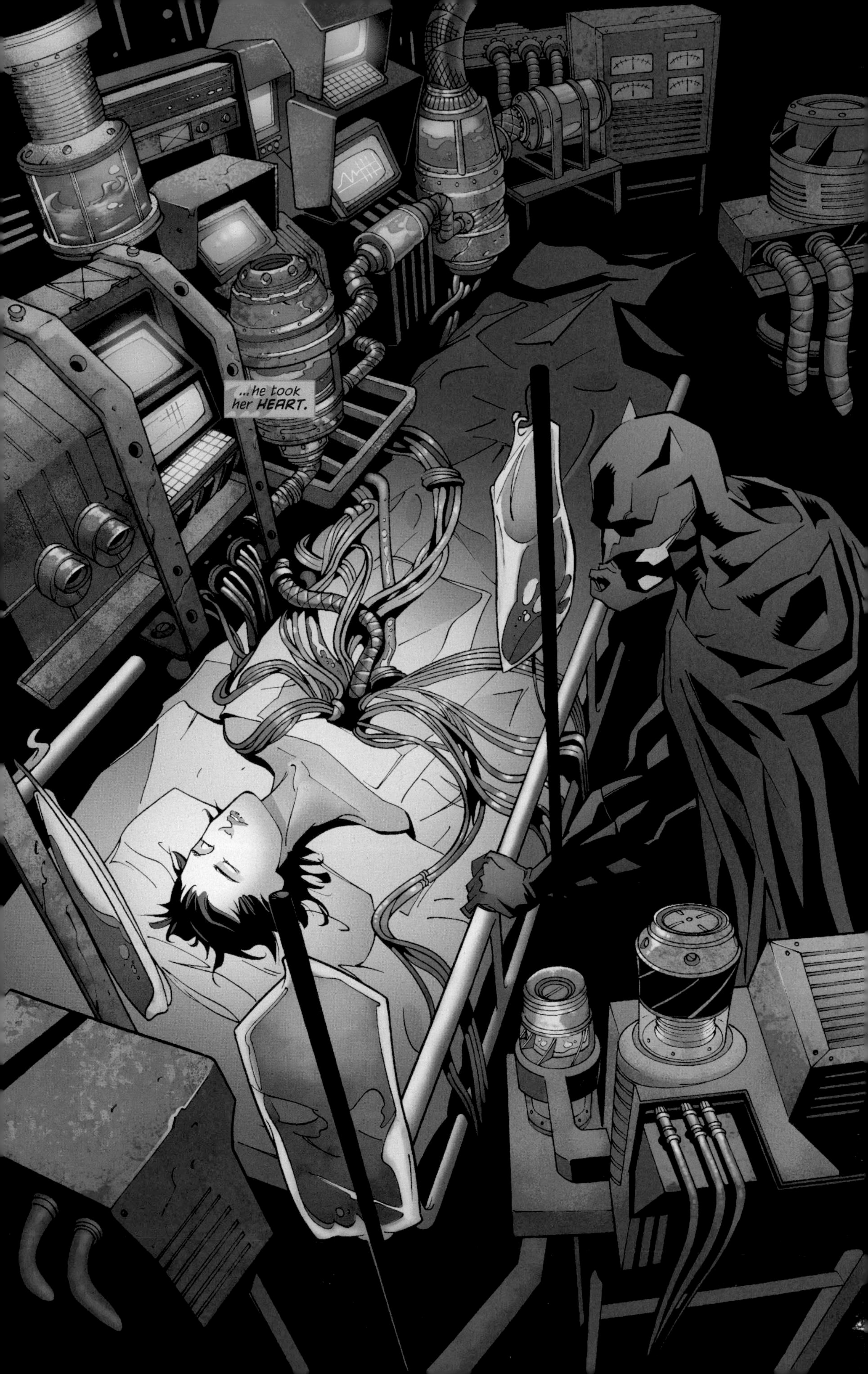
...he took her HEART.

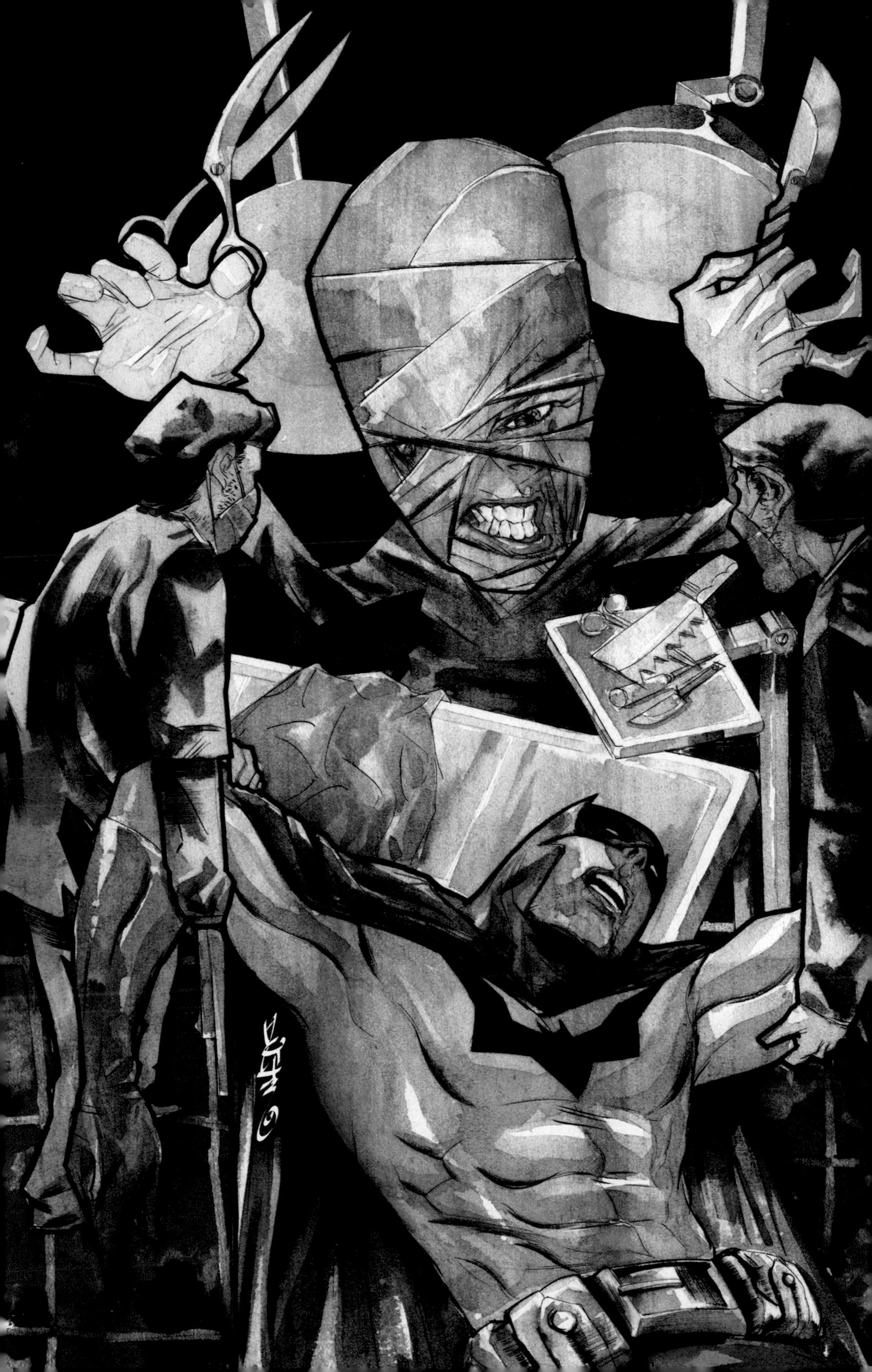

"Patience is bitter, but its fruit is sweet."

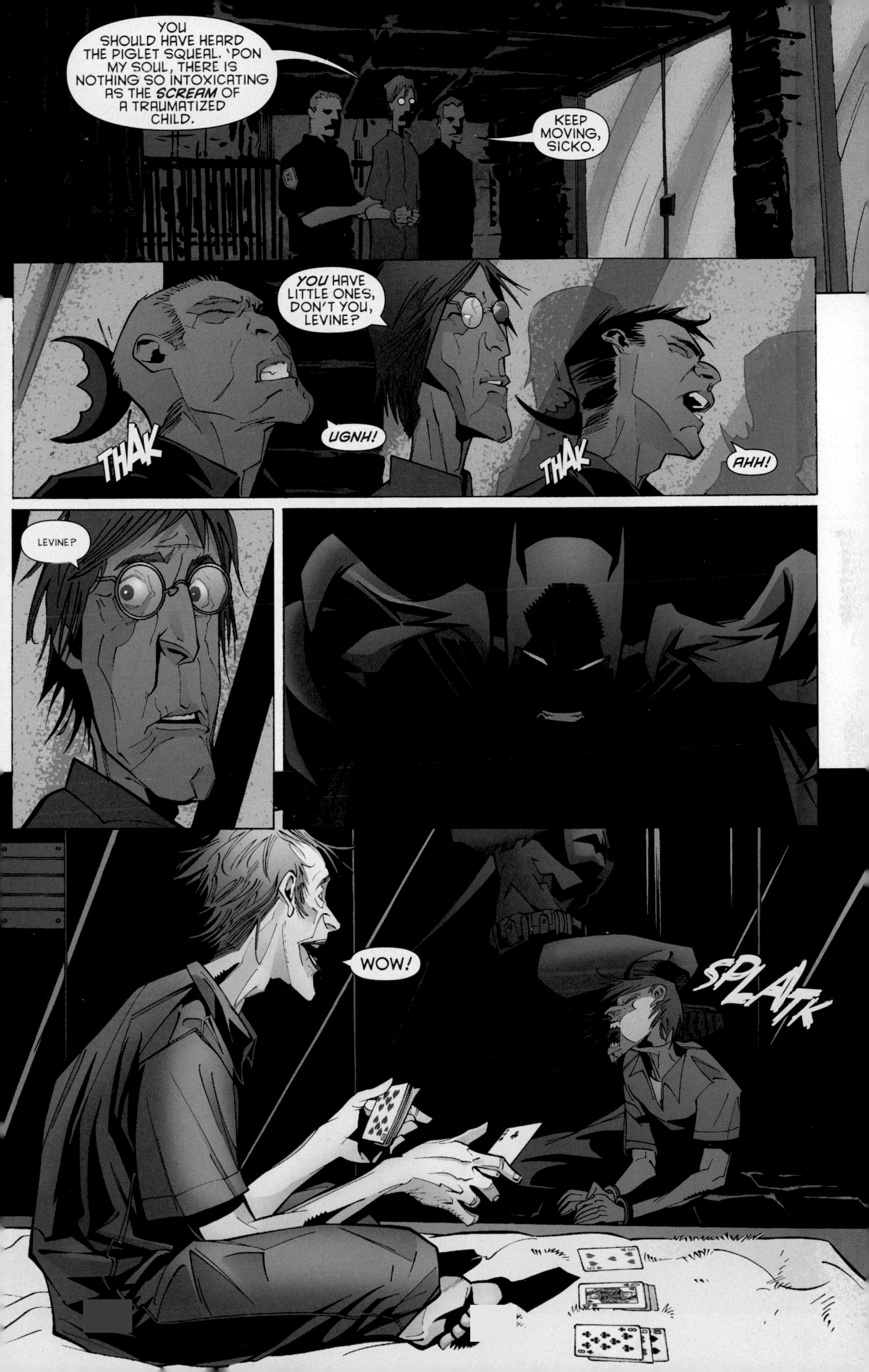

YOU SHOULD HAVE HEARD THE PIGLET SQUEAL. 'PON MY SOUL, THERE IS NOTHING SO INTOXICATING AS THE *SCREAM* OF A TRAUMATIZED CHILD.
KEEP MOVING, SICKO.
YOU HAVE LITTLE ONES, DON'T YOU, LEVINE?
THAK
UGNH!
THAK
AHH!
LEVINE?
WOW!
SPLATK

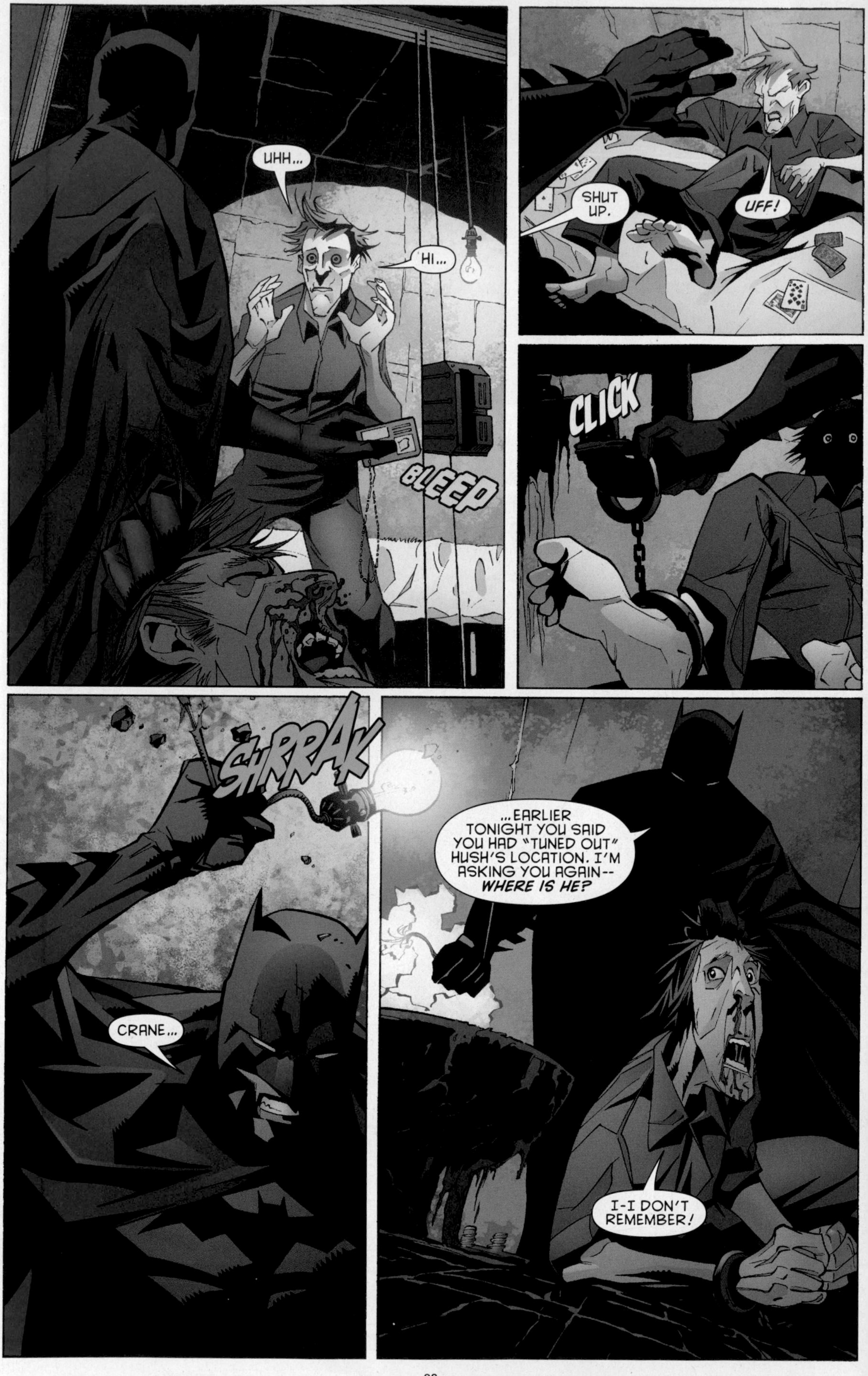
UHH...
HI...
BLEEP
SHUT UP.
UFF!
CLICK
SHRRAK
CRANE...
...EARLIER TONIGHT YOU SAID YOU HAD "TUNED OUT" HUSH'S LOCATION. I'M ASKING YOU AGAIN-- *WHERE IS HE?*
I-I DON'T REMEMBER!

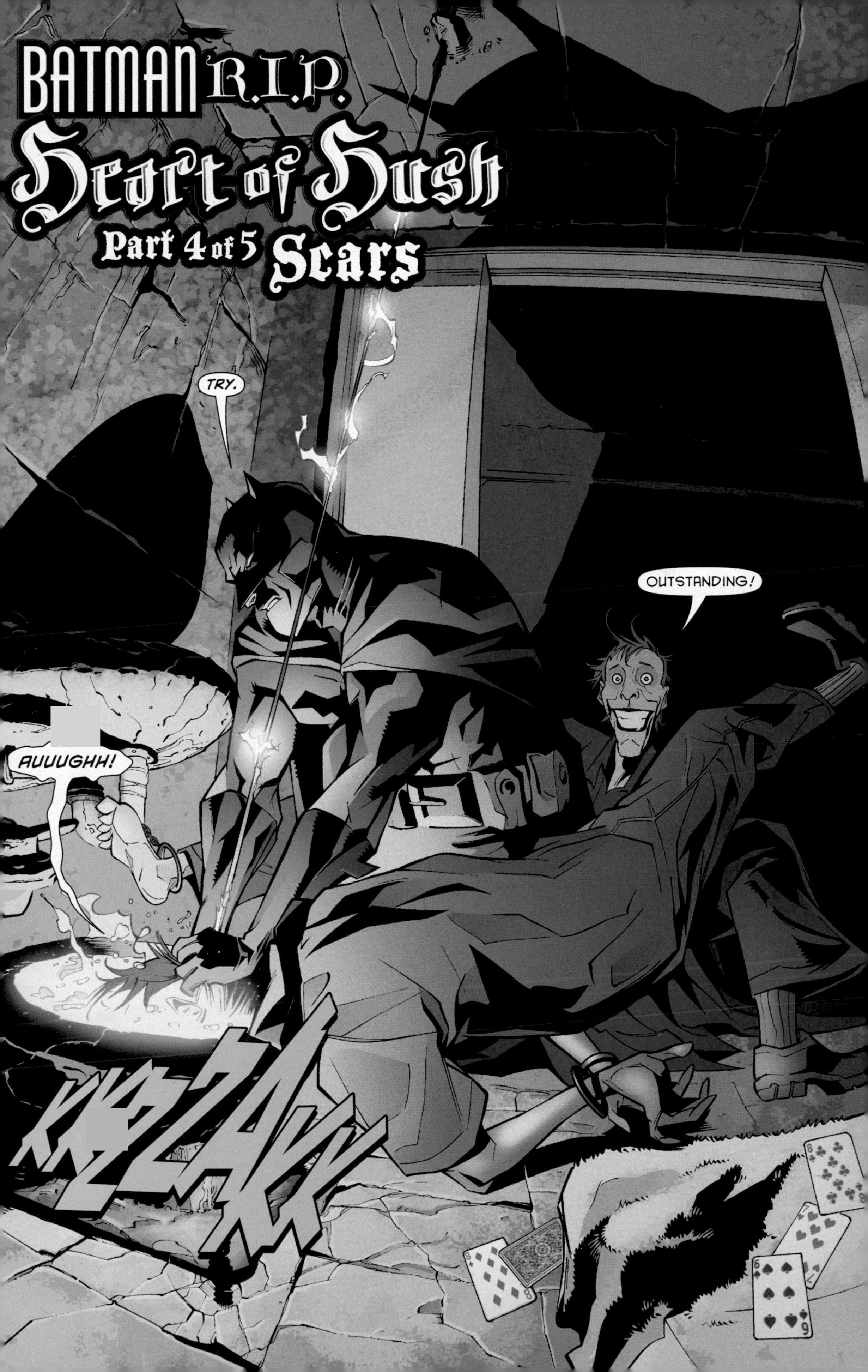
BATMAN R.I.P.
Heart of Hush
Part 4 of 5 Scars
TRY.
OUTSTANDING!
AUUUGHH!

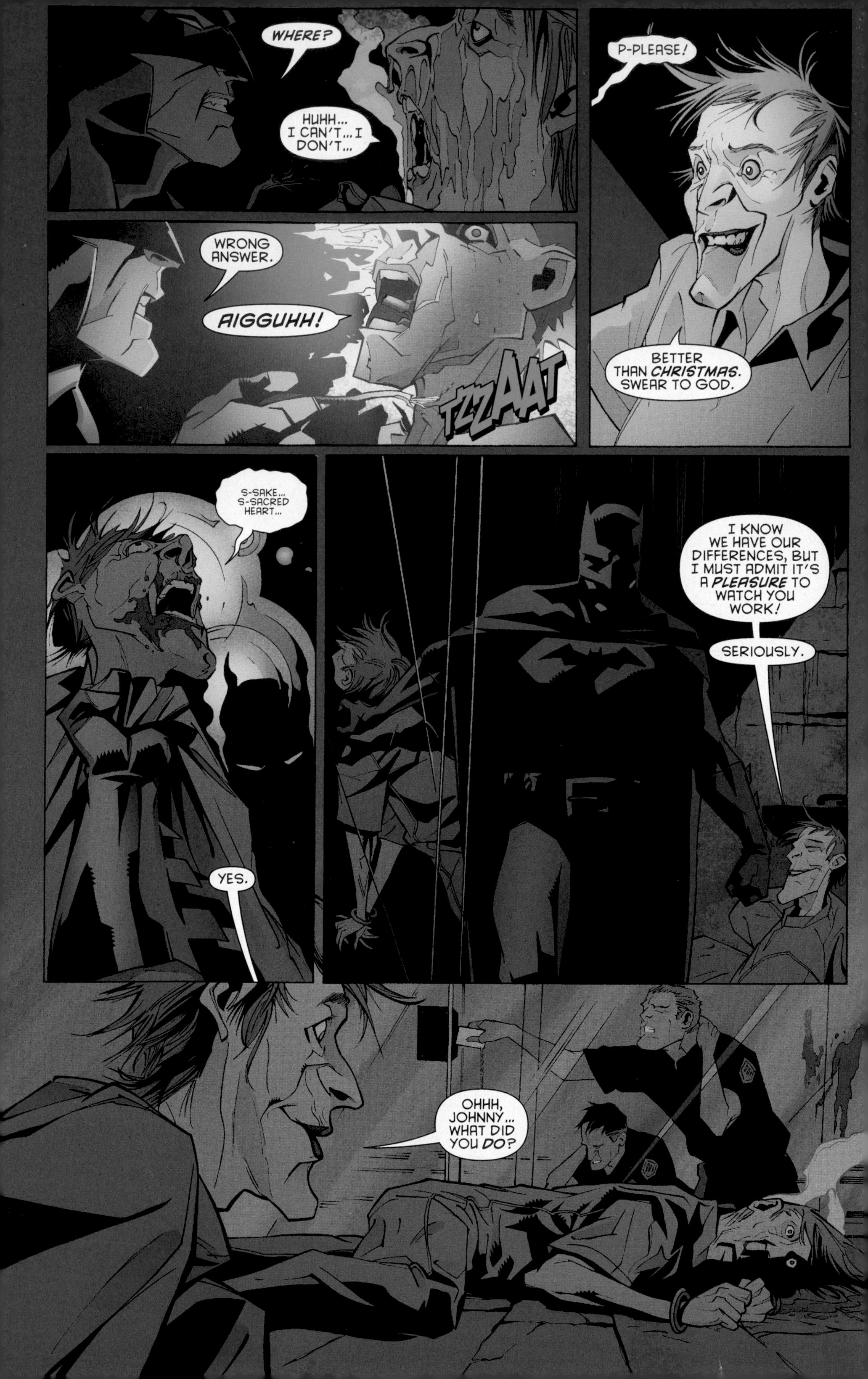
WHERE?
HUHH... I CAN'T... I DON'T...
P-PLEASE!
WRONG ANSWER.
AIGGUHH!
TZZAAT
BETTER THAN CHRISTMAS. SWEAR TO GOD.
S-SAKE... S-SACRED HEART...
YES.
I KNOW WE HAVE OUR DIFFERENCES, BUT I MUST ADMIT IT'S A PLEASURE TO WATCH YOU WORK!
SERIOUSLY.
OHHH, JOHNNY... WHAT DID YOU DO?

MID-NITE. HOW IS SHE?

SELINA'S VITAL SIGNS ARE STABLE. THE MACHINE IS KEEPING HER ALIVE, BUT I'M NOT SURE *HOW*, OR FOR HOW *LONG.*

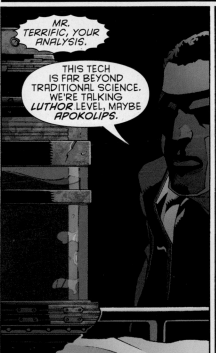

MR. TERRIFIC, YOUR ANALYSIS.

THIS TECH IS FAR BEYOND TRADITIONAL SCIENCE. WE'RE TALKING *LUTHOR* LEVEL, MAYBE *APOKOLIPS.*

I HEARD THOMAS ELLIOT WAS A GIFTED SURGEON, BUT I NEVER SUSPECTED HE HAD *THIS* IN HIM.

HE HAD *HELP.* HIS HATRED OF ME PROVIDED THE SPARK, SOMEONE ELSE DID THE HEAVY WORK.

IF IT'S ANY CONSOLATION, SELINA SEEMS TO BE FREE FROM PAIN. WE'LL DO WHAT WE CAN TO SEE SHE STAYS THAT WAY.

YOU NEED ANY BACKUP? SAY THE WORD, AND I'LL HAVE BOTH THE JLA *AND* THE SOCIETY--

NO.

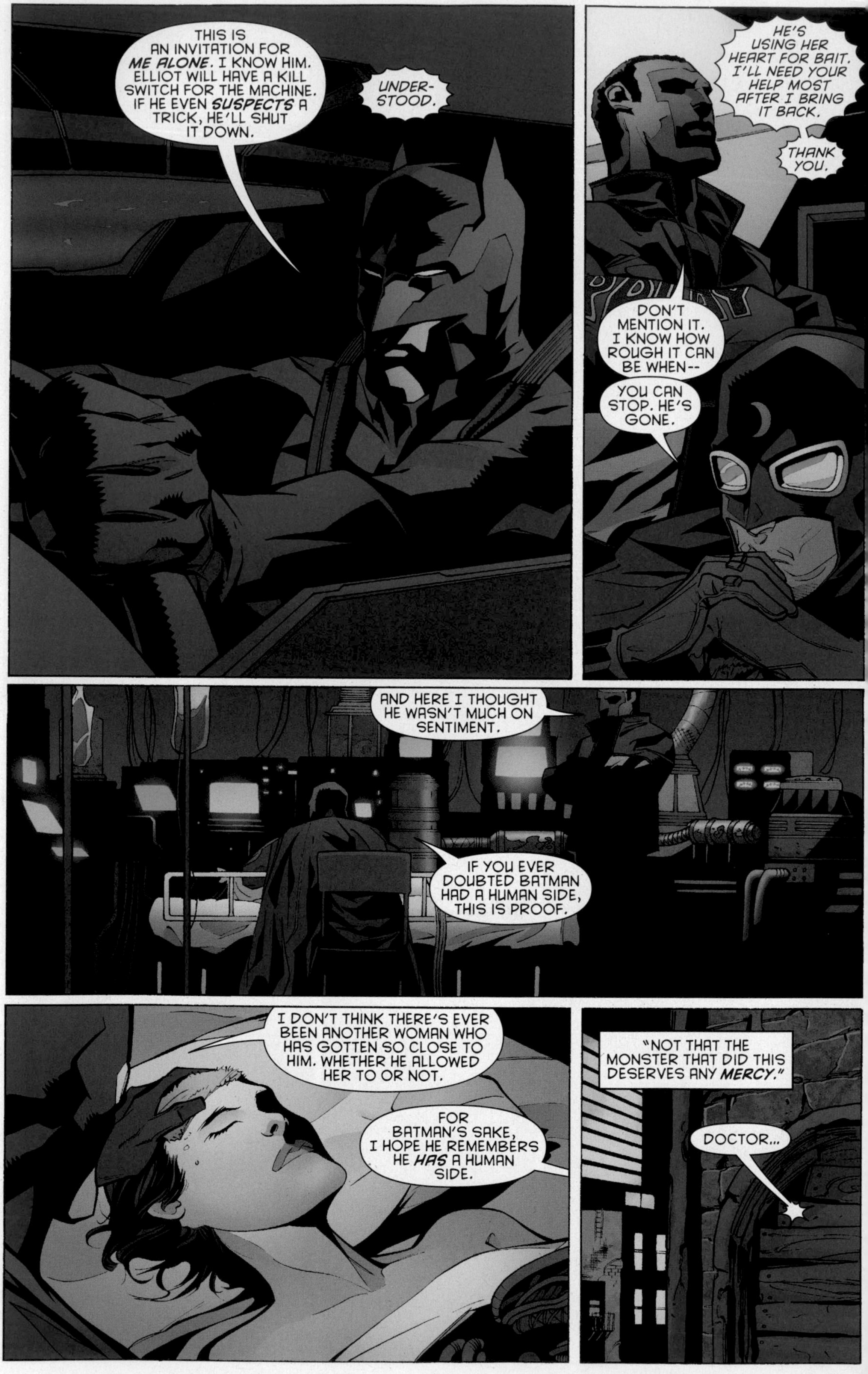
THIS IS AN INVITATION FOR ME ALONE. I KNOW HIM. ELLIOT WILL HAVE A KILL SWITCH FOR THE MACHINE. IF HE EVEN SUSPECTS A TRICK, HE'LL SHUT IT DOWN.
UNDER-STOOD.
HE'S USING HER HEART FOR BAIT. I'LL NEED YOUR HELP MOST AFTER I BRING IT BACK.
THANK YOU.
DON'T MENTION IT. I KNOW HOW ROUGH IT CAN BE WHEN--
YOU CAN STOP. HE'S GONE.
AND HERE I THOUGHT HE WASN'T MUCH ON SENTIMENT.
IF YOU EVER DOUBTED BATMAN HAD A HUMAN SIDE, THIS IS PROOF.
I DON'T THINK THERE'S EVER BEEN ANOTHER WOMAN WHO HAS GOTTEN SO CLOSE TO HIM. WHETHER HE ALLOWED HER TO OR NOT.
FOR BATMAN'S SAKE, I HOPE HE REMEMBERS HE HAS A HUMAN SIDE.
"NOT THAT THE MONSTER THAT DID THIS DESERVES ANY MERCY."
DOCTOR...

OUR PEOPLE CALLED. THEY'VE SEEN THE CAR. HE'S HEADED THIS WAY *FAST*.

I ANTICIPATED AS MUCH. THANK YOU, NURSE.

TELL THE STAFF TO TAKE THEIR PLACES AT ALL ENTRANCES. BY EVERY DOOR, UNDER EVERY SKYLIGHT. HE'S OUT FOR BLOOD AND WILL BE MAKING A BIG, SCARY ENTRANCE.

YES, DOCTOR.

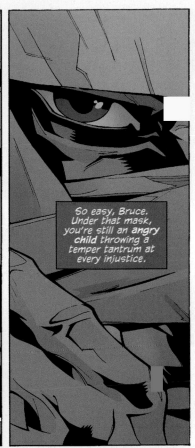

So easy, Bruce. Under that mask, you're still an *angry child* throwing a temper tantrum at every injustice.

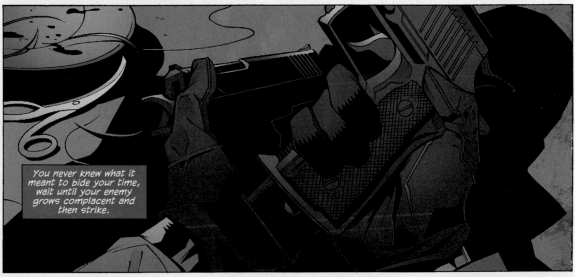

You never knew what it meant to bide your time, wait until your enemy grows complacent and then strike.

As Aristotle said, "Patience is bitter, but its fruit is sweet."

I'VE GONE OVER THE DOCTOR'S REPORT IN DETAIL, MOTHER. YOUR CANCER IS IN FULL REMISSION. YOU SHOULD BE COMPLETELY HEALED WITHIN A MONTH.

DON'T *LIE* TO ME, TOMMY. I'M A SICK WOMAN. I NEED TWENTY-FOUR HOUR ATTENTION.

ON THE CONTRARY. I MAY BE JUST STARTING MED SCHOOL, BUT I THINK A FEW NIGHTS ALONE WOULD DO YOU A WORLD OF GOOD.

IT'S THAT *GIRL*, ISN'T IT? THAT *CRIMINAL'S* DAUGHTER.

YOU DON'T EVEN *KNOW* PEYTON.

WE'VE BEEN DATING FOUR MONTHS AND YOU STILL WON'T DEIGN TO MEET HER.

I DON'T NEED TO MEET HER. SHE'S *TRASH*, HER AND HER WHOLE THIEVING FAMILY!

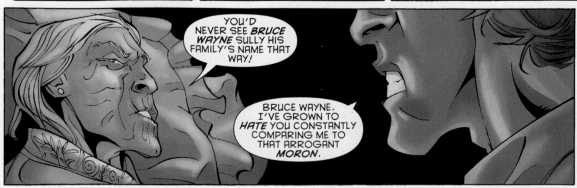

YOU'D NEVER SEE *BRUCE WAYNE* SULLY HIS FAMILY'S NAME THAT WAY!

BRUCE WAYNE. I'VE GROWN TO *HATE* YOU CONSTANTLY COMPARING ME TO THAT ARROGANT *MORON*.

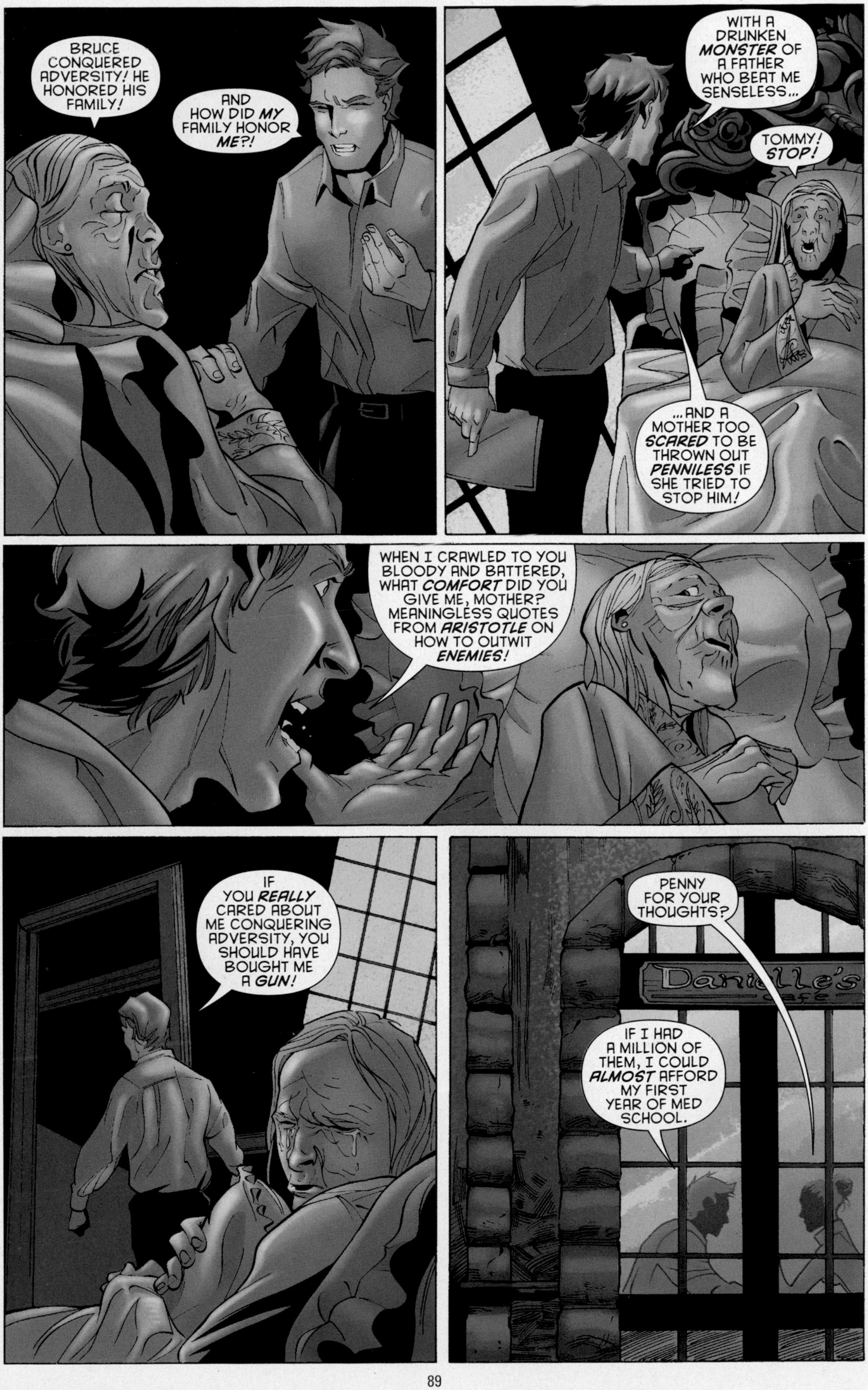

BRUCE CONQUERED ADVERSITY! HE HONORED HIS FAMILY!
AND HOW DID *MY* FAMILY HONOR *ME*?!
WITH A DRUNKEN *MONSTER* OF A FATHER WHO BEAT ME SENSELESS...
TOMMY! *STOP!*
...AND A MOTHER TOO *SCARED* TO BE THROWN OUT *PENNILESS* IF SHE TRIED TO STOP HIM!
WHEN I CRAWLED TO YOU BLOODY AND BATTERED, WHAT *COMFORT* DID YOU GIVE ME, MOTHER? MEANINGLESS QUOTES FROM *ARISTOTLE* ON HOW TO OUTWIT *ENEMIES!*
IF YOU *REALLY* CARED ABOUT ME CONQUERING ADVERSITY, YOU SHOULD HAVE BOUGHT ME A *GUN!*
PENNY FOR YOUR THOUGHTS?
Danielle's
cafe
IF I HAD A MILLION OF THEM, I COULD *ALMOST* AFFORD MY FIRST YEAR OF MED SCHOOL.

YOU'RE NOT THE ONLY ONE WITH PARENT ISSUES, TOM. GANGSTER'S DAUGHTER, HELLO?

THE OLD MAN ISN'T THRILLED ABOUT ME DATING ANYONE OUTSIDE "THE BUSINESS"...

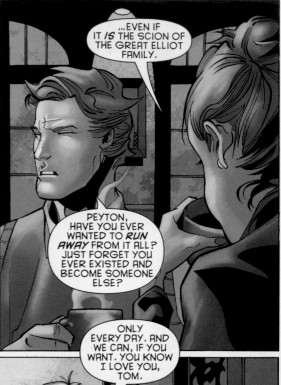

...EVEN IF IT *IS* THE SCION OF THE GREAT ELLIOT FAMILY.

PEYTON, HAVE YOU EVER WANTED TO *RUN AWAY* FROM IT ALL? JUST FORGET YOU EVER EXISTED AND BECOME SOMEONE ELSE?

ONLY EVERY DAY. AND WE CAN, IF YOU WANT. YOU KNOW I LOVE YOU, TOM.

I KNOW...

BUT THAT WOULD MEAN YOU GIVING UP ON MEDICINE. THAT'S BEEN YOUR DREAM.

I WON'T MAKE IT WITHOUT MOTHER'S MONEY. IT'S THE ONLY THING THAT'S BEEN KEEPING ME TOGETHER THESE LAST FEW YEARS.

WELL, *ONE* OF THE ONLY THINGS.

WHY DON'T YOU LET *ME* TALK TO MOMMY DEAREST? WHO KNOWS? THE OLD BIRD AND I MIGHT HIT IT OFF.

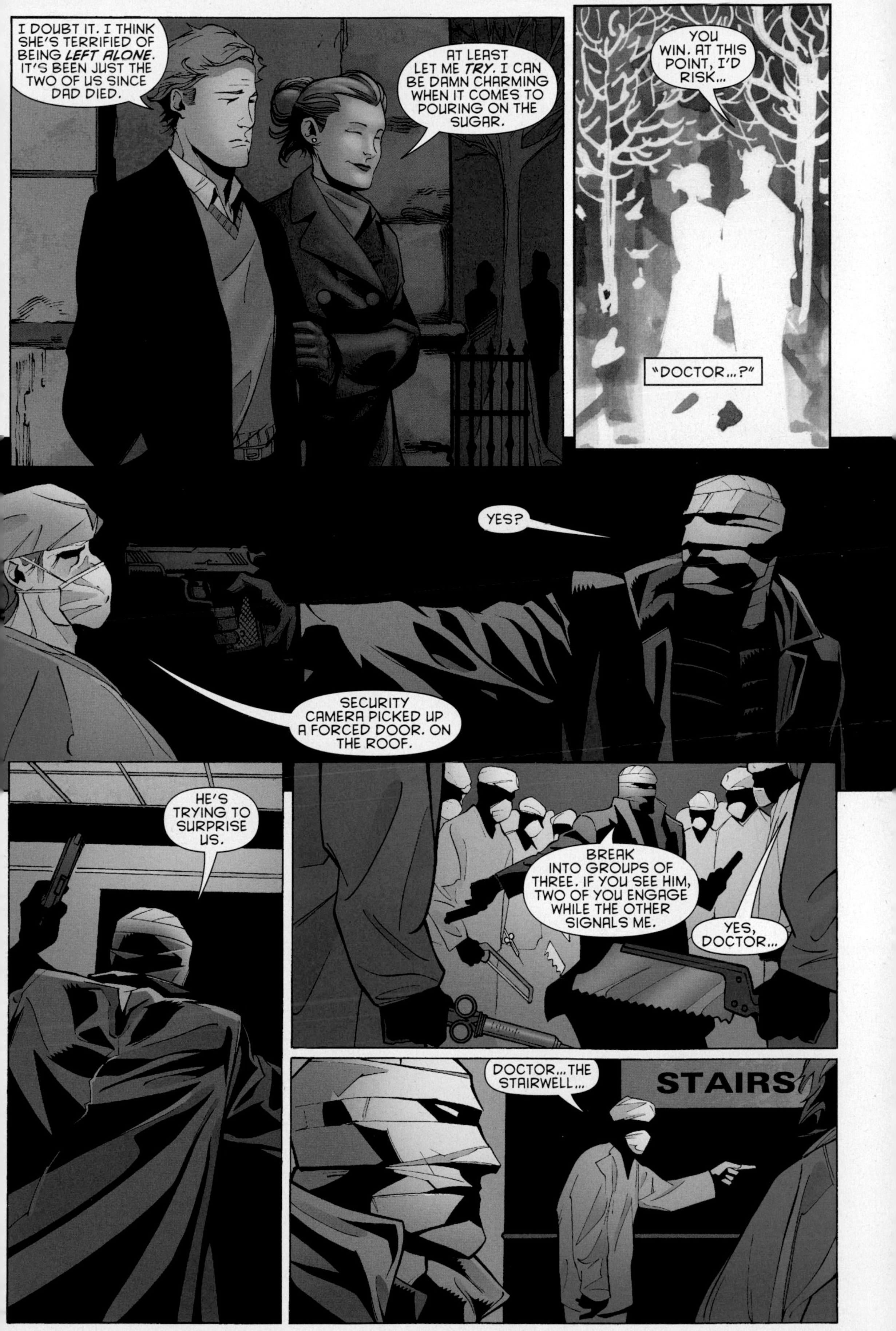
I DOUBT IT. I THINK SHE'S TERRIFIED OF BEING LEFT ALONE. IT'S BEEN JUST THE TWO OF US SINCE DAD DIED.
AT LEAST LET ME TRY. I CAN BE DAMN CHARMING WHEN IT COMES TO POURING ON THE SUGAR.
YOU WIN. AT THIS POINT, I'D RISK...
"DOCTOR...?"
YES?
SECURITY CAMERA PICKED UP A FORCED DOOR. ON THE ROOF.
HE'S TRYING TO SURPRISE US.
BREAK INTO GROUPS OF THREE. IF YOU SEE HIM, TWO OF YOU ENGAGE WHILE THE OTHER SIGNALS ME.
YES, DOCTOR...
DOCTOR... THE STAIRWELL...
STAIRS

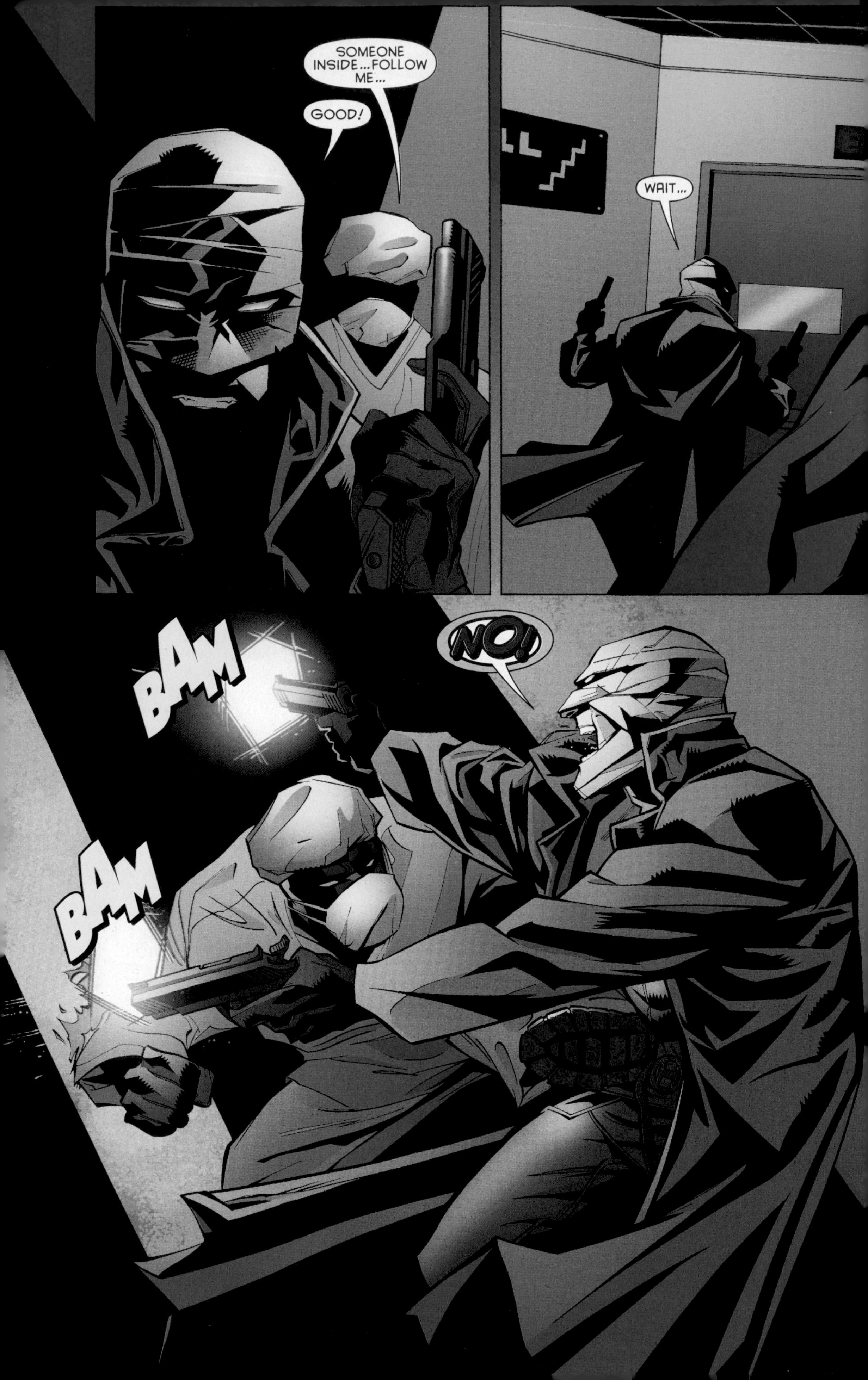

SOMEONE INSIDE...FOLLOW ME...
GOOD!
WAIT...
BAM
NO!
BAM

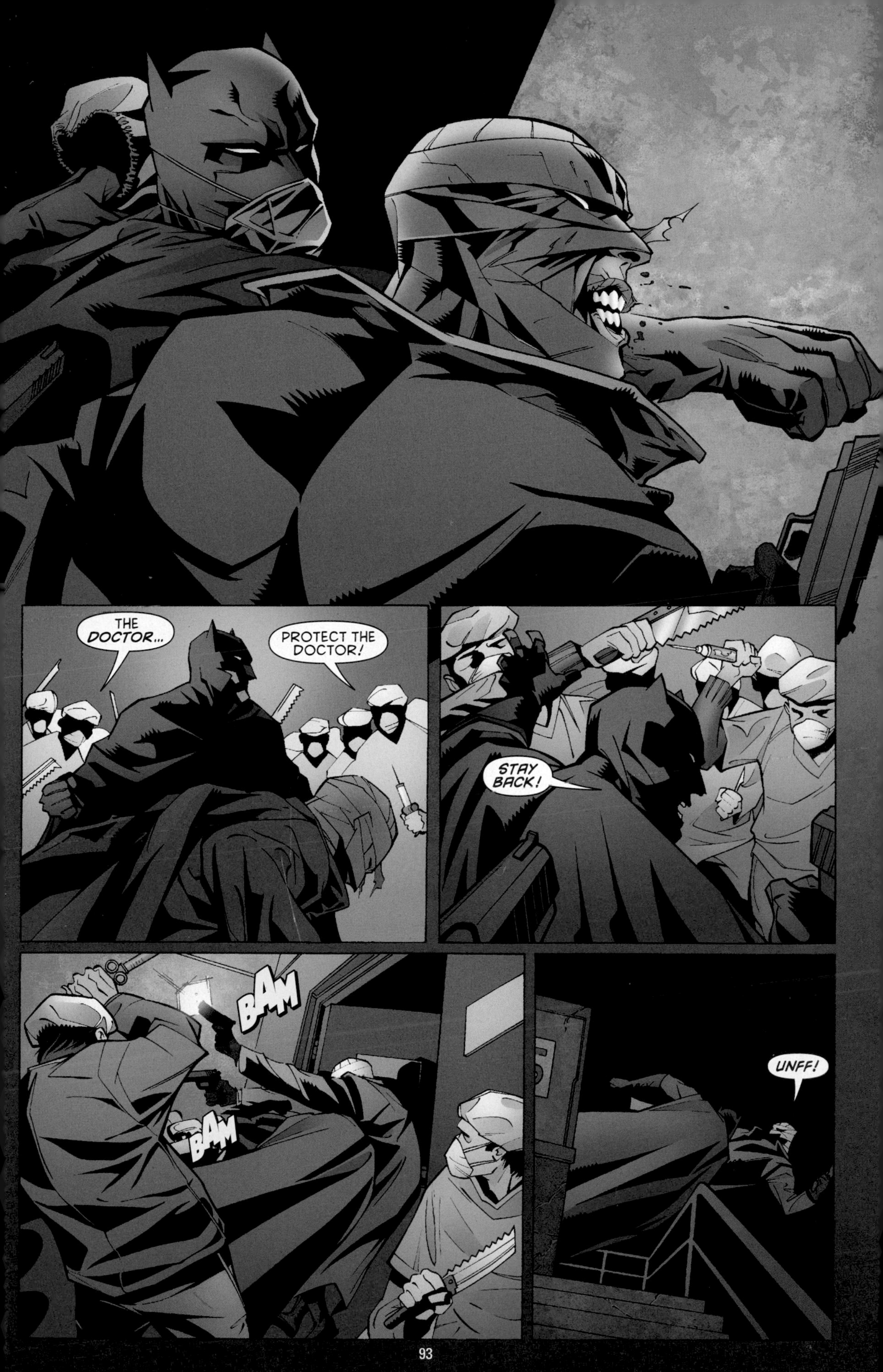
THE DOCTOR...
PROTECT THE DOCTOR!
STAY BACK!
BAM
BAM
UNFF!

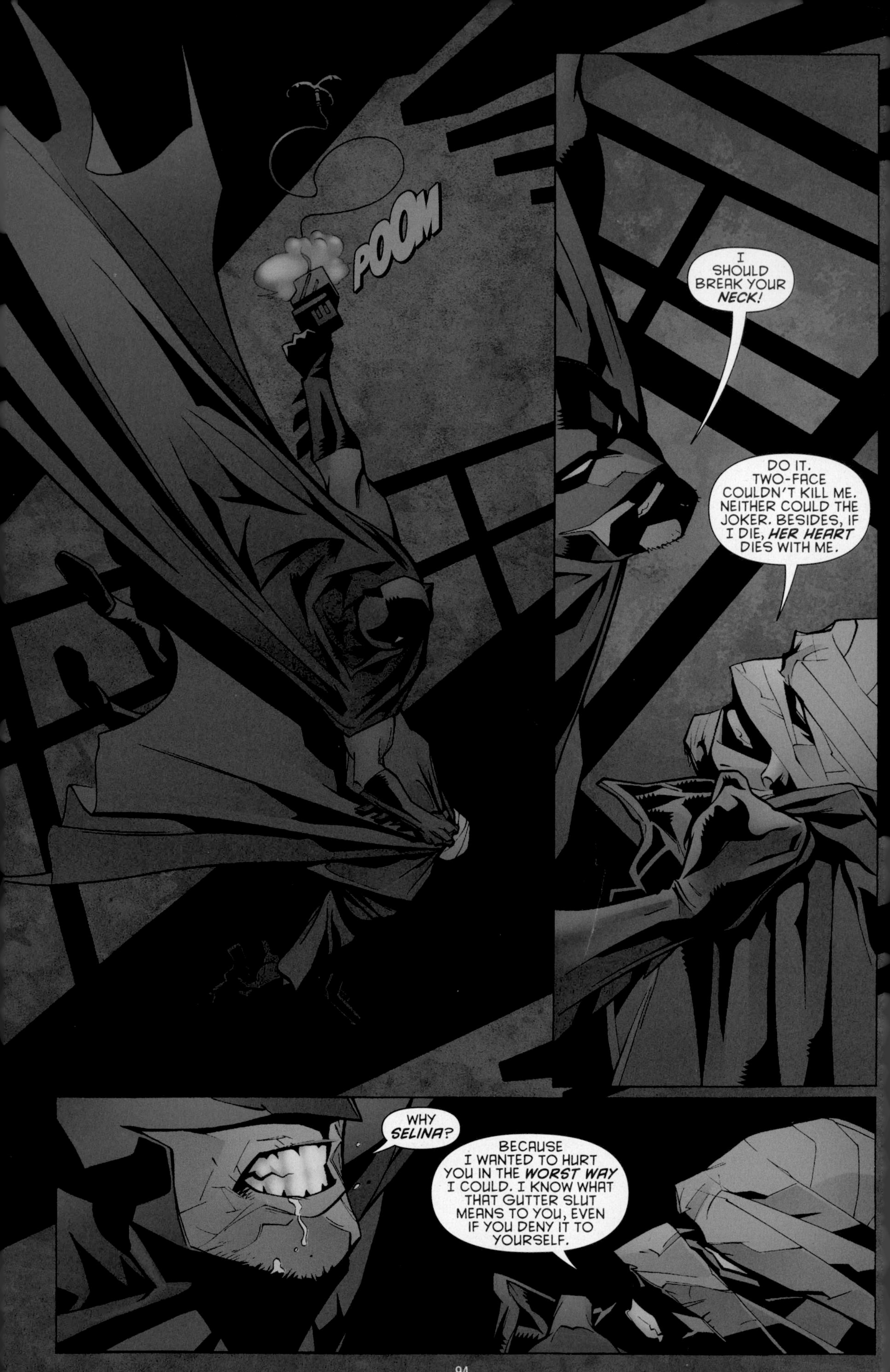
POOM
I SHOULD BREAK YOUR *NECK!*
DO IT. TWO-FACE COULDN'T KILL ME. NEITHER COULD THE JOKER. BESIDES, IF I DIE, *HER HEART* DIES WITH ME.
WHY *SELINA?*
BECAUSE I WANTED TO HURT YOU IN THE *WORST WAY* I COULD. I KNOW WHAT THAT GUTTER SLUT MEANS TO YOU, EVEN IF YOU DENY IT TO YOURSELF.

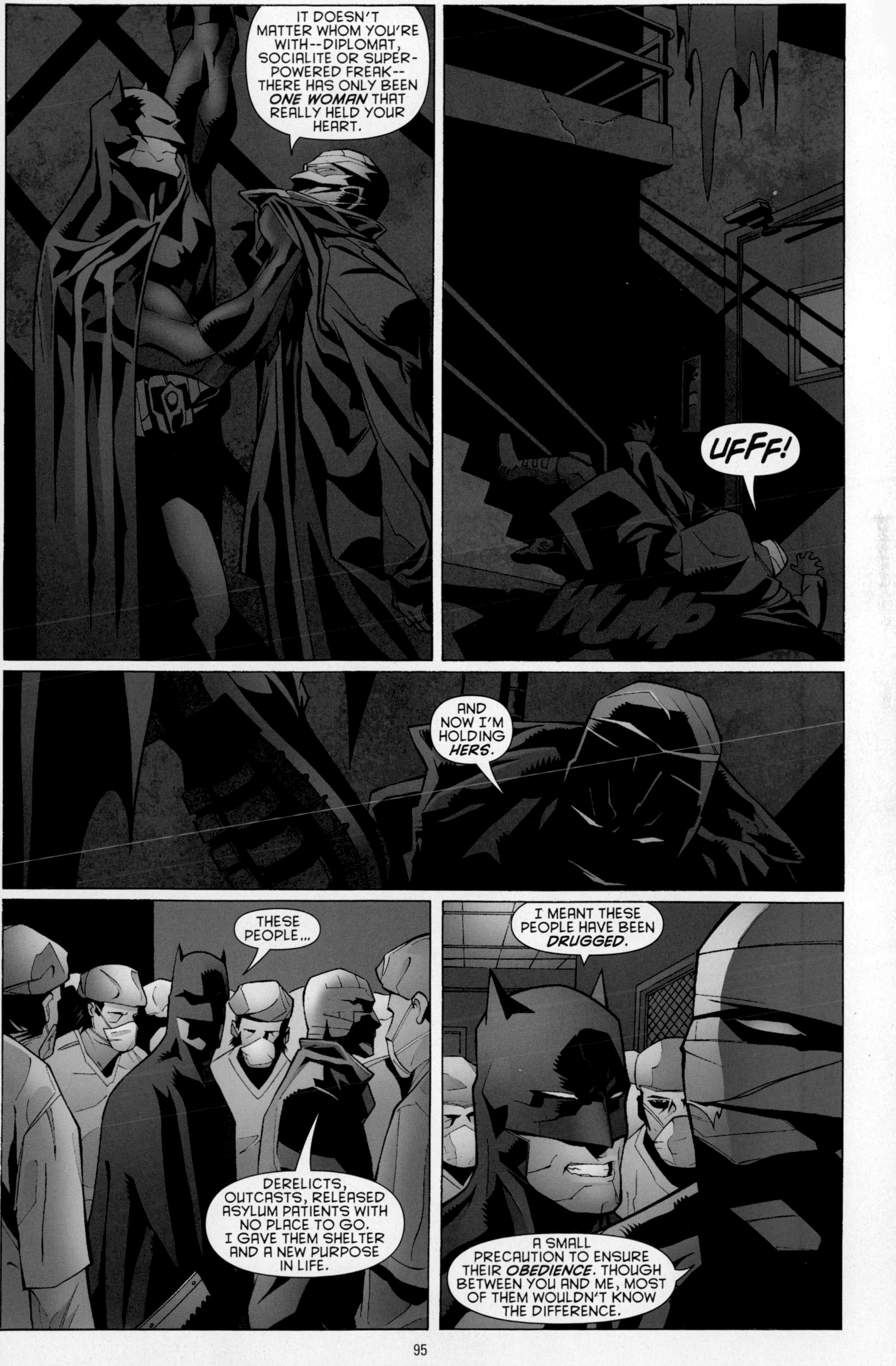
IT DOESN'T MATTER WHOM YOU'RE WITH--DIPLOMAT, SOCIALITE OR SUPER-POWERED FREAK--THERE HAS ONLY BEEN ONE WOMAN THAT REALLY HELD YOUR HEART.
UFFF!
WUMP
AND NOW I'M HOLDING HERS.
THESE PEOPLE...
DERELICTS, OUTCASTS, RELEASED ASYLUM PATIENTS WITH NO PLACE TO GO. I GAVE THEM SHELTER AND A NEW PURPOSE IN LIFE.
I MEANT THESE PEOPLE HAVE BEEN DRUGGED.
A SMALL PRECAUTION TO ENSURE THEIR OBEDIENCE. THOUGH BETWEEN YOU AND ME, MOST OF THEM WOULDN'T KNOW THE DIFFERENCE.

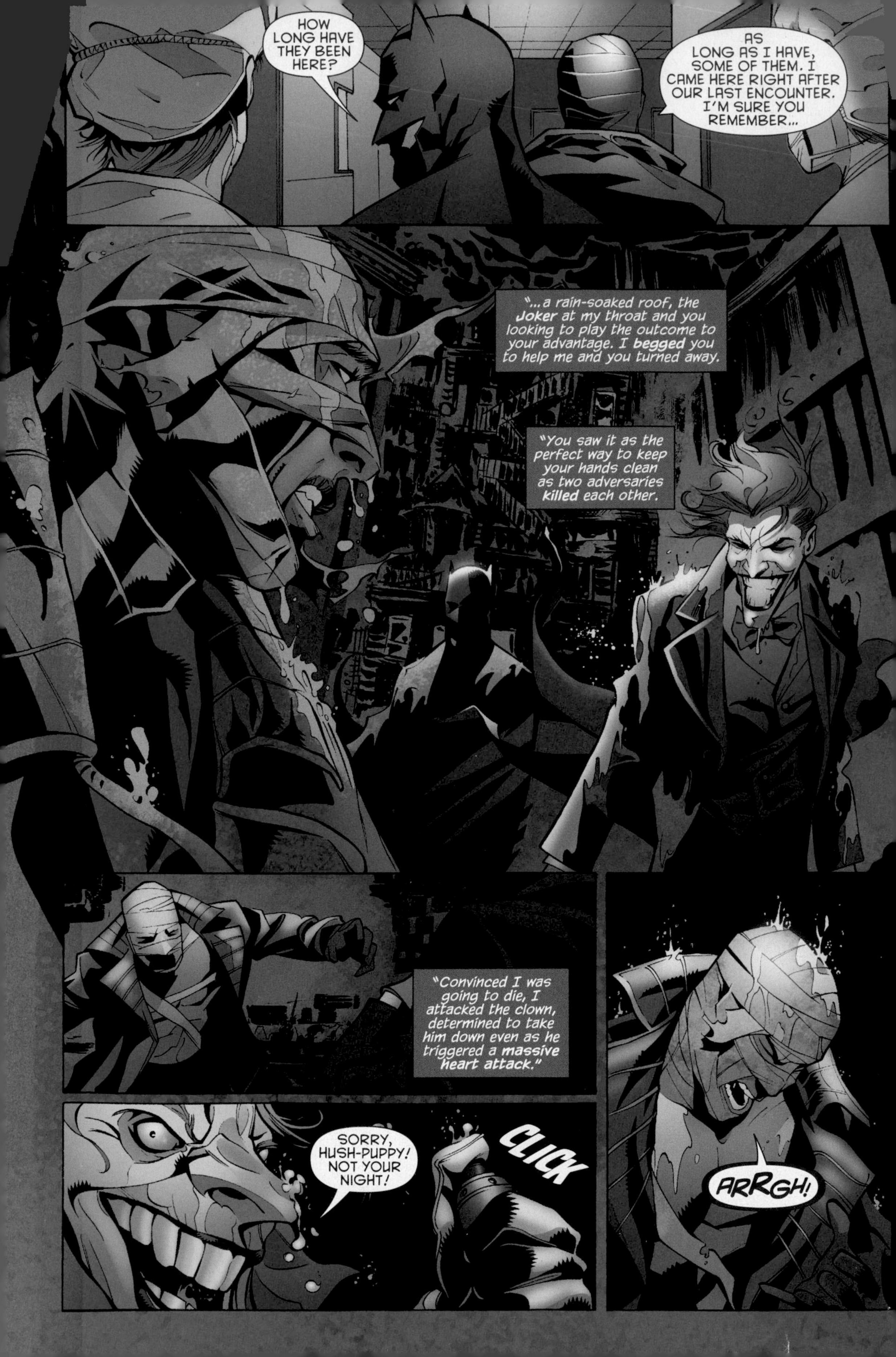
HOW LONG HAVE THEY BEEN HERE?
AS LONG AS I HAVE, SOME OF THEM. I CAME HERE RIGHT AFTER OUR LAST ENCOUNTER. I'M SURE YOU REMEMBER...
"...a rain-soaked roof, the Joker at my throat and you looking to play the outcome to your advantage. I begged you to help me and you turned away.
"You saw it as the perfect way to keep your hands clean as two adversaries killed each other.
"Convinced I was going to die, I attacked the clown, determined to take him down even as he triggered a massive heart attack."
SORRY, HUSH-PUPPY! NOT YOUR NIGHT!
CLICK
ARRGH!

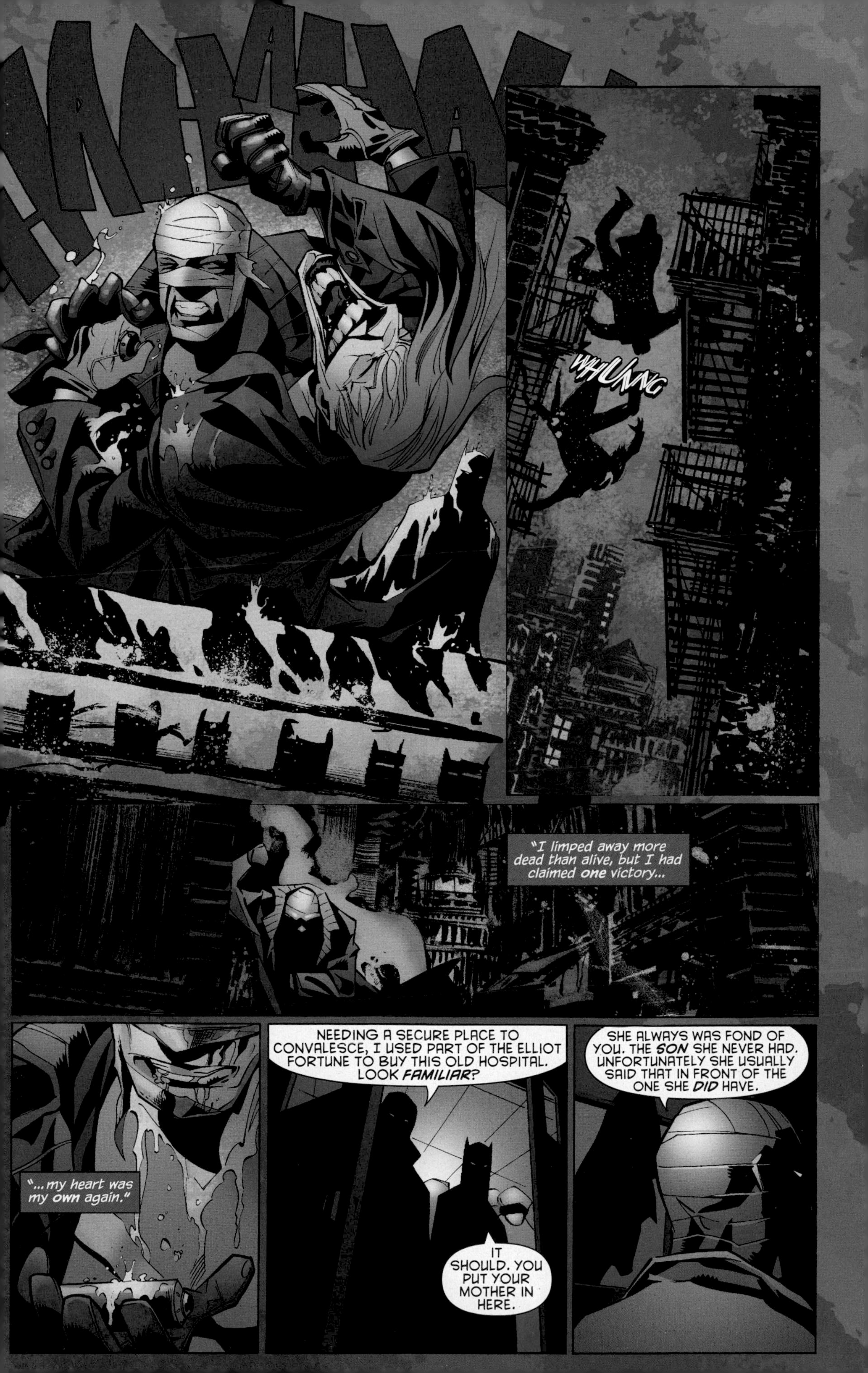
WHUNNG
"I limped away more dead than alive, but I had claimed one victory...
"...my heart was my own again."
NEEDING A SECURE PLACE TO CONVALESCE, I USED PART OF THE ELLIOT FORTUNE TO BUY THIS OLD HOSPITAL. LOOK FAMILIAR?
IT SHOULD. YOU PUT YOUR MOTHER IN HERE.
SHE ALWAYS WAS FOND OF YOU. THE SON SHE NEVER HAD. UNFORTUNATELY SHE USUALLY SAID THAT IN FRONT OF THE ONE SHE DID HAVE.

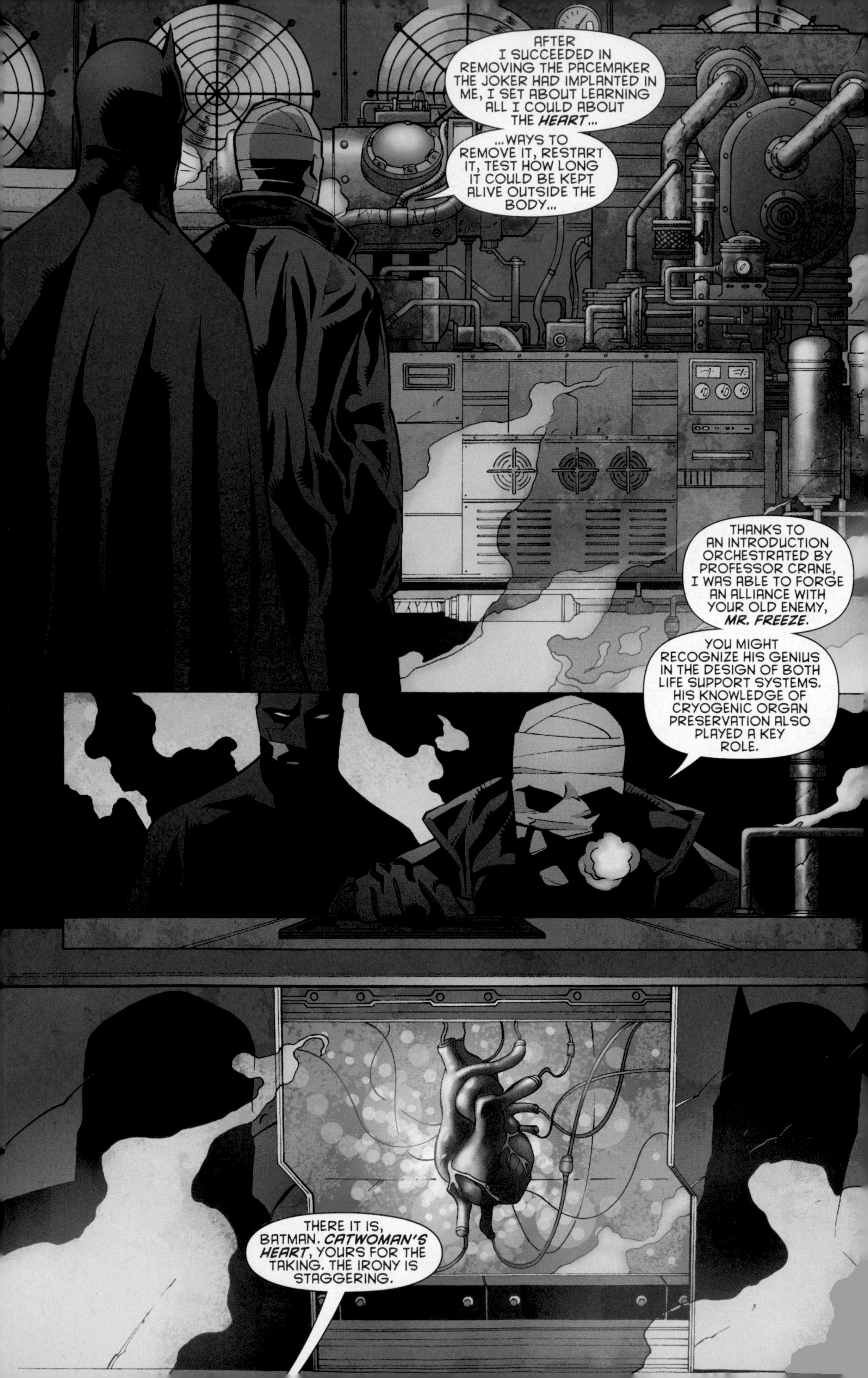
AFTER I SUCCEEDED IN REMOVING THE PACEMAKER THE JOKER HAD IMPLANTED IN ME, I SET ABOUT LEARNING ALL I COULD ABOUT THE HEART...
...WAYS TO REMOVE IT, RESTART IT, TEST HOW LONG IT COULD BE KEPT ALIVE OUTSIDE THE BODY...
THANKS TO AN INTRODUCTION ORCHESTRATED BY PROFESSOR CRANE, I WAS ABLE TO FORGE AN ALLIANCE WITH YOUR OLD ENEMY, MR. FREEZE.
YOU MIGHT RECOGNIZE HIS GENIUS IN THE DESIGN OF BOTH LIFE SUPPORT SYSTEMS. HIS KNOWLEDGE OF CRYOGENIC ORGAN PRESERVATION ALSO PLAYED A KEY ROLE.
THERE IT IS, BATMAN. CATWOMAN'S HEART, YOURS FOR THE TAKING. THE IRONY IS STAGGERING.

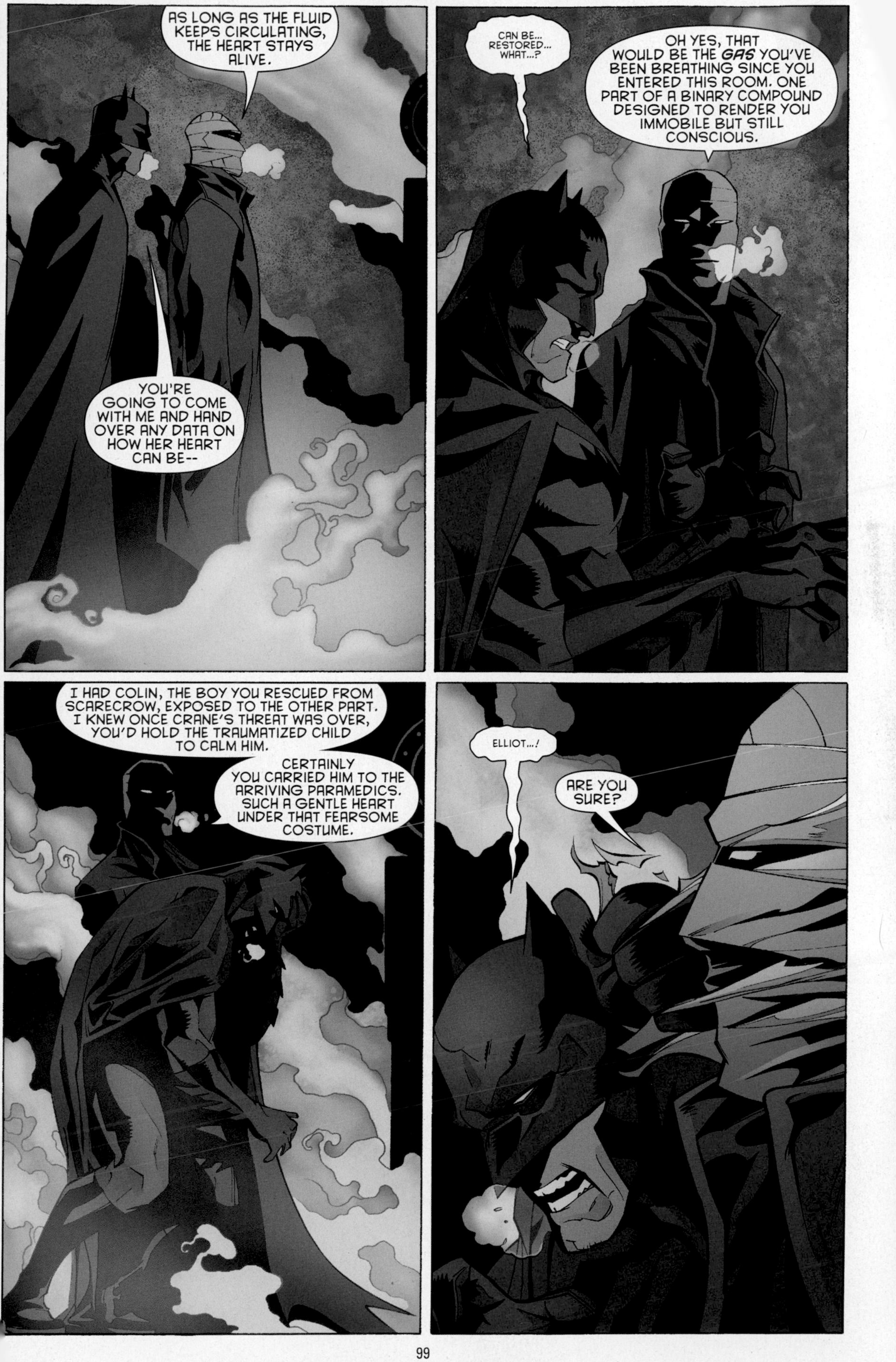
AS LONG AS THE FLUID KEEPS CIRCULATING, THE HEART STAYS ALIVE.
YOU'RE GOING TO COME WITH ME AND HAND OVER ANY DATA ON HOW HER HEART CAN BE--
CAN BE... RESTORED... WHAT...?
OH YES, THAT WOULD BE THE GAS YOU'VE BEEN BREATHING SINCE YOU ENTERED THIS ROOM. ONE PART OF A BINARY COMPOUND DESIGNED TO RENDER YOU IMMOBILE BUT STILL CONSCIOUS.
I HAD COLIN, THE BOY YOU RESCUED FROM SCARECROW, EXPOSED TO THE OTHER PART. I KNEW ONCE CRANE'S THREAT WAS OVER, YOU'D HOLD THE TRAUMATIZED CHILD TO CALM HIM.
CERTAINLY YOU CARRIED HIM TO THE ARRIVING PARAMEDICS. SUCH A GENTLE HEART UNDER THAT FEARSOME COSTUME.
ELLIOT...!
ARE YOU SURE?

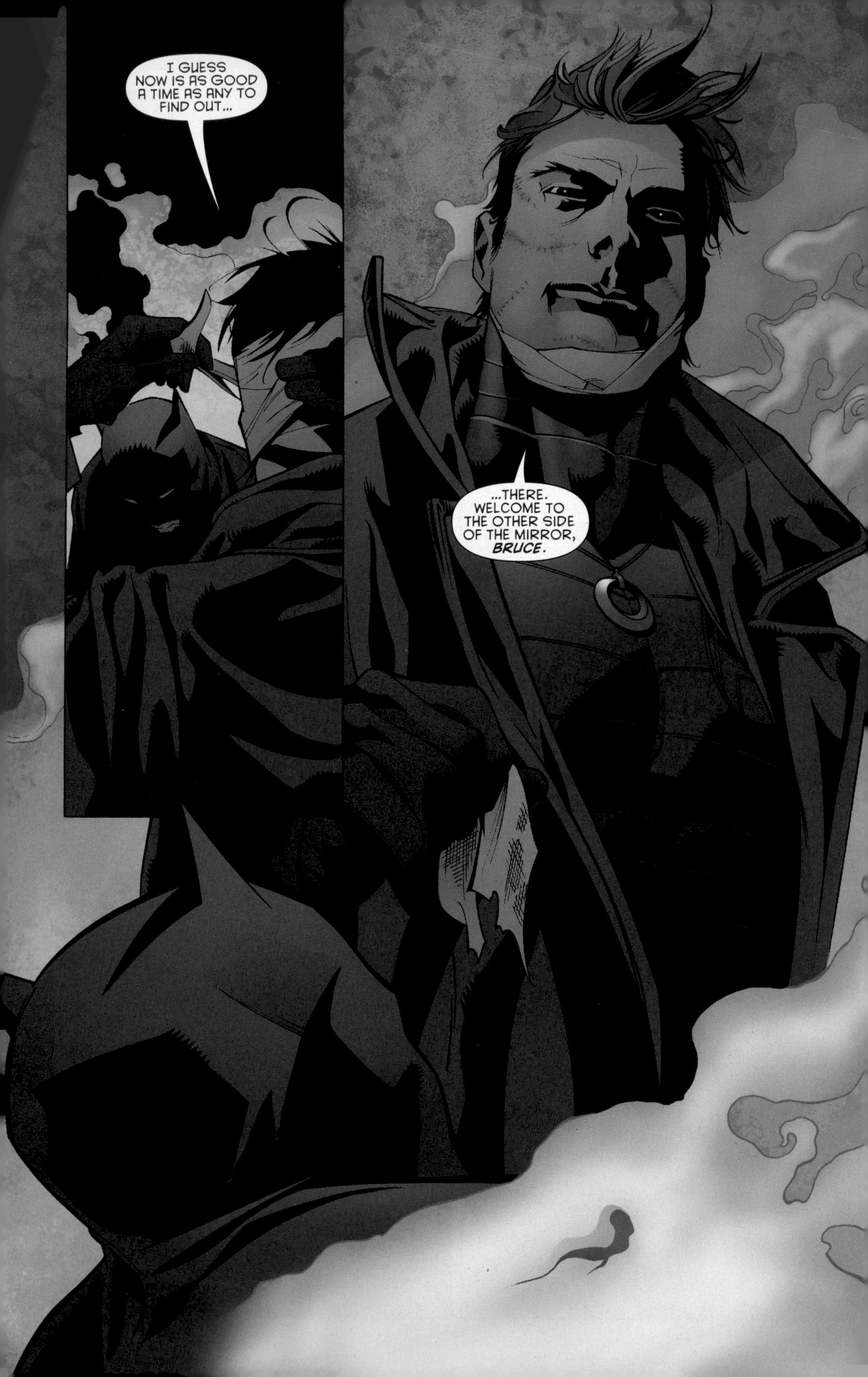
I GUESS NOW IS AS GOOD A TIME AS ANY TO FIND OUT...
...THERE. WELCOME TO THE OTHER SIDE OF THE MIRROR, *BRUCE*.

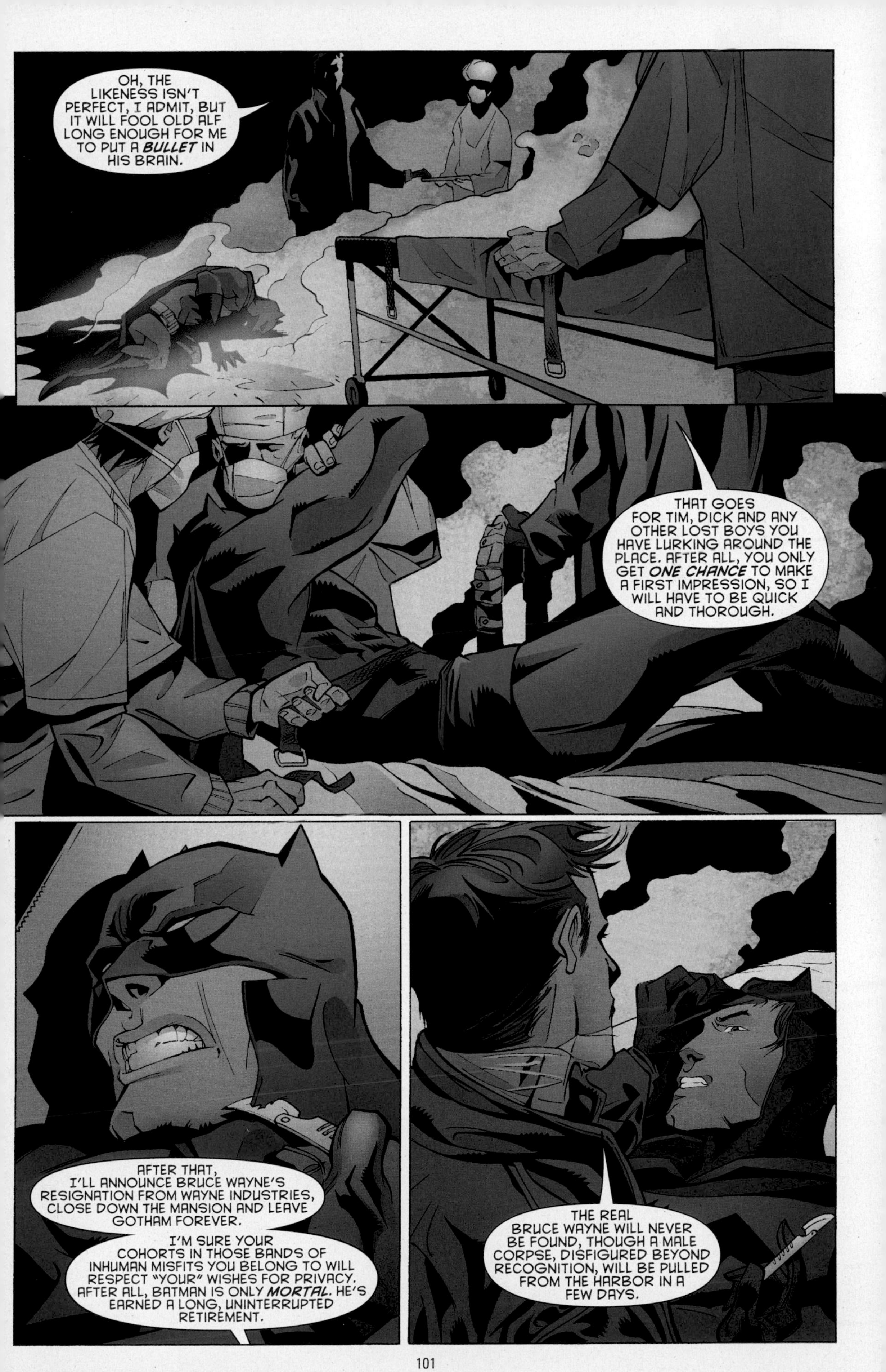
OH, THE LIKENESS ISN'T PERFECT, I ADMIT, BUT IT WILL FOOL OLD ALF LONG ENOUGH FOR ME TO PUT A BULLET IN HIS BRAIN.
THAT GOES FOR TIM, DICK AND ANY OTHER LOST BOYS YOU HAVE LURKING AROUND THE PLACE. AFTER ALL, YOU ONLY GET ONE CHANCE TO MAKE A FIRST IMPRESSION, SO I WILL HAVE TO BE QUICK AND THOROUGH.
AFTER THAT, I'LL ANNOUNCE BRUCE WAYNE'S RESIGNATION FROM WAYNE INDUSTRIES, CLOSE DOWN THE MANSION AND LEAVE GOTHAM FOREVER.
I'M SURE YOUR COHORTS IN THOSE BANDS OF INHUMAN MISFITS YOU BELONG TO WILL RESPECT "YOUR" WISHES FOR PRIVACY. AFTER ALL, BATMAN IS ONLY MORTAL. HE'S EARNED A LONG, UNINTERRUPTED RETIREMENT.
THE REAL BRUCE WAYNE WILL NEVER BE FOUND, THOUGH A MALE CORPSE, DISFIGURED BEYOND RECOGNITION, WILL BE PULLED FROM THE HARBOR IN A FEW DAYS.

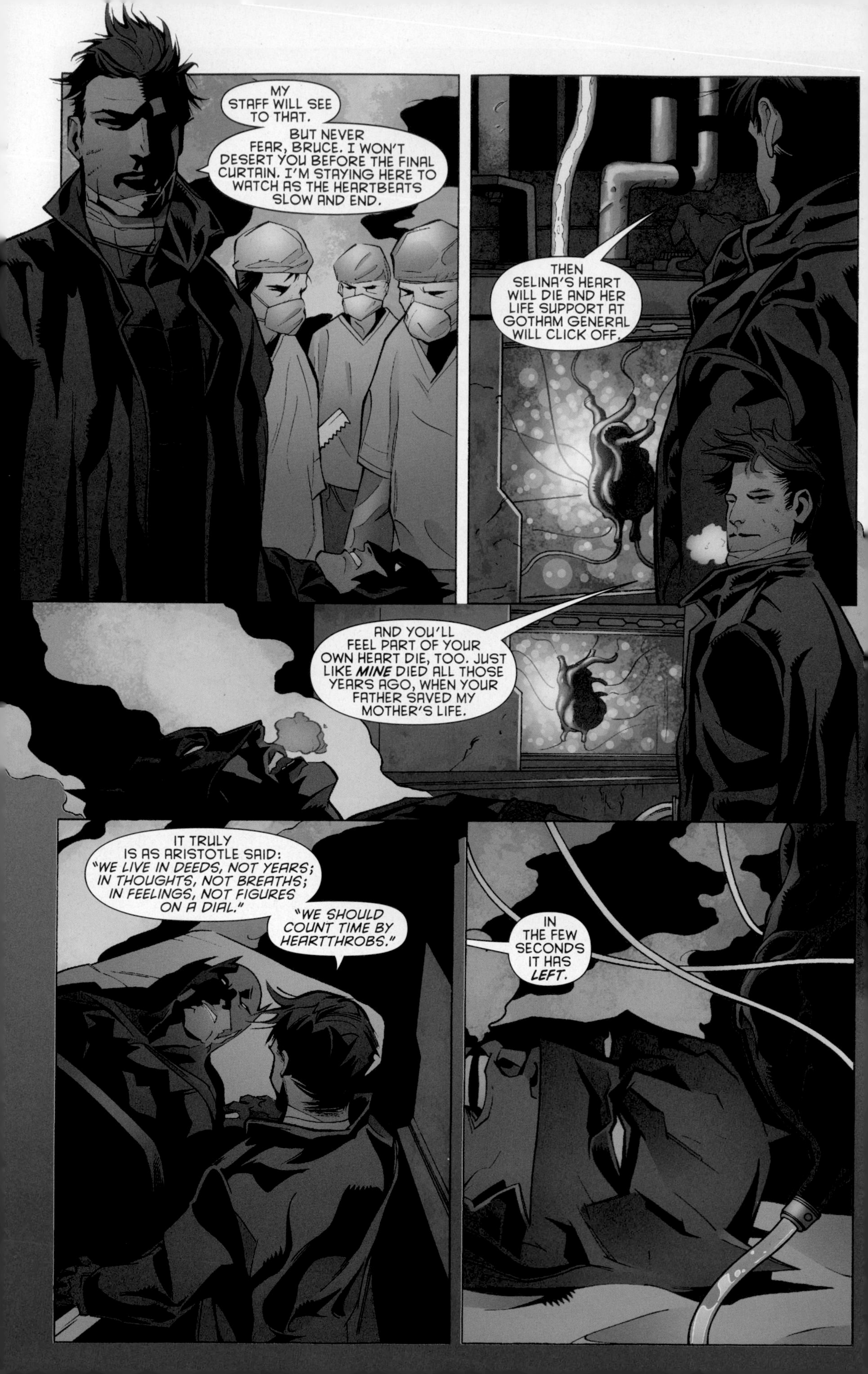
MY STAFF WILL SEE TO THAT.
BUT NEVER FEAR, BRUCE. I WON'T DESERT YOU BEFORE THE FINAL CURTAIN. I'M STAYING HERE TO WATCH AS THE HEARTBEATS SLOW AND END.
THEN SELINA'S HEART WILL DIE AND HER LIFE SUPPORT AT GOTHAM GENERAL WILL CLICK OFF.
AND YOU'LL FEEL PART OF YOUR OWN HEART DIE, TOO. JUST LIKE *MINE* DIED ALL THOSE YEARS AGO, WHEN YOUR FATHER SAVED MY MOTHER'S LIFE.
IT TRULY IS AS ARISTOTLE SAID: *"WE LIVE IN DEEDS, NOT YEARS; IN THOUGHTS, NOT BREATHS; IN FEELINGS, NOT FIGURES ON A DIAL."*
"WE SHOULD COUNT TIME BY HEARTTHROBS."
IN THE FEW SECONDS IT HAS *LEFT*.

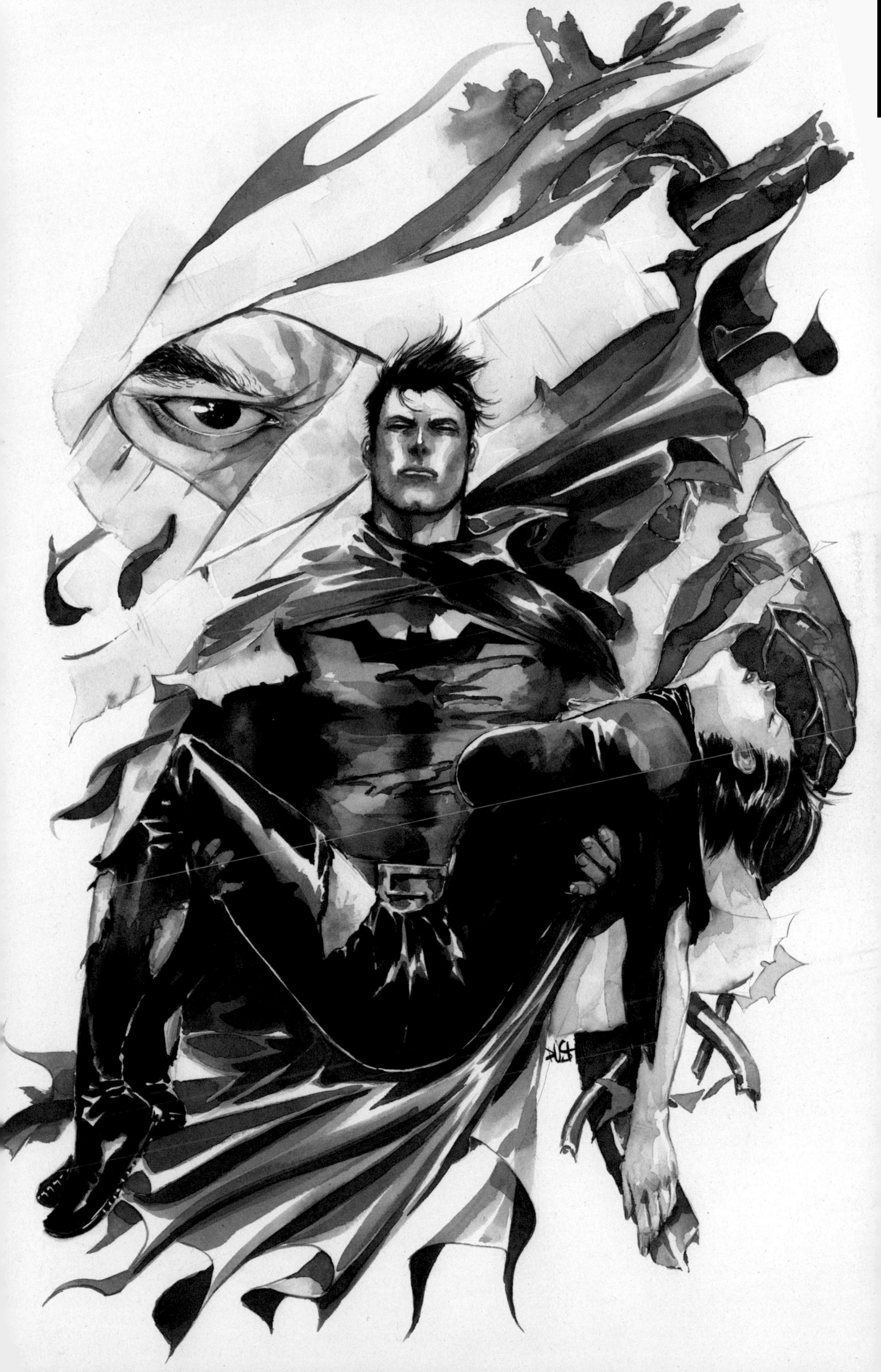

"We live in deeds, not years..."

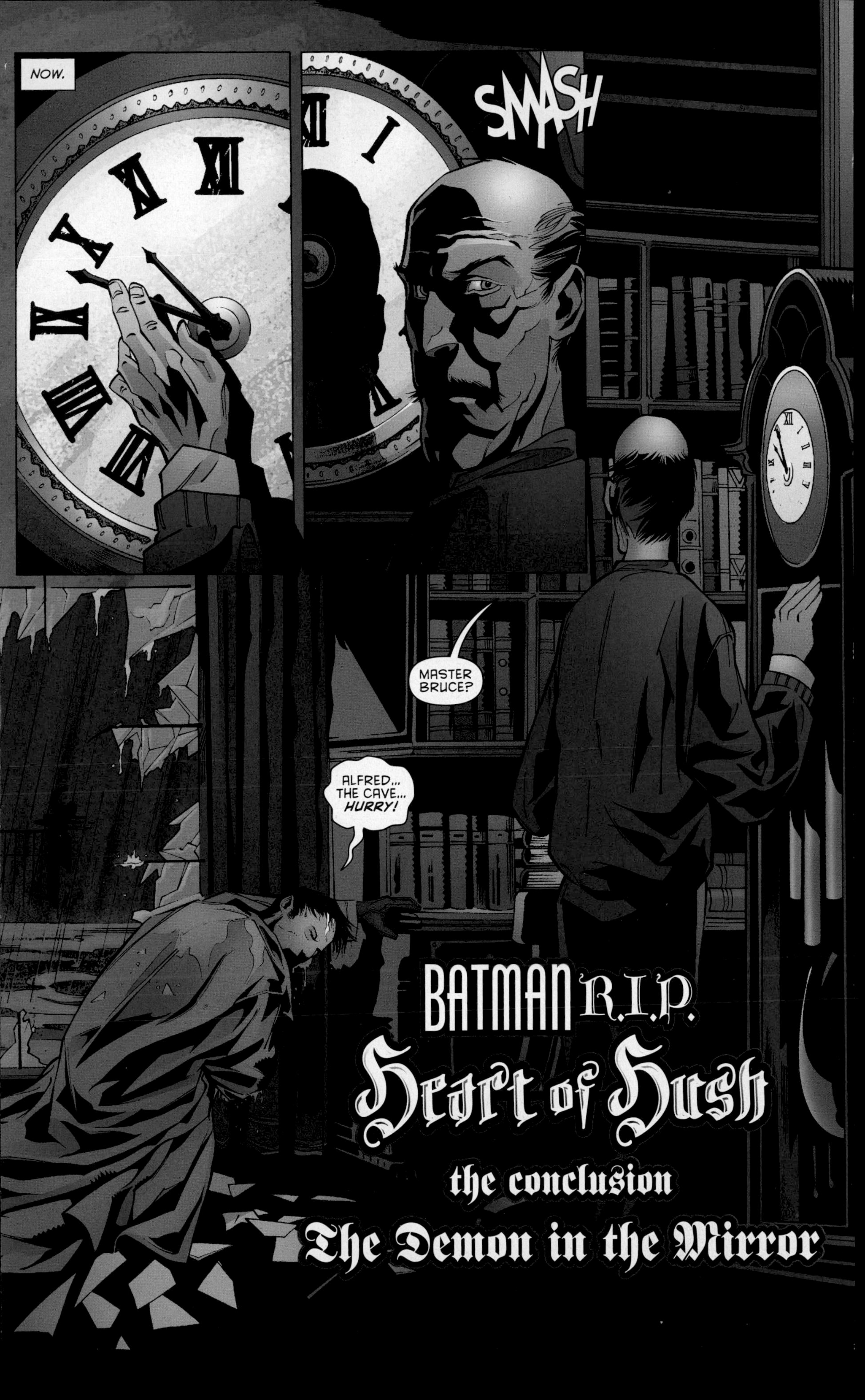
NOW.
SMASH
MASTER BRUCE?
ALFRED... THE CAVE... HURRY!
BATMAN R.I.P.
Heart of Hush
the conclusion
The Demon in the Mirror

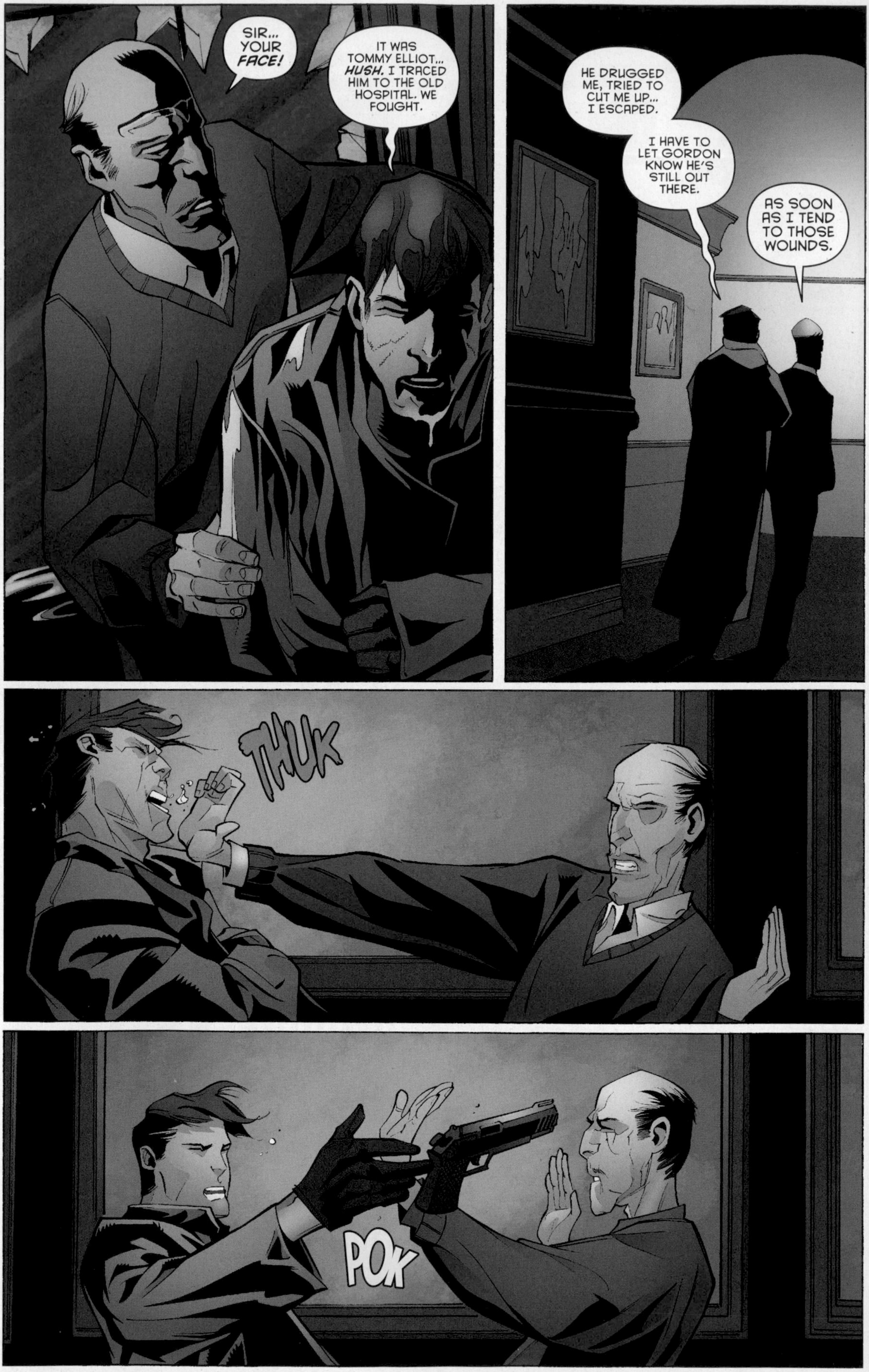

SIR... YOUR FACE!
IT WAS TOMMY ELLIOT... HUSH. I TRACED HIM TO THE OLD HOSPITAL. WE FOUGHT.
HE DRUGGED ME, TRIED TO CUT ME UP... I ESCAPED.
I HAVE TO LET GORDON KNOW HE'S STILL OUT THERE.
AS SOON AS I TEND TO THOSE WOUNDS.
THUK
POK

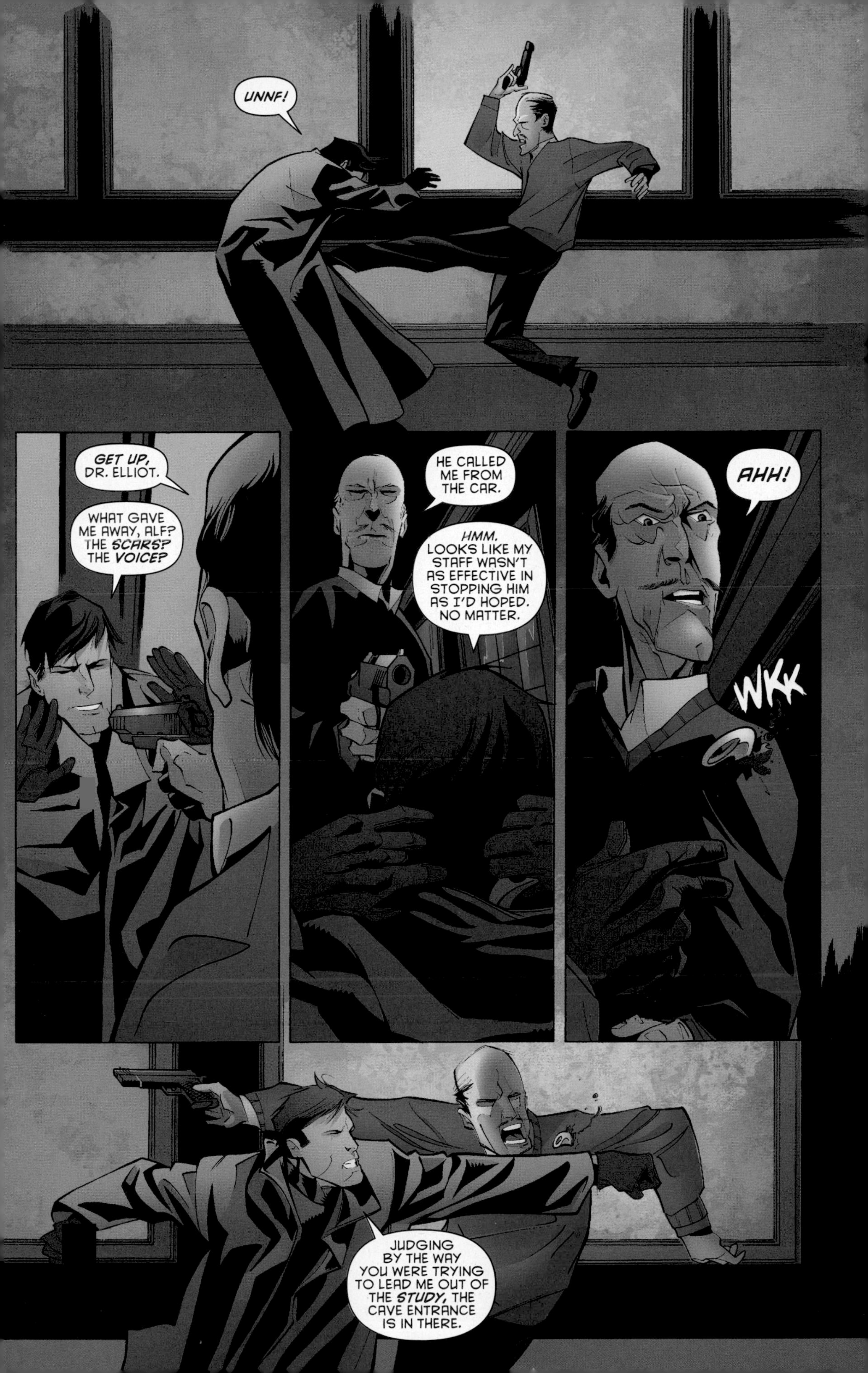
UNNF!
GET UP, DR. ELLIOT.
WHAT GAVE ME AWAY, ALF? THE SCARS? THE VOICE?
HE CALLED ME FROM THE CAR.
HMM. LOOKS LIKE MY STAFF WASN'T AS EFFECTIVE IN STOPPING HIM AS I'D HOPED. NO MATTER.
AHH!
WKK
JUDGING BY THE WAY YOU WERE TRYING TO LEAD ME OUT OF THE STUDY, THE CAVE ENTRANCE IS IN THERE.

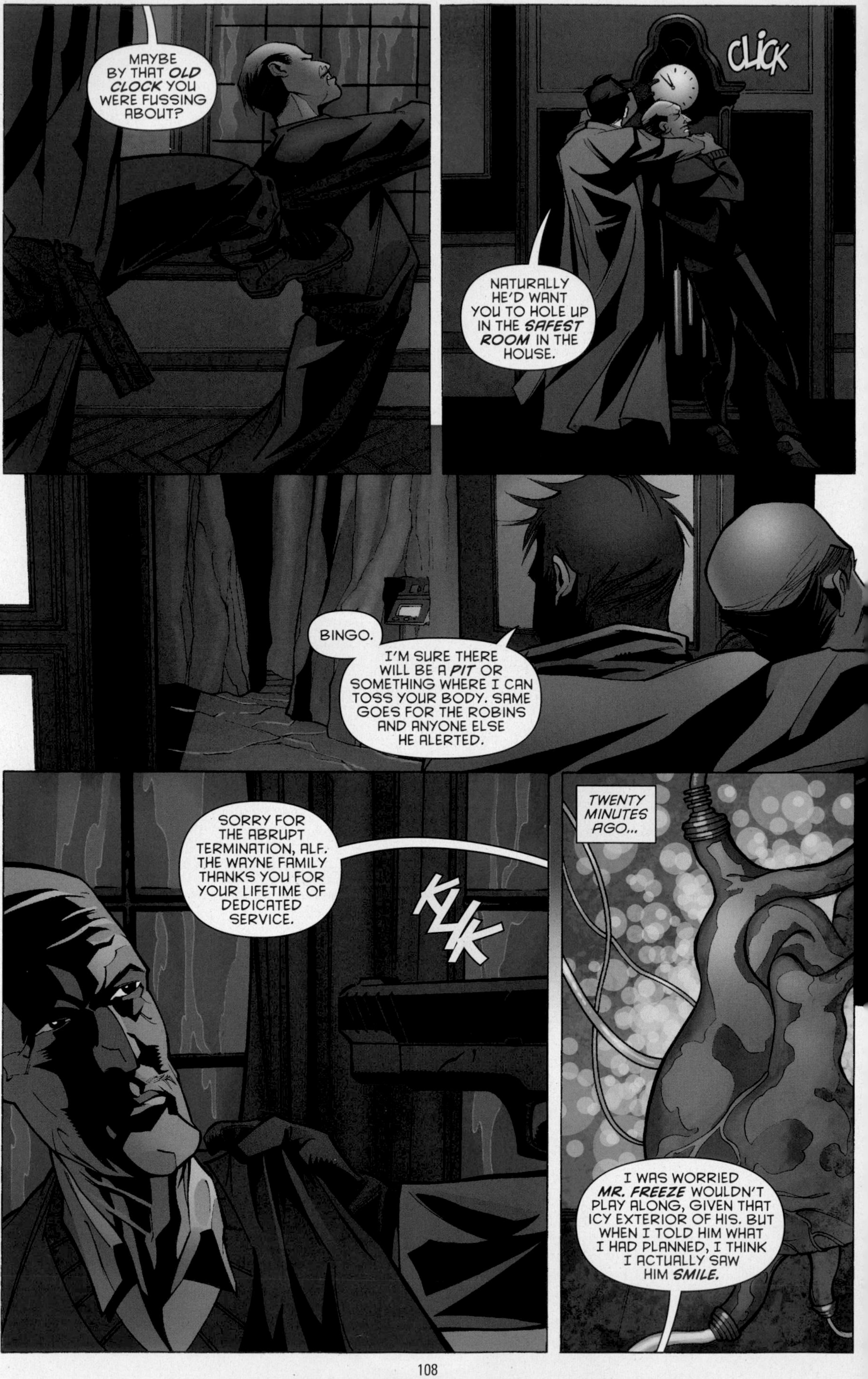
MAYBE BY THAT OLD CLOCK YOU WERE FUSSING ABOUT?
CLICK
NATURALLY HE'D WANT YOU TO HOLE UP IN THE SAFEST ROOM IN THE HOUSE.
BINGO.
I'M SURE THERE WILL BE A PIT OR SOMETHING WHERE I CAN TOSS YOUR BODY. SAME GOES FOR THE ROBINS AND ANYONE ELSE HE ALERTED.
SORRY FOR THE ABRUPT TERMINATION, ALF. THE WAYNE FAMILY THANKS YOU FOR YOUR LIFETIME OF DEDICATED SERVICE.
KLIK
TWENTY MINUTES AGO...
I WAS WORRIED MR. FREEZE WOULDN'T PLAY ALONG, GIVEN THAT ICY EXTERIOR OF HIS. BUT WHEN I TOLD HIM WHAT I HAD PLANNED, I THINK I ACTUALLY SAW HIM SMILE.

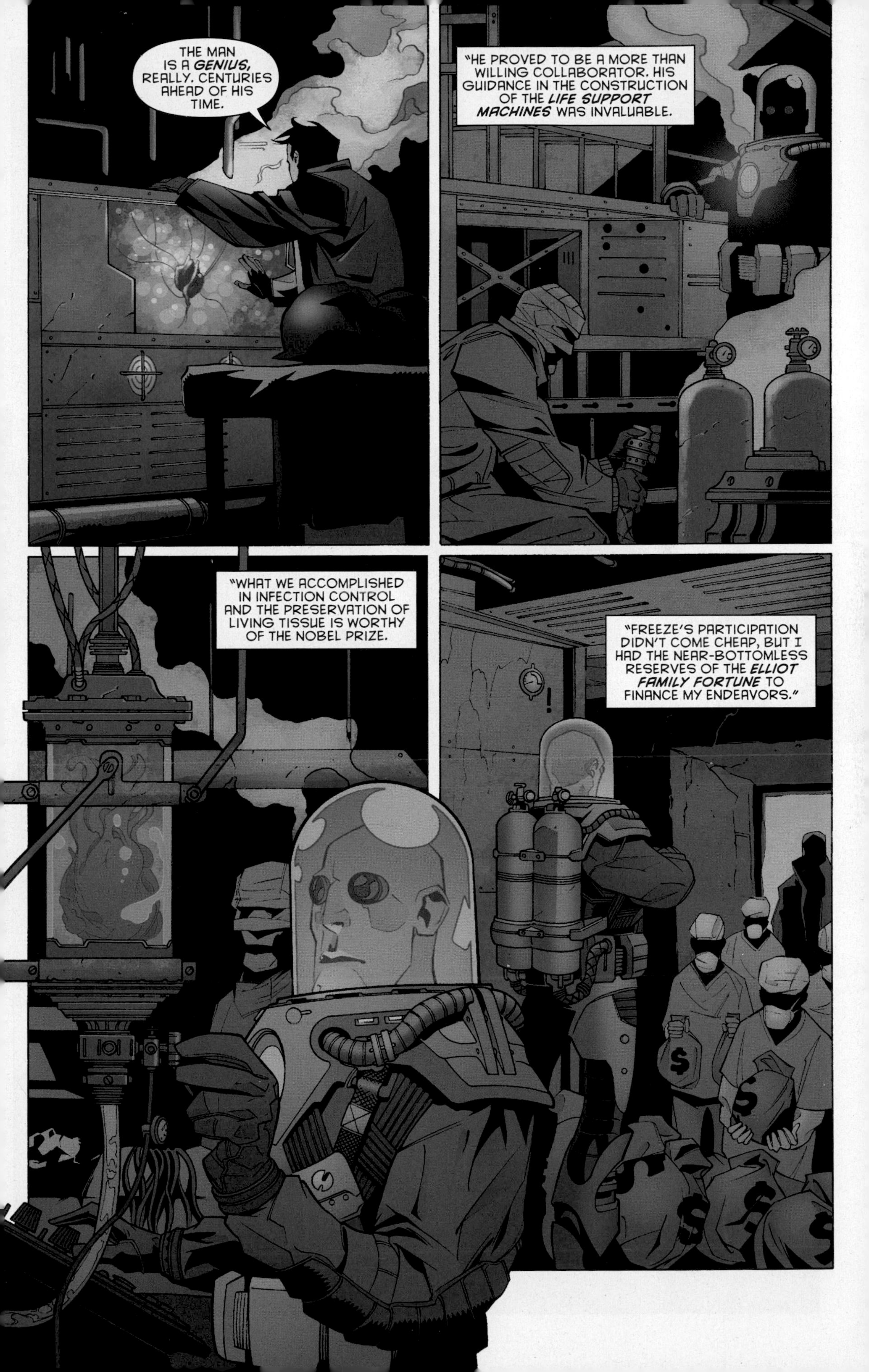
THE MAN IS A GENIUS, REALLY. CENTURIES AHEAD OF HIS TIME.
"HE PROVED TO BE A MORE THAN WILLING COLLABORATOR. HIS GUIDANCE IN THE CONSTRUCTION OF THE LIFE SUPPORT MACHINES WAS INVALUABLE.
"WHAT WE ACCOMPLISHED IN INFECTION CONTROL AND THE PRESERVATION OF LIVING TISSUE IS WORTHY OF THE NOBEL PRIZE.
"FREEZE'S PARTICIPATION DIDN'T COME CHEAP, BUT I HAD THE NEAR-BOTTOMLESS RESERVES OF THE ELLIOT FAMILY FORTUNE TO FINANCE MY ENDEAVORS."

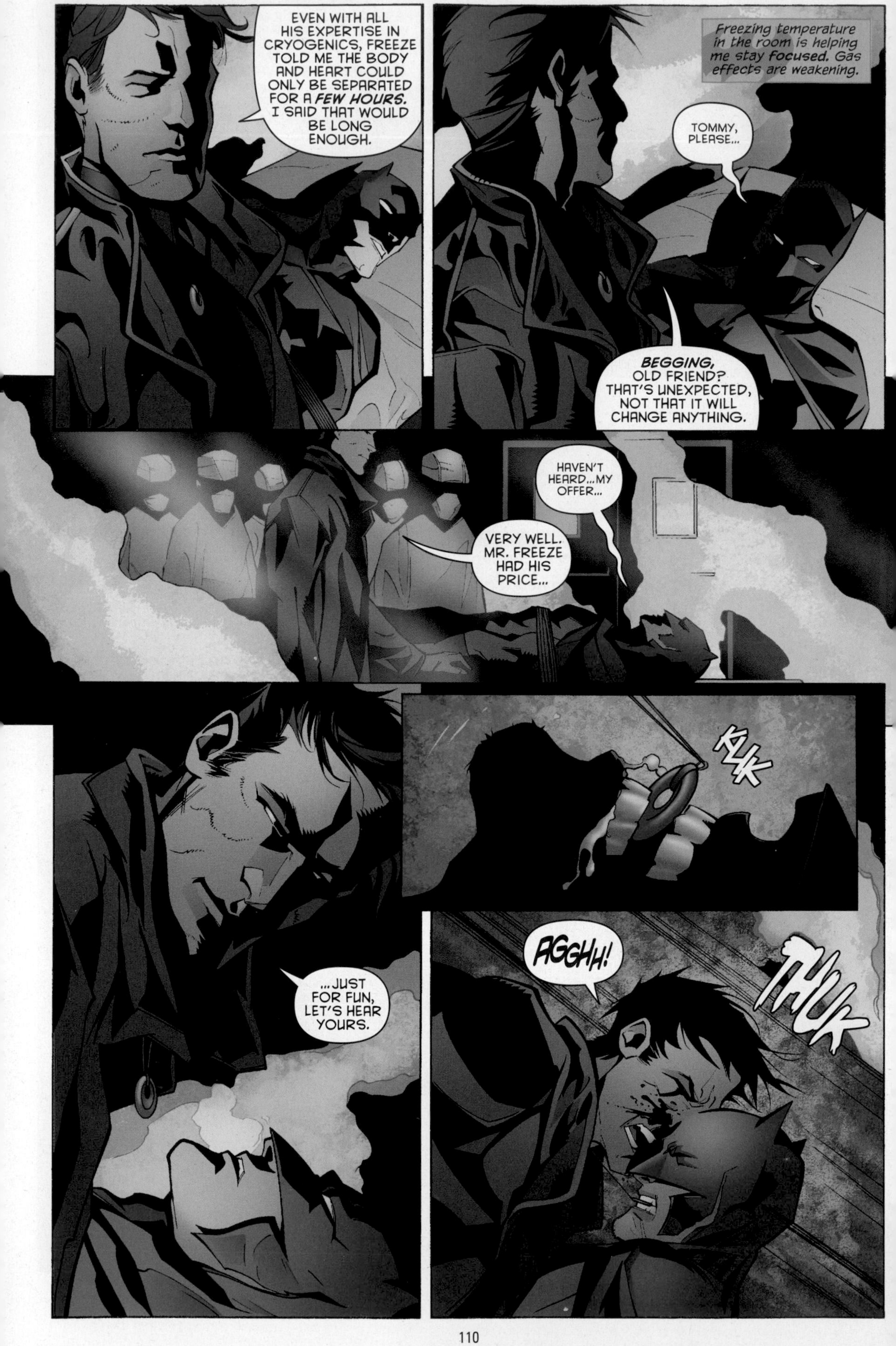
EVEN WITH ALL HIS EXPERTISE IN CRYOGENICS, FREEZE TOLD ME THE BODY AND HEART COULD ONLY BE SEPARATED FOR A FEW HOURS. I SAID THAT WOULD BE LONG ENOUGH.
Freezing temperature in the room is helping me stay focused. Gas effects are weakening.
TOMMY, PLEASE...
BEGGING, OLD FRIEND? THAT'S UNEXPECTED, NOT THAT IT WILL CHANGE ANYTHING.
HAVEN'T HEARD...MY OFFER...
VERY WELL. MR. FREEZE HAD HIS PRICE...
...JUST FOR FUN, LET'S HEAR YOURS.
KLIK
AGGHH!
THUK

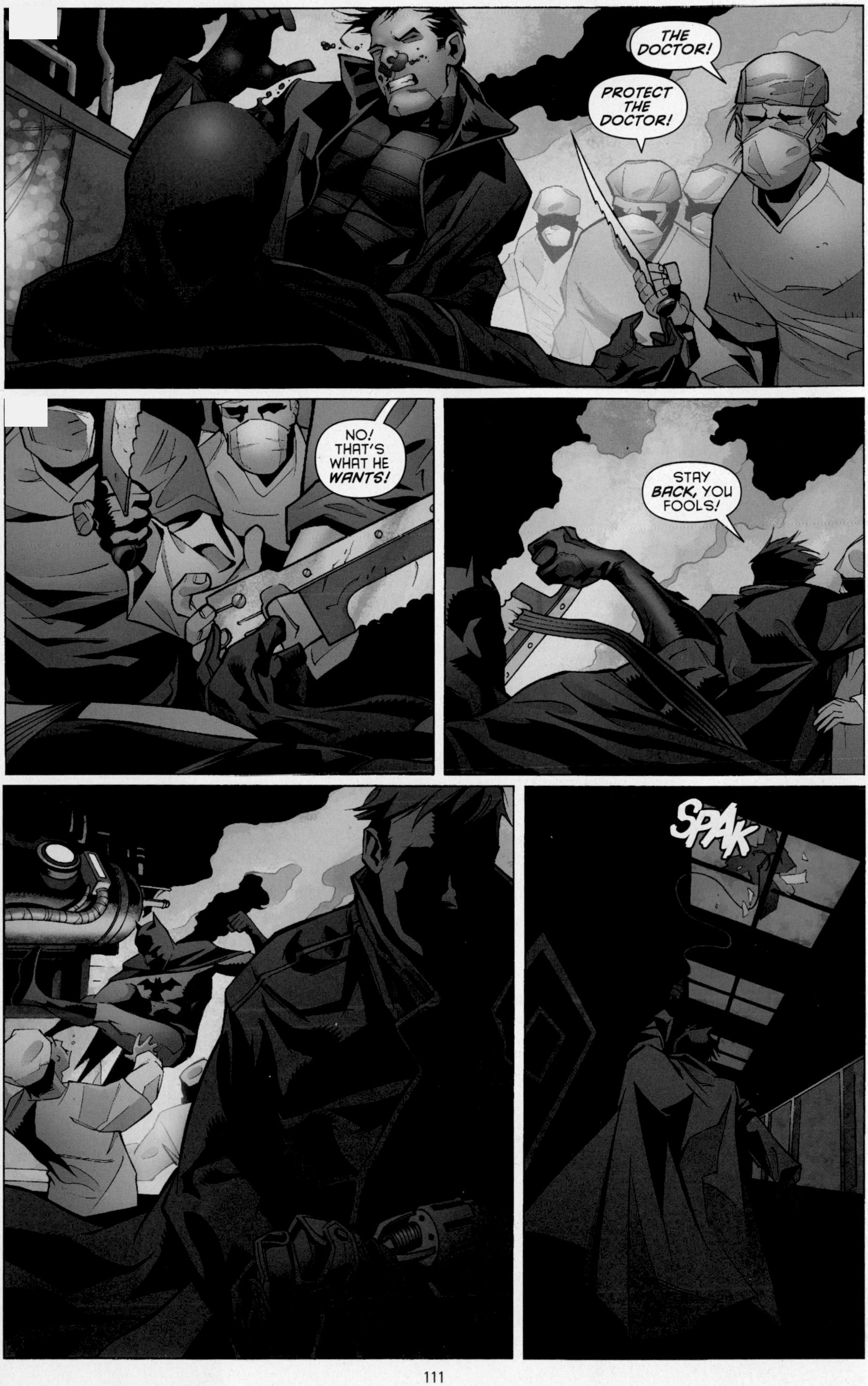
THE DOCTOR!
PROTECT THE DOCTOR!
NO! THAT'S WHAT HE WANTS!
STAY BACK, YOU FOOLS!
SPAK

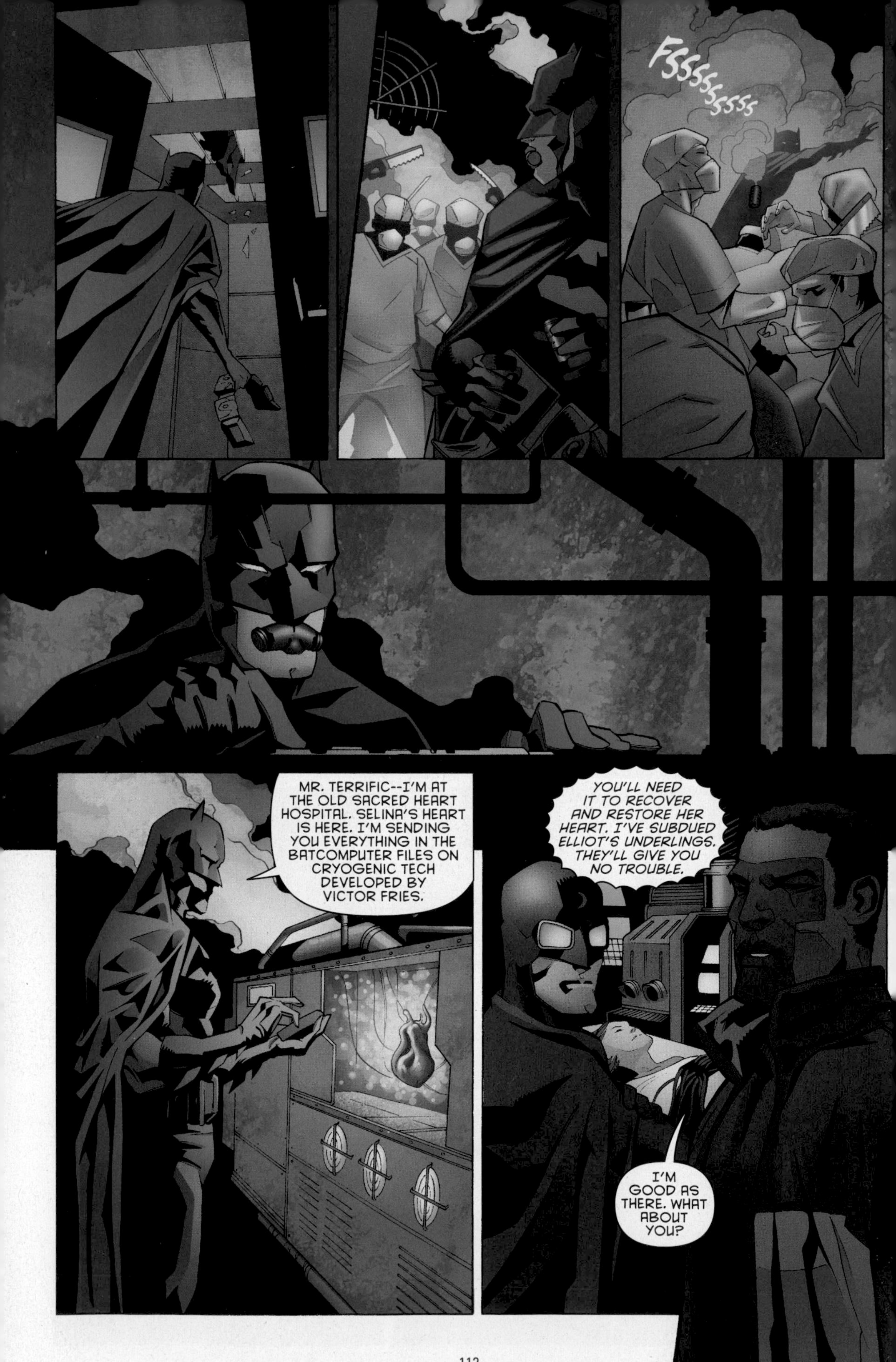
FSSSSSSSSS
MR. TERRIFIC--I'M AT THE OLD SACRED HEART HOSPITAL. SELINA'S HEART IS HERE. I'M SENDING YOU EVERYTHING IN THE BATCOMPUTER FILES ON CRYOGENIC TECH DEVELOPED BY VICTOR FRIES.
YOU'LL NEED IT TO RECOVER AND RESTORE HER HEART. I'VE SUBDUED ELLIOT'S UNDERLINGS. THEY'LL GIVE YOU NO TROUBLE.
I'M GOOD AS THERE. WHAT ABOUT YOU?

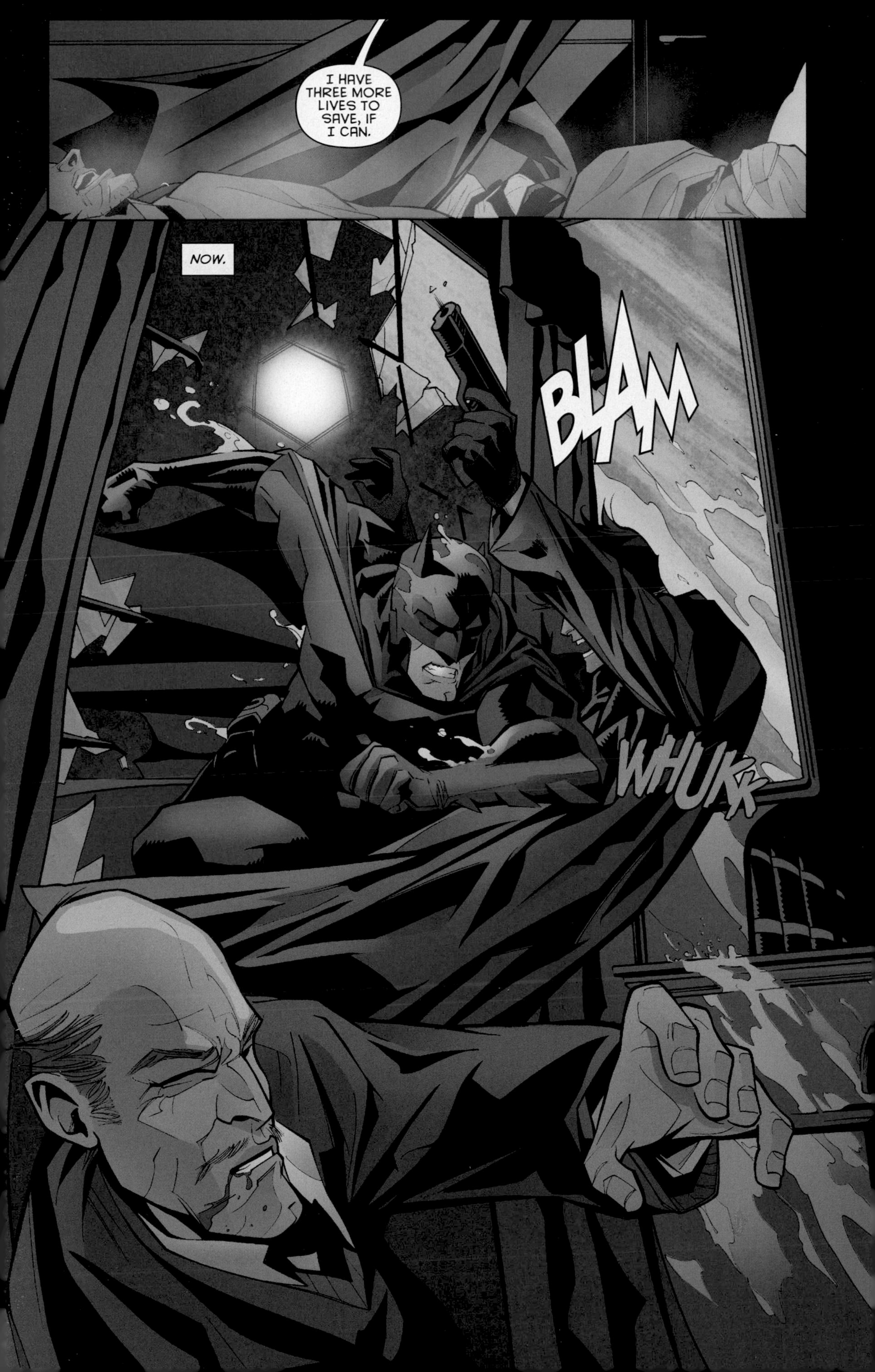
I HAVE THREE MORE LIVES TO SAVE, IF I CAN.
NOW.
BLAM
WHUKK

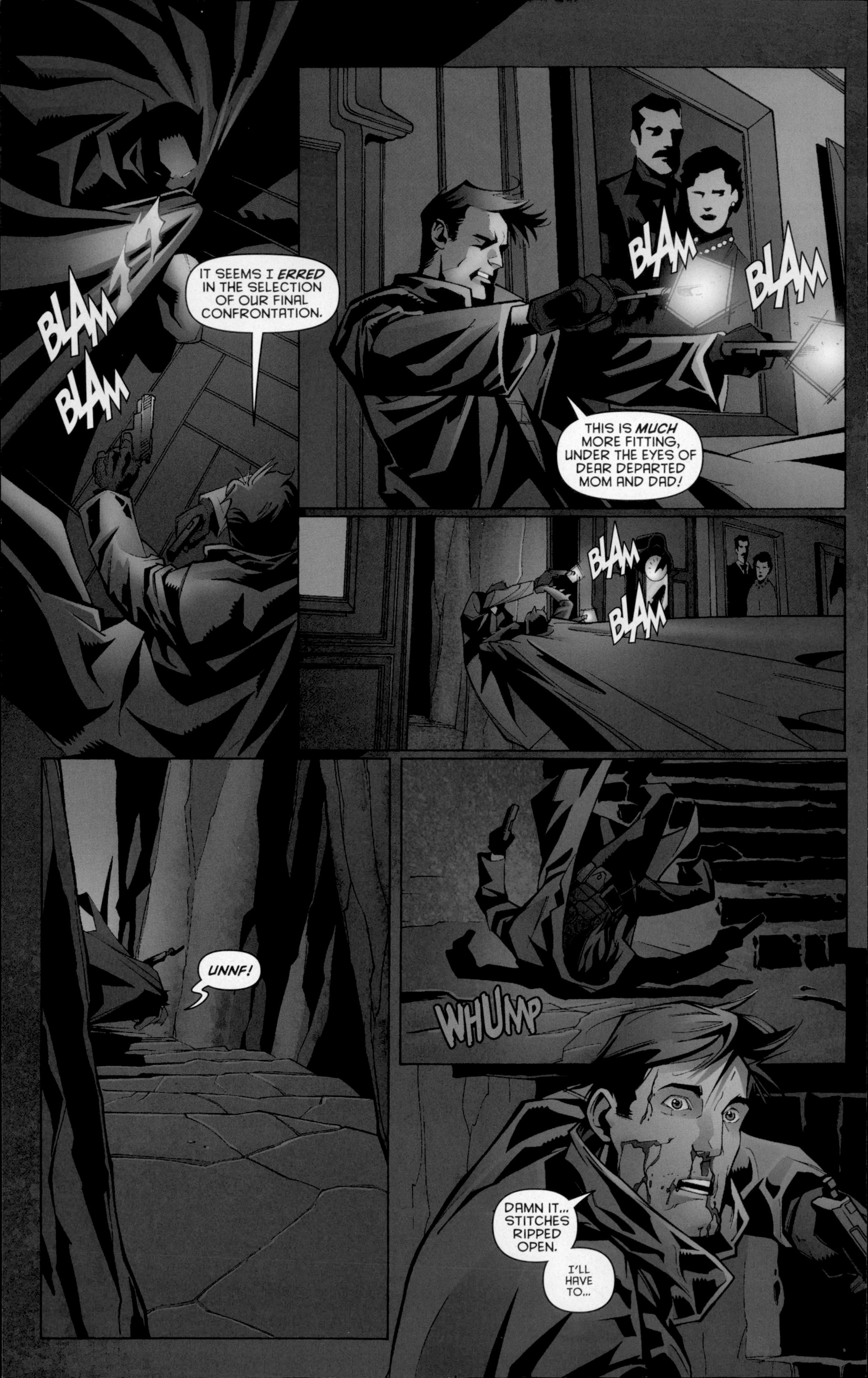
BLAM
BLAM
IT SEEMS I *ERRED* IN THE SELECTION OF OUR FINAL CONFRONTATION.
BLAM
BLAM
THIS IS *MUCH* MORE FITTING, UNDER THE EYES OF DEAR DEPARTED MOM AND DAD!
BLAM
BLAM
UNNF!
WHUMP
DAMN IT... STITCHES RIPPED OPEN.
I'LL HAVE TO...

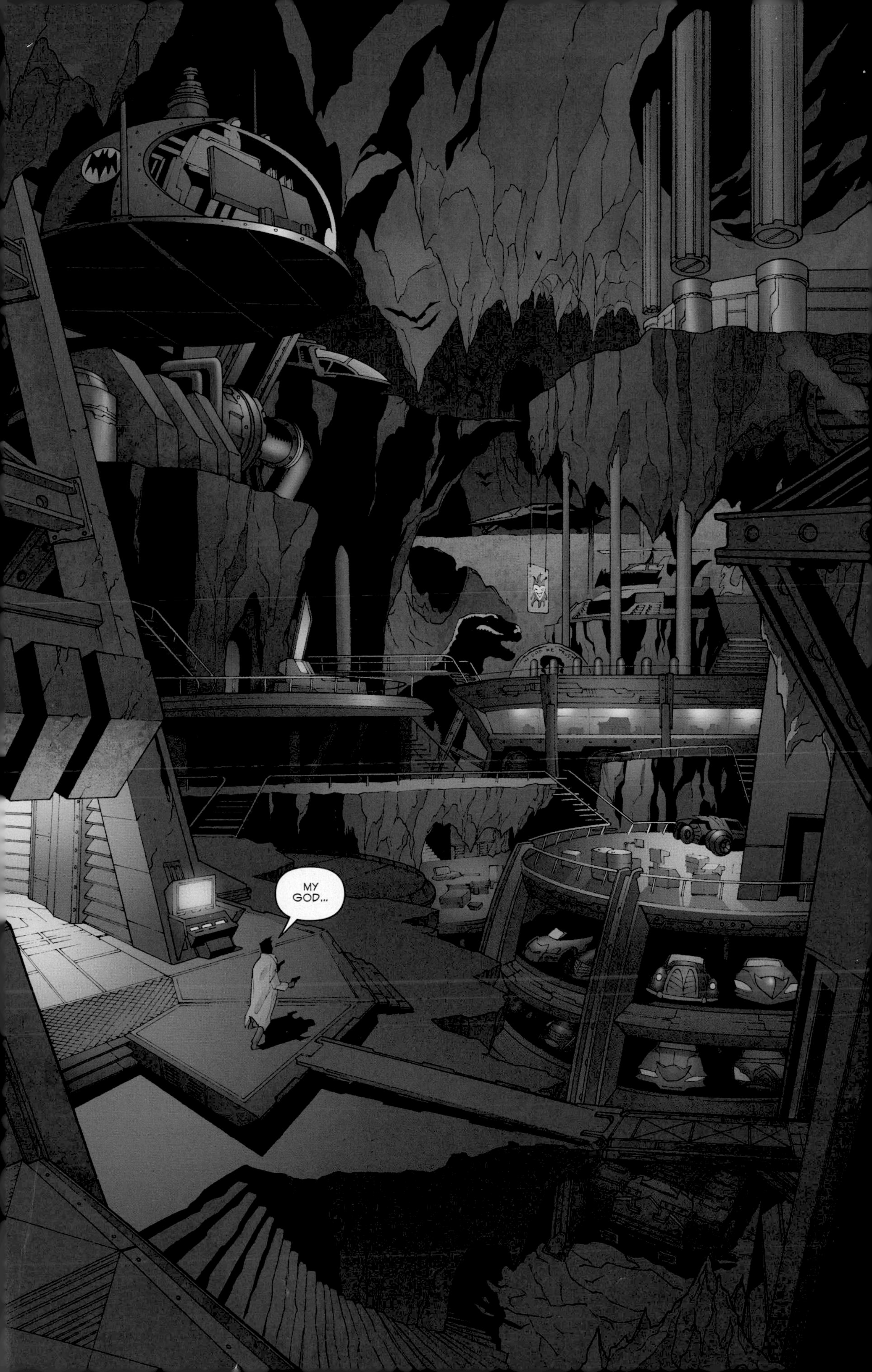
MY GOD...

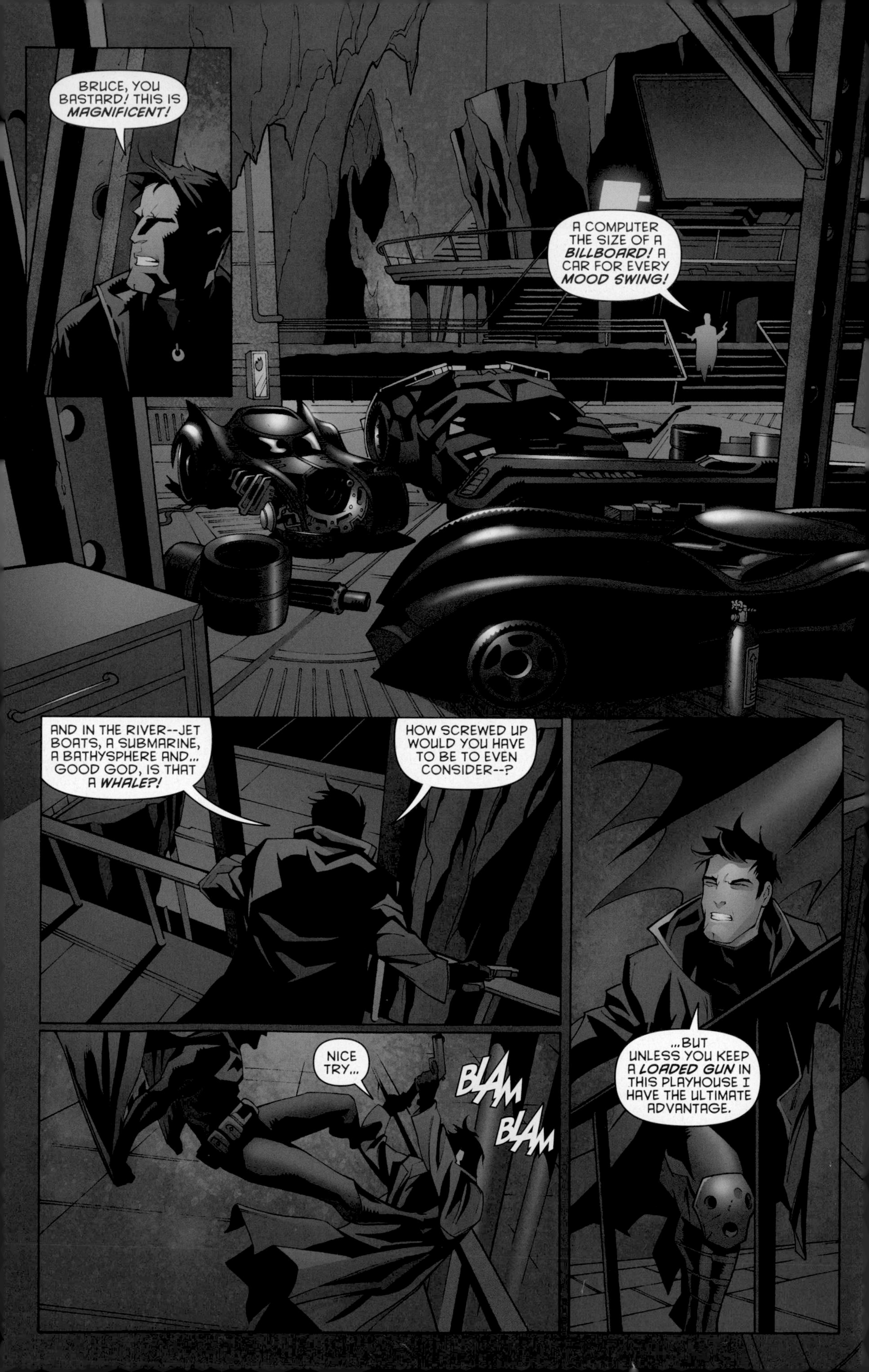
BRUCE, YOU BASTARD! THIS IS MAGNIFICENT!
A COMPUTER THE SIZE OF A BILLBOARD! A CAR FOR EVERY MOOD SWING!
AND IN THE RIVER--JET BOATS, A SUBMARINE, A BATHYSPHERE AND... GOOD GOD, IS THAT A WHALE?!
HOW SCREWED UP WOULD YOU HAVE TO BE TO EVEN CONSIDER--?
...BUT UNLESS YOU KEEP A LOADED GUN IN THIS PLAYHOUSE I HAVE THE ULTIMATE ADVANTAGE.
NICE TRY...
BLAM
BLAM

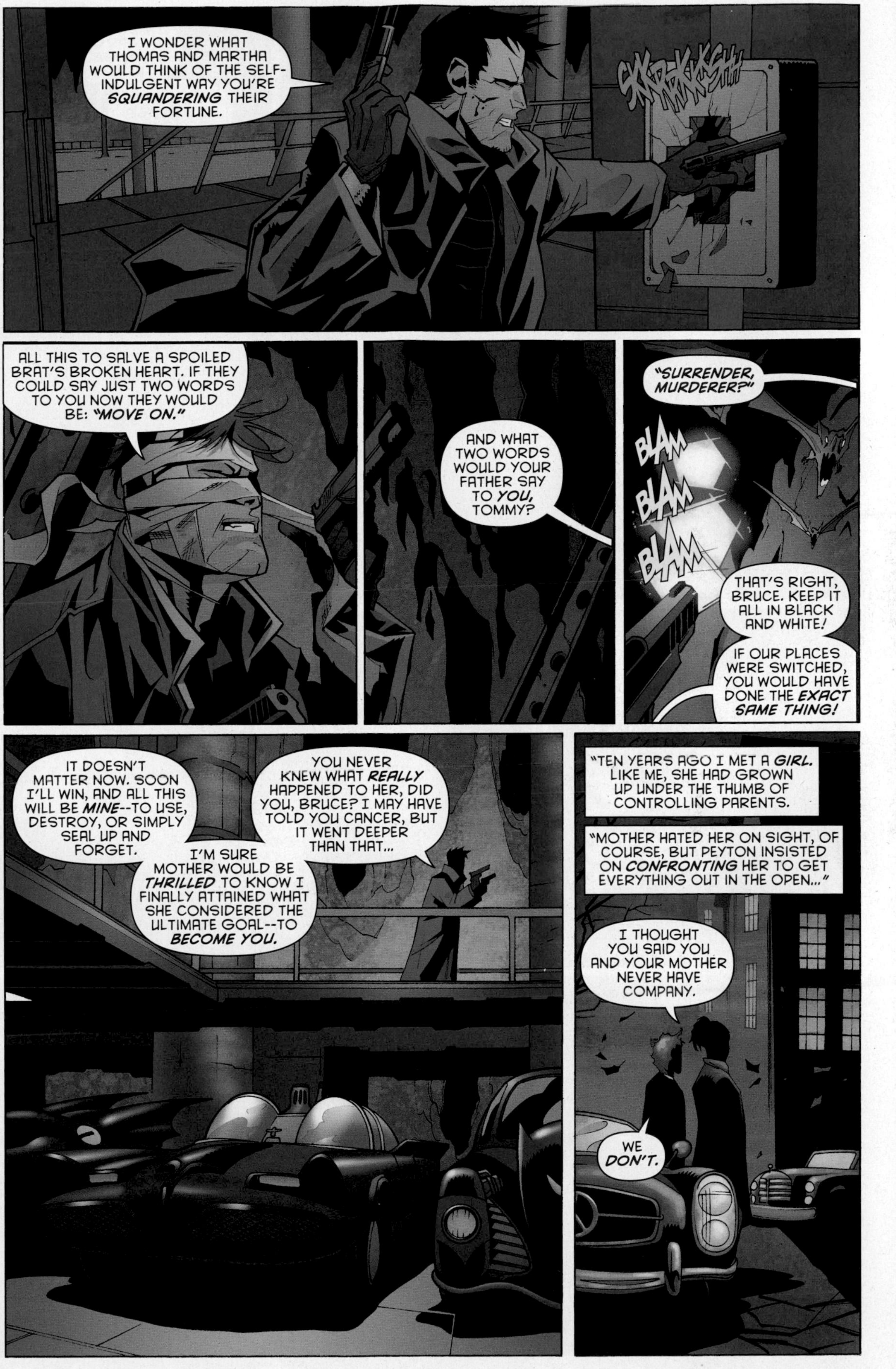
I WONDER WHAT THOMAS AND MARTHA WOULD THINK OF THE SELF-INDULGENT WAY YOU'RE *SQUANDERING* THEIR FORTUNE.
SKRRKKSSH
ALL THIS TO SALVE A SPOILED BRAT'S BROKEN HEART. IF THEY COULD SAY JUST TWO WORDS TO YOU NOW THEY WOULD BE: *"MOVE ON."*
AND WHAT TWO WORDS WOULD YOUR FATHER SAY TO *YOU,* TOMMY?
"SURRENDER, MURDERER?"
BLAM
BLAM
BLAM
THAT'S RIGHT, BRUCE. KEEP IT ALL IN BLACK AND WHITE!
IF OUR PLACES WERE SWITCHED, YOU WOULD HAVE DONE THE *EXACT SAME THING!*
IT DOESN'T MATTER NOW. SOON I'LL WIN, AND ALL THIS WILL BE *MINE*--TO USE, DESTROY, OR SIMPLY SEAL UP AND FORGET.
I'M SURE MOTHER WOULD BE *THRILLED* TO KNOW I FINALLY ATTAINED WHAT SHE CONSIDERED THE ULTIMATE GOAL--TO *BECOME YOU.*
YOU NEVER KNEW WHAT *REALLY* HAPPENED TO HER, DID YOU, BRUCE? I MAY HAVE TOLD YOU CANCER, BUT IT WENT DEEPER THAN THAT...
"TEN YEARS AGO I MET A *GIRL.* LIKE ME, SHE HAD GROWN UP UNDER THE THUMB OF CONTROLLING PARENTS.
"MOTHER HATED HER ON SIGHT, OF COURSE, BUT PEYTON INSISTED ON *CONFRONTING* HER TO GET EVERYTHING OUT IN THE OPEN..."
I THOUGHT YOU SAID YOU AND YOUR MOTHER NEVER HAVE COMPANY.
WE *DON'T.*

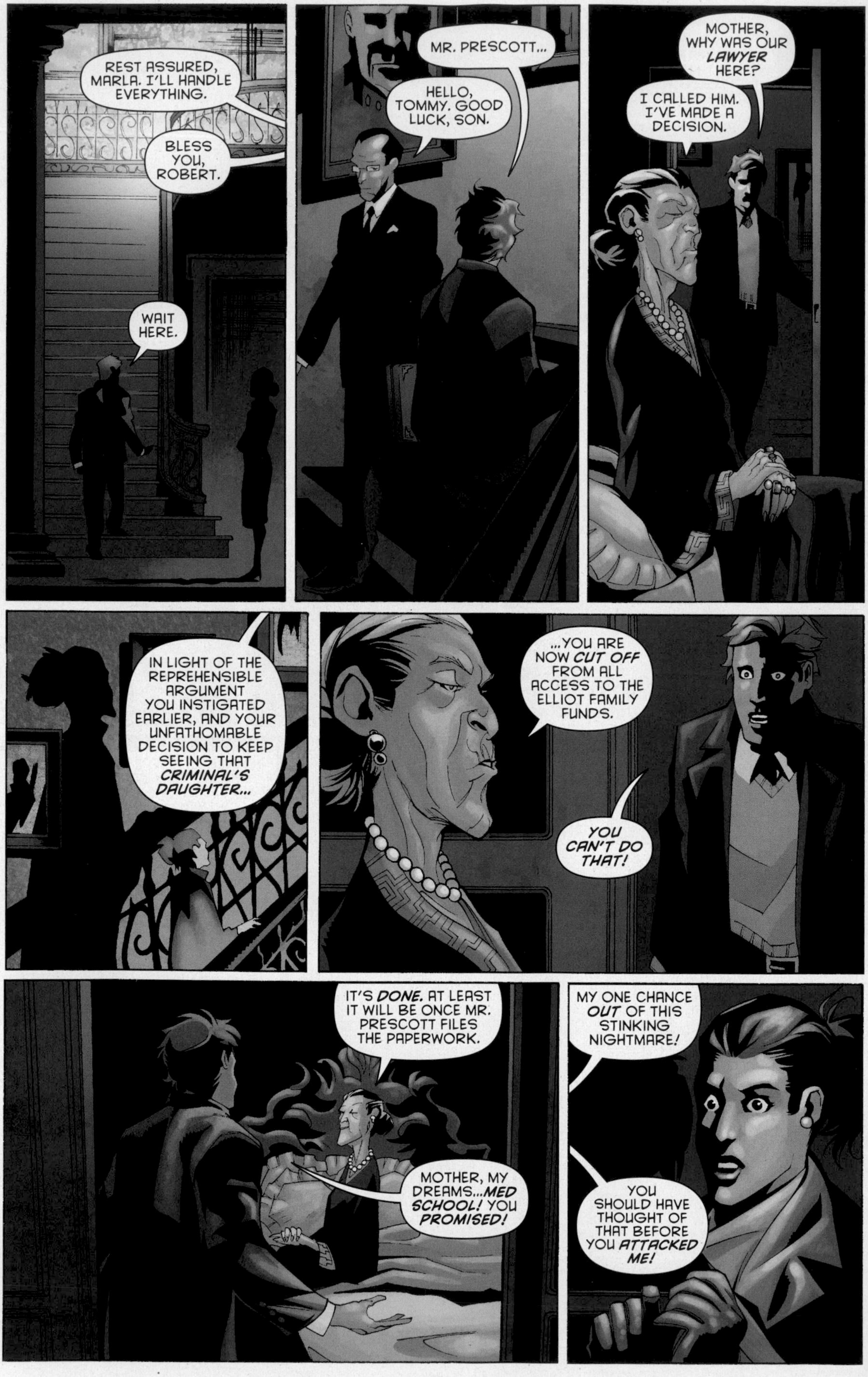
REST ASSURED, MARLA. I'LL HANDLE EVERYTHING.
BLESS YOU, ROBERT.
WAIT HERE.
MR. PRESCOTT...
HELLO, TOMMY. GOOD LUCK, SON.
MOTHER, WHY WAS OUR LAWYER HERE?
I CALLED HIM. I'VE MADE A DECISION.
IN LIGHT OF THE REPREHENSIBLE ARGUMENT YOU INSTIGATED EARLIER, AND YOUR UNFATHOMABLE DECISION TO KEEP SEEING THAT CRIMINAL'S DAUGHTER...
...YOU ARE NOW CUT OFF FROM ALL ACCESS TO THE ELLIOT FAMILY FUNDS.
YOU CAN'T DO THAT!
IT'S DONE. AT LEAST IT WILL BE ONCE MR. PRESCOTT FILES THE PAPERWORK.
MOTHER, MY DREAMS...MED SCHOOL! YOU PROMISED!
MY ONE CHANCE OUT OF THIS STINKING NIGHTMARE!
YOU SHOULD HAVE THOUGHT OF THAT BEFORE YOU ATTACKED ME!

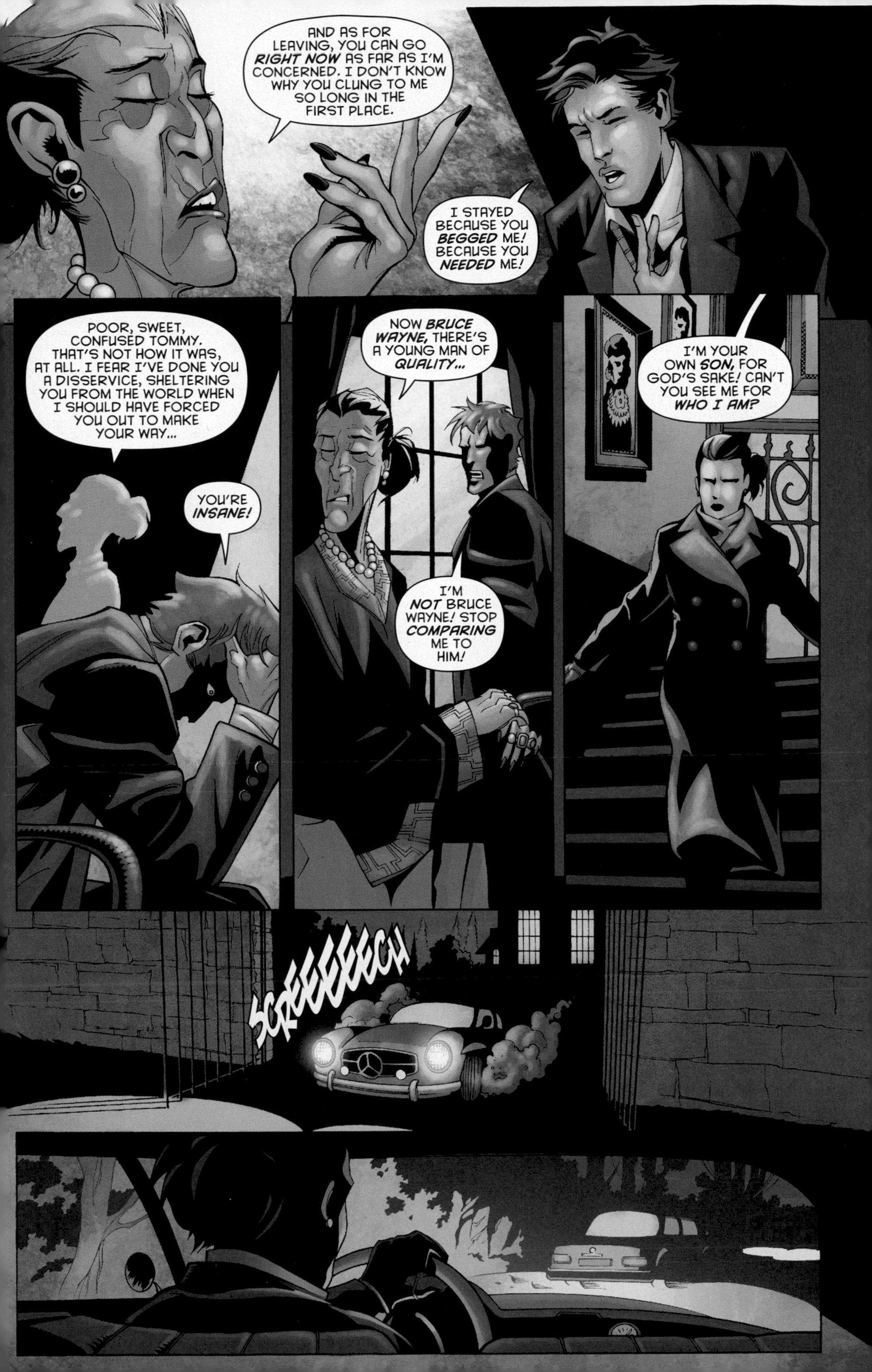
AND AS FOR LEAVING, YOU CAN GO RIGHT NOW AS FAR AS I'M CONCERNED. I DON'T KNOW WHY YOU CLUNG TO ME SO LONG IN THE FIRST PLACE.
I STAYED BECAUSE YOU BEGGED ME! BECAUSE YOU NEEDED ME!
POOR, SWEET, CONFUSED TOMMY. THAT'S NOT HOW IT WAS, AT ALL. I FEAR I'VE DONE YOU A DISSERVICE, SHELTERING YOU FROM THE WORLD WHEN I SHOULD HAVE FORCED YOU OUT TO MAKE YOUR WAY...
YOU'RE INSANE!
NOW BRUCE WAYNE, THERE'S A YOUNG MAN OF QUALITY...
I'M NOT BRUCE WAYNE! STOP COMPARING ME TO HIM!
I'M YOUR OWN SON, FOR GOD'S SAKE! CAN'T YOU SEE ME FOR WHO I AM?
SCREEEEECH

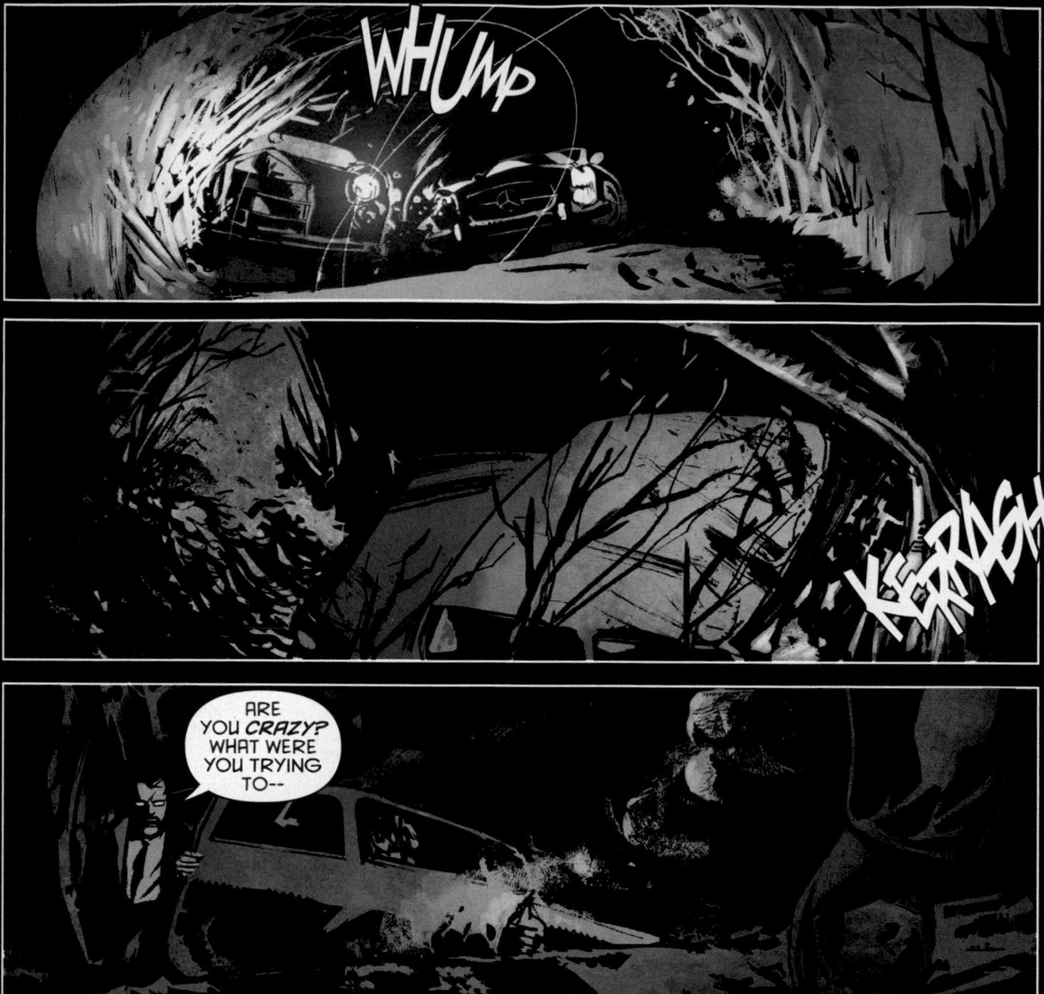
WHUMP
KERRASH
ARE YOU CRAZY? WHAT WERE YOU TRYING TO--

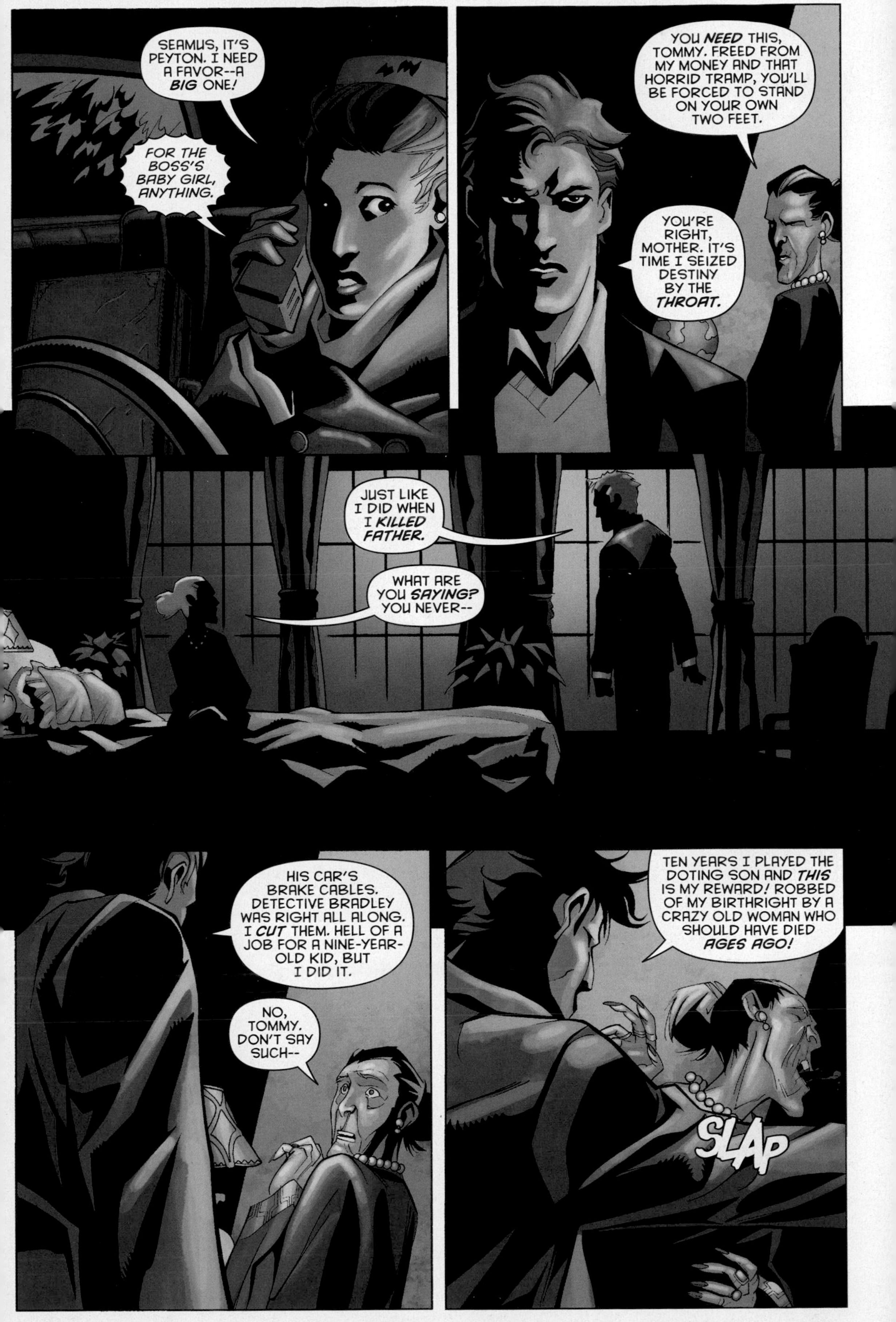
SEAMUS, IT'S PEYTON. I NEED A FAVOR--A BIG ONE!
FOR THE BOSS'S BABY GIRL, ANYTHING.
YOU NEED THIS, TOMMY. FREED FROM MY MONEY AND THAT HORRID TRAMP, YOU'LL BE FORCED TO STAND ON YOUR OWN TWO FEET.
YOU'RE RIGHT, MOTHER. IT'S TIME I SEIZED DESTINY BY THE THROAT.
JUST LIKE I DID WHEN I KILLED FATHER.
WHAT ARE YOU SAYING? YOU NEVER--
HIS CAR'S BRAKE CABLES. DETECTIVE BRADLEY WAS RIGHT ALL ALONG. I CUT THEM. HELL OF A JOB FOR A NINE-YEAR-OLD KID, BUT I DID IT.
NO, TOMMY. DON'T SAY SUCH--
TEN YEARS I PLAYED THE DOTING SON AND THIS IS MY REWARD! ROBBED OF MY BIRTHRIGHT BY A CRAZY OLD WOMAN WHO SHOULD HAVE DIED AGES AGO!
SLAP

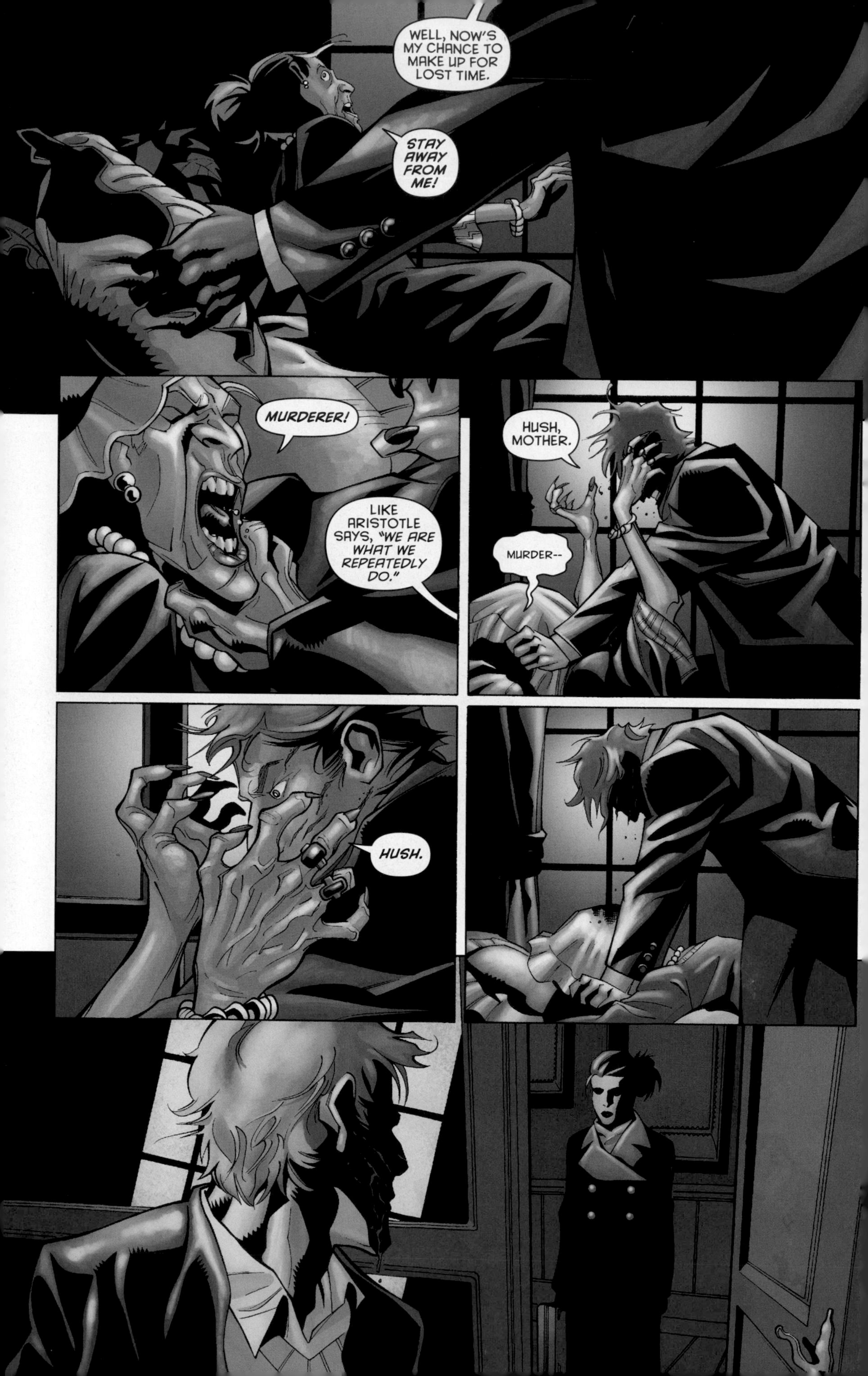
WELL, NOW'S MY CHANCE TO MAKE UP FOR LOST TIME.
STAY AWAY FROM ME!
MURDERER!
LIKE ARISTOTLE SAYS, "WE ARE WHAT WE REPEATEDLY DO."
HUSH, MOTHER.
MURDER--
HUSH.

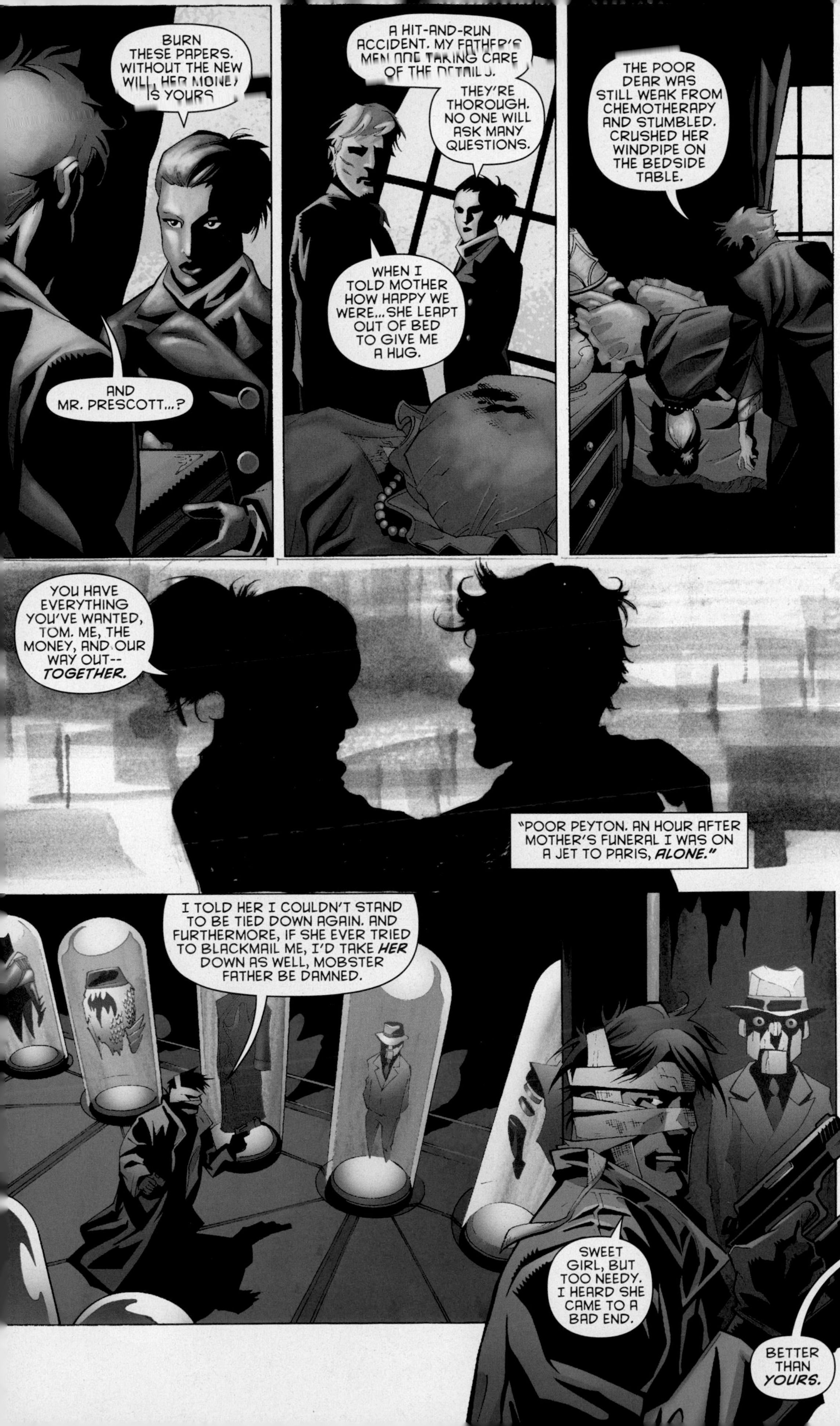
BURN THESE PAPERS. WITHOUT THE NEW WILL, HER MONEY IS YOURS.
AND MR. PRESCOTT...?
A HIT-AND-RUN ACCIDENT. MY FATHER'S MEN ARE TAKING CARE OF THE DETAILS.
THEY'RE THOROUGH. NO ONE WILL ASK MANY QUESTIONS.
WHEN I TOLD MOTHER HOW HAPPY WE WERE... SHE LEAPT OUT OF BED TO GIVE ME A HUG.
THE POOR DEAR WAS STILL WEAK FROM CHEMOTHERAPY AND STUMBLED. CRUSHED HER WINDPIPE ON THE BEDSIDE TABLE.
YOU HAVE EVERYTHING YOU'VE WANTED, TOM. ME, THE MONEY, AND OUR WAY OUT-- *TOGETHER.*
"POOR PEYTON. AN HOUR AFTER MOTHER'S FUNERAL I WAS ON A JET TO PARIS, *ALONE.*"
I TOLD HER I COULDN'T STAND TO BE TIED DOWN AGAIN. AND FURTHERMORE, IF SHE EVER TRIED TO BLACKMAIL ME, I'D TAKE *HER* DOWN AS WELL, MOBSTER FATHER BE DAMNED.
SWEET GIRL, BUT TOO NEEDY. I HEARD SHE CAME TO A BAD END.
BETTER THAN *YOURS.*

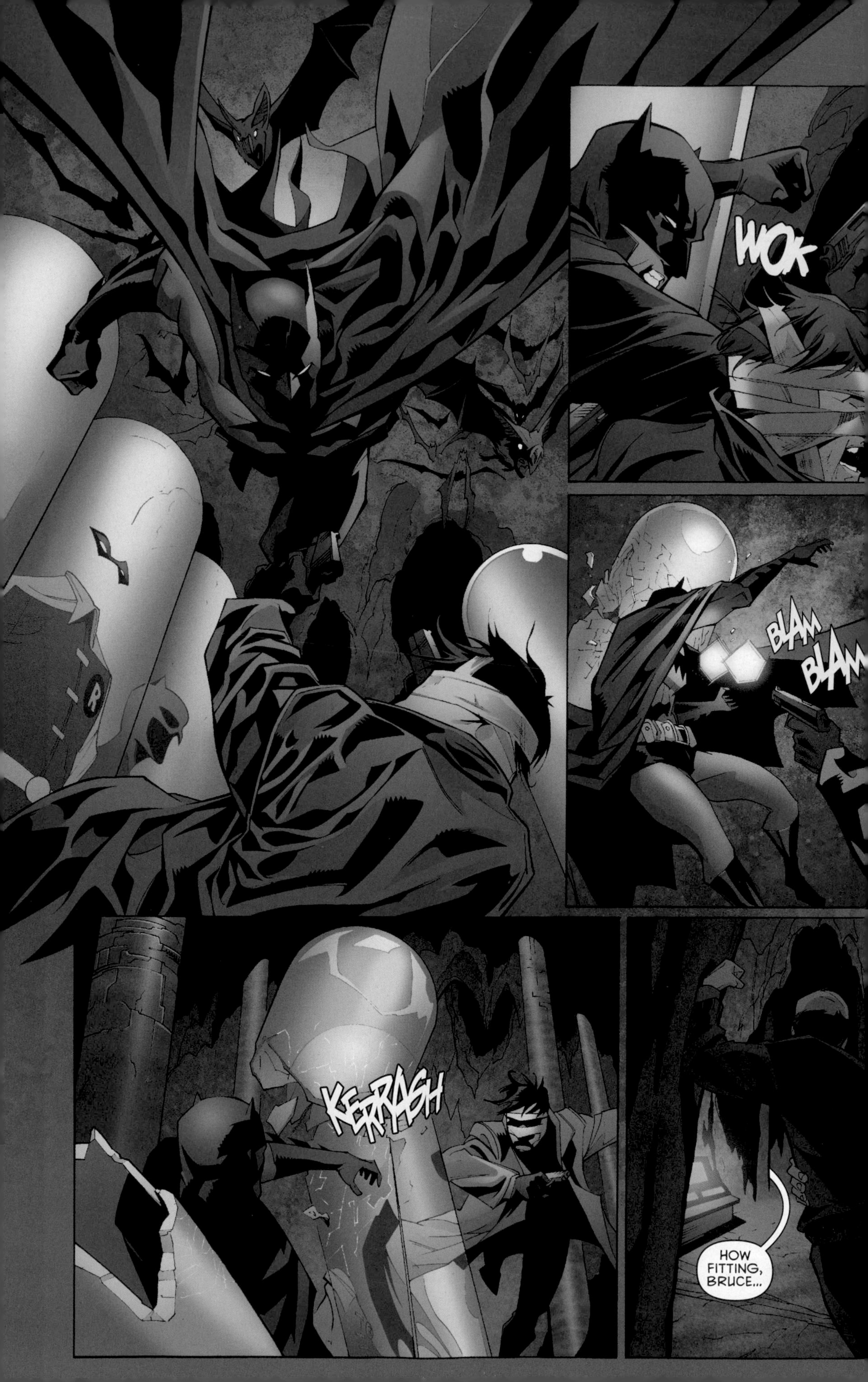
WOK
BLAM
BLAM
KERRASH
HOW FITTING, BRUCE...

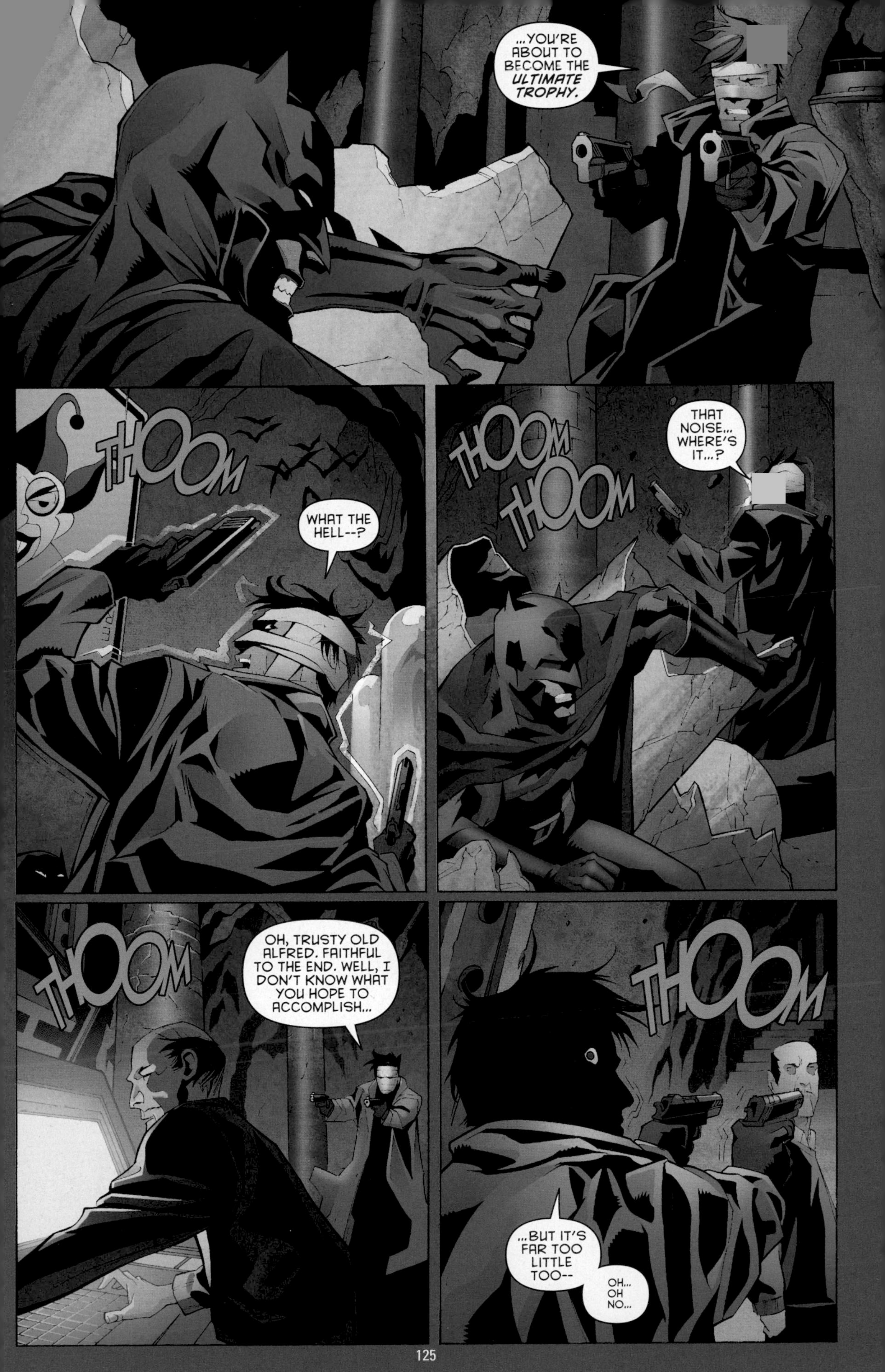
...YOU'RE ABOUT TO BECOME THE *ULTIMATE TROPHY.*
THOOM
WHAT THE HELL--?
THOOM
THOOM
THAT NOISE... WHERE'S IT...?
THOOM
OH, TRUSTY OLD ALFRED. FAITHFUL TO THE END. WELL, I DON'T KNOW WHAT YOU HOPE TO ACCOMPLISH...
THOOM
...BUT IT'S FAR TOO LITTLE TOO--
OH... OH NO...

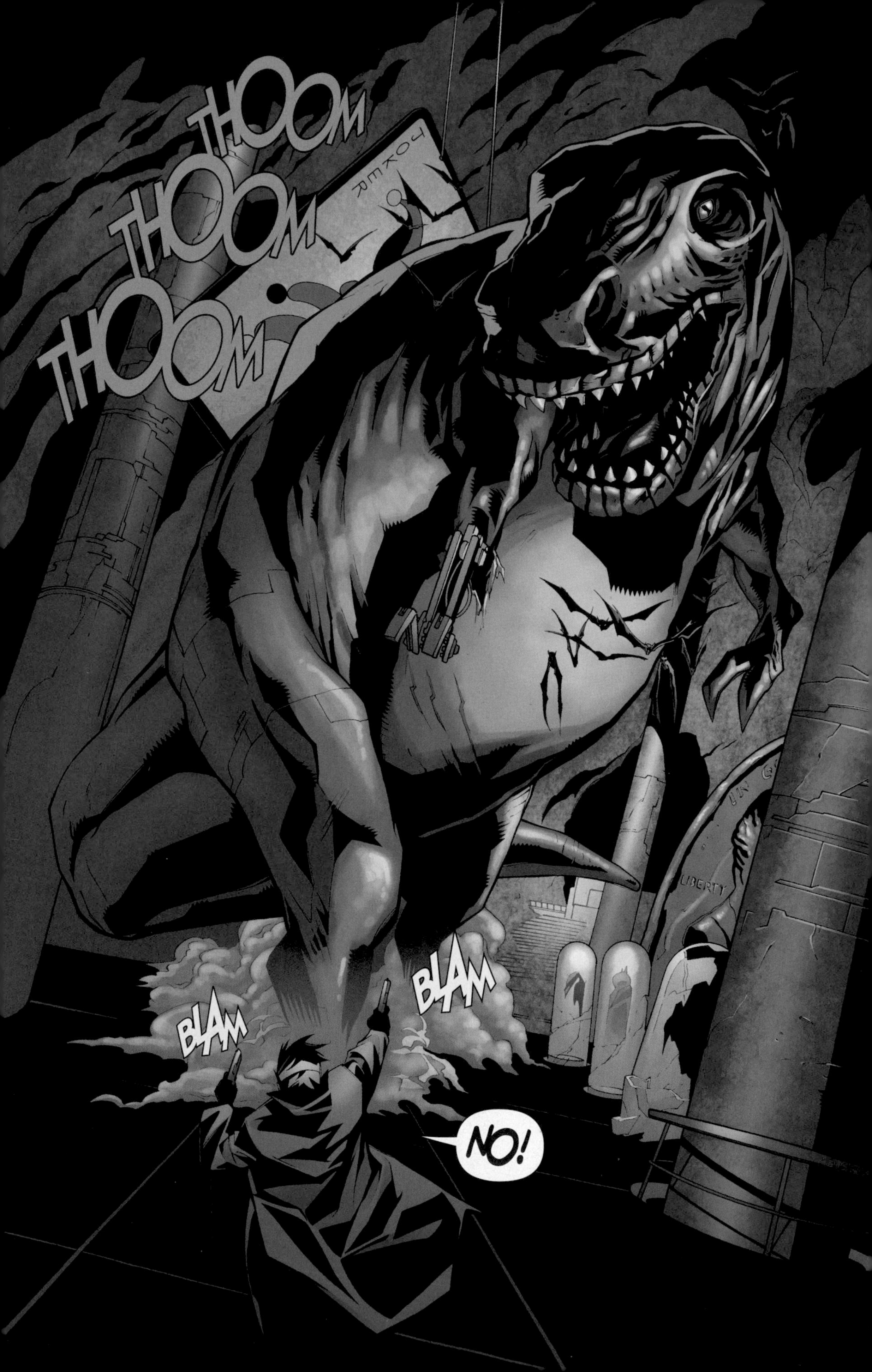
THOOM
THOOM
THOOM
JOKER
BLAM
BLAM
NO!
LIBERTY

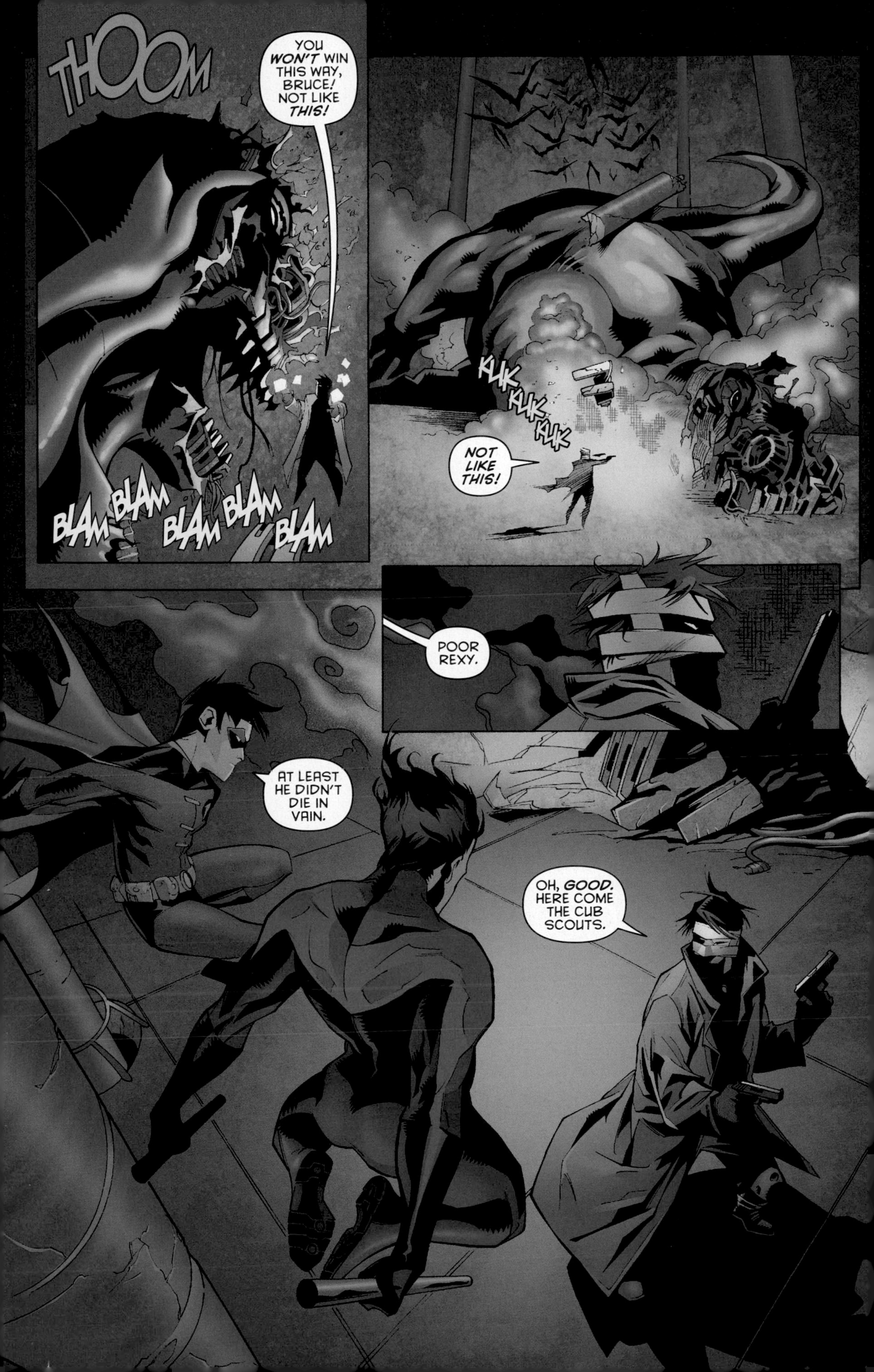
THOOM
YOU WON'T WIN THIS WAY, BRUCE! NOT LIKE THIS!
BLAM BLAM BLAM BLAM BLAM
KUK KUK KUK
NOT LIKE THIS!
POOR REXY.
AT LEAST HE DIDN'T DIE IN VAIN.
OH, GOOD. HERE COME THE CUB SCOUTS.

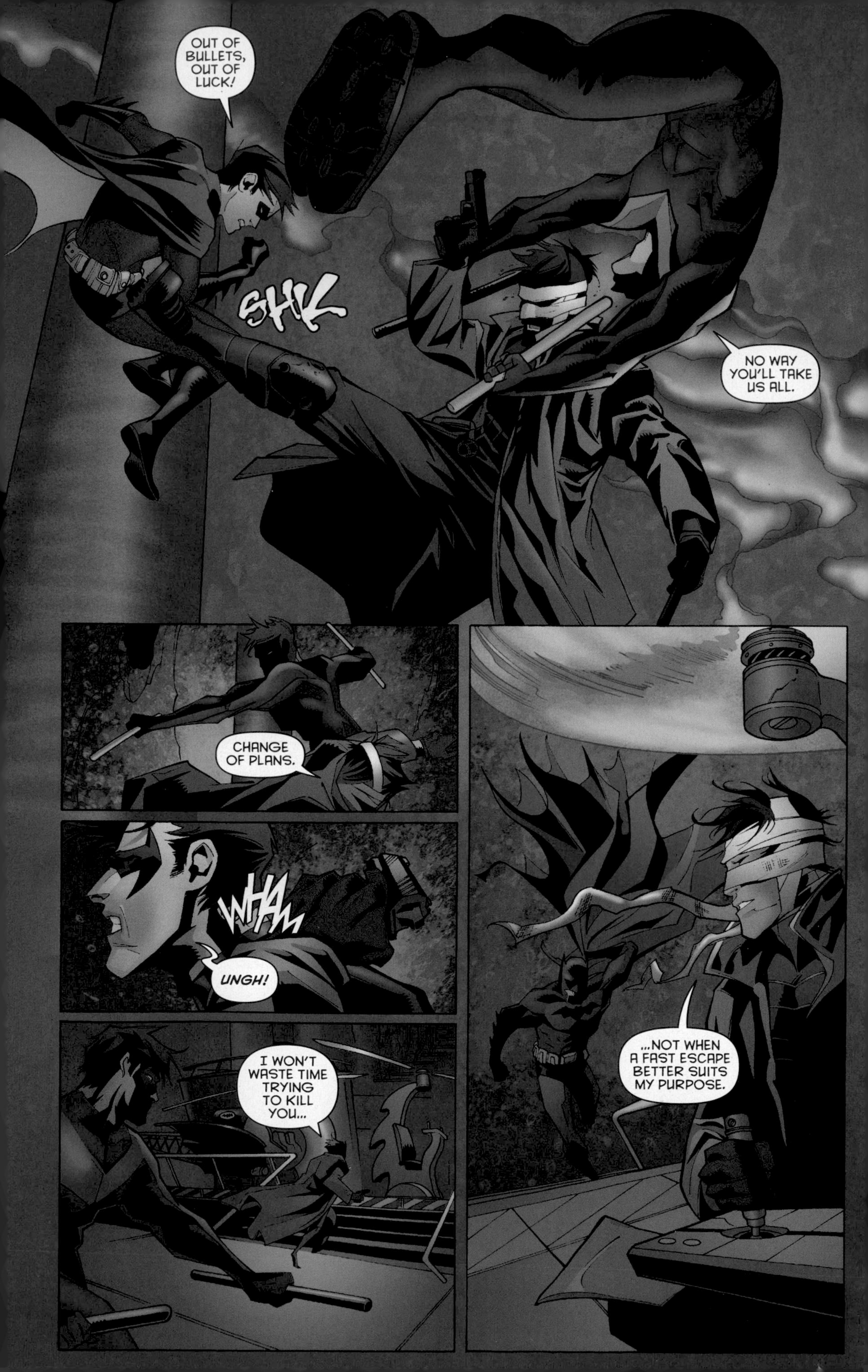
OUT OF BULLETS, OUT OF LUCK!
SHIK
NO WAY YOU'LL TAKE US ALL.
CHANGE OF PLANS.
WHAM
UNGH!
I WON'T WASTE TIME TRYING TO KILL YOU...
...NOT WHEN A FAST ESCAPE BETTER SUITS MY PURPOSE.

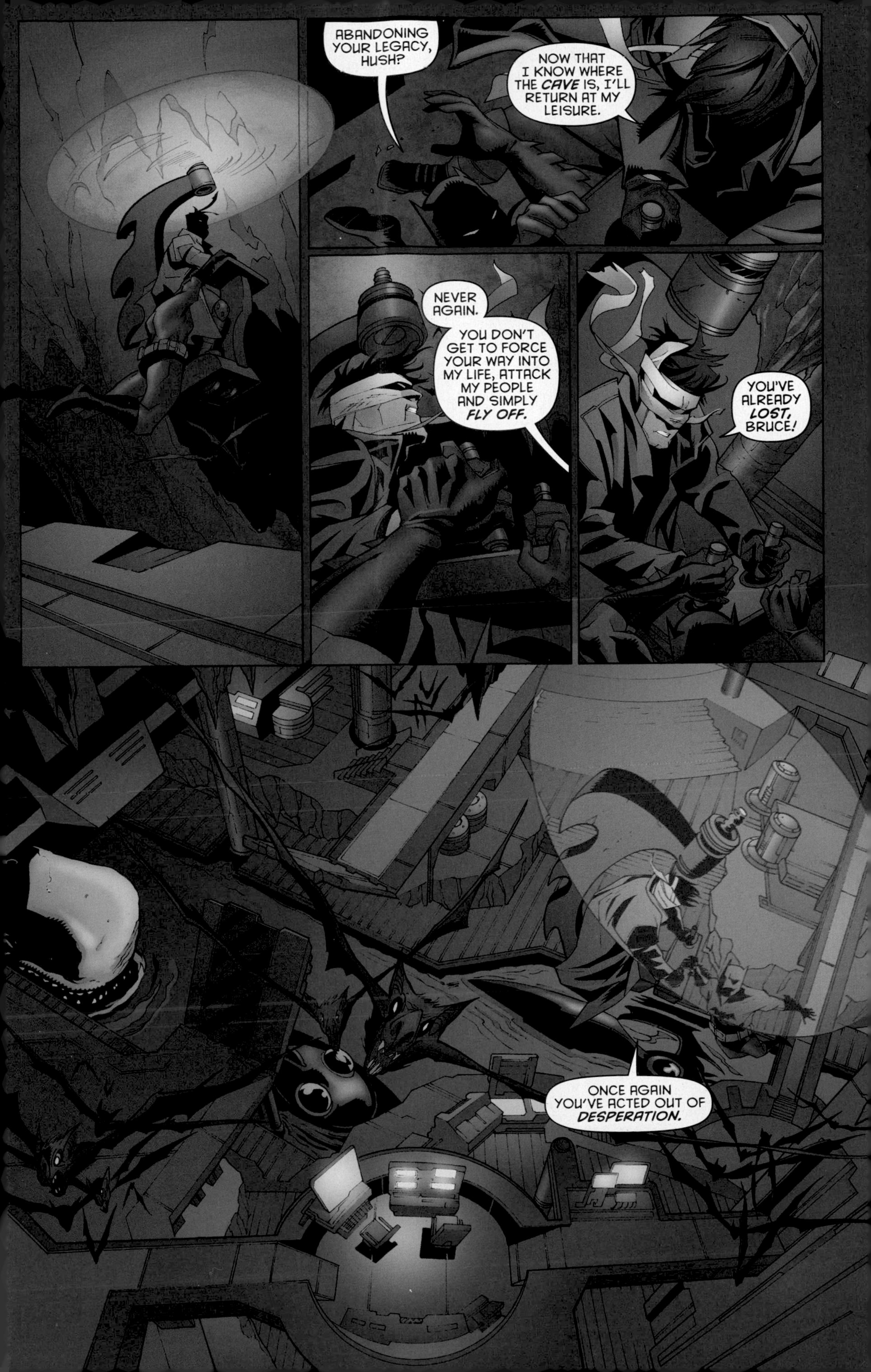
ABANDONING YOUR LEGACY, HUSH?
NOW THAT I KNOW WHERE THE CAVE IS, I'LL RETURN AT MY LEISURE.
NEVER AGAIN.
YOU DON'T GET TO FORCE YOUR WAY INTO MY LIFE, ATTACK MY PEOPLE AND SIMPLY FLY OFF.
YOU'VE ALREADY LOST, BRUCE!
ONCE AGAIN YOU'VE ACTED OUT OF DESPERATION.

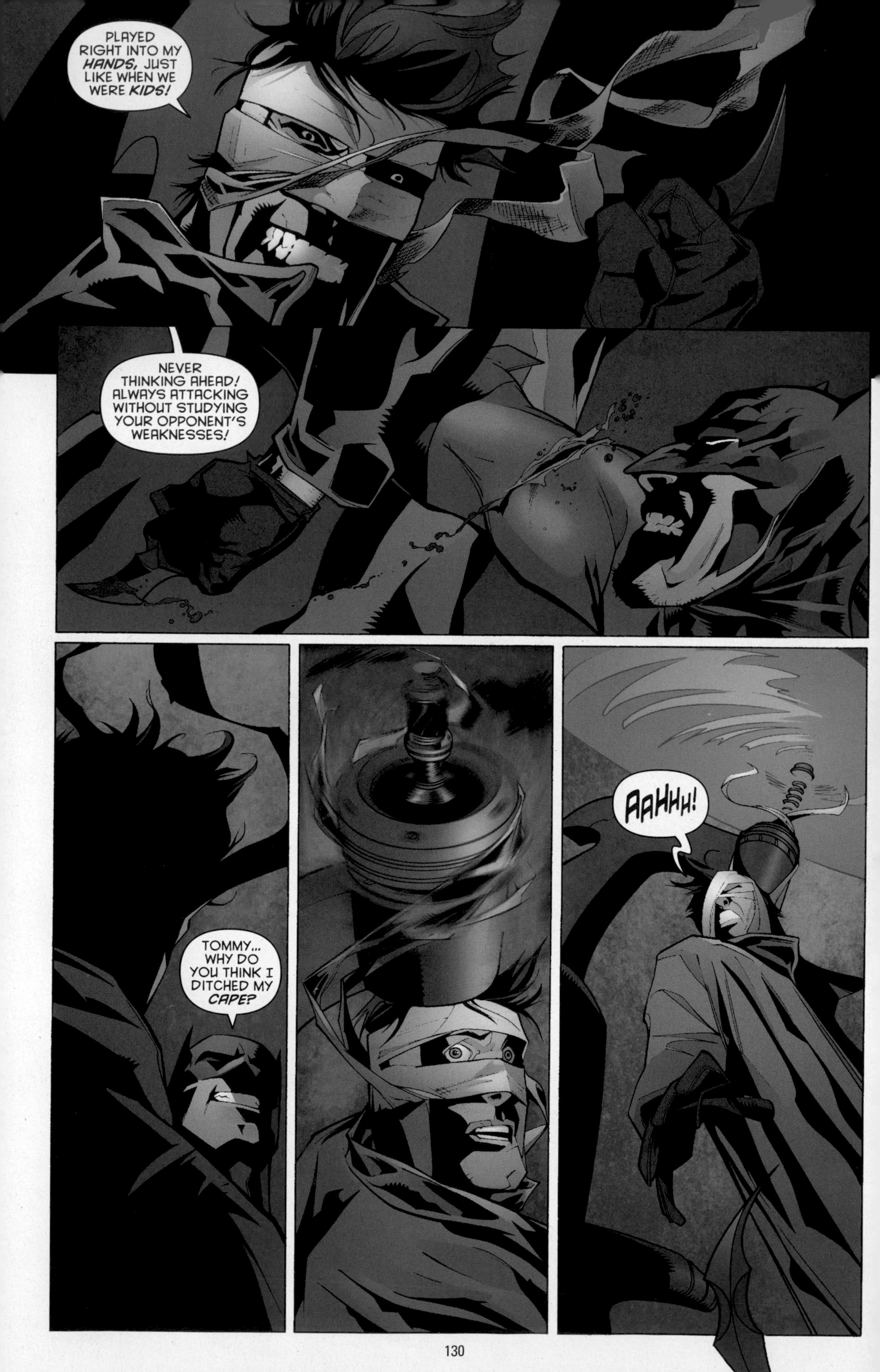
PLAYED RIGHT INTO MY HANDS, JUST LIKE WHEN WE WERE KIDS!
NEVER THINKING AHEAD! ALWAYS ATTACKING WITHOUT STUDYING YOUR OPPONENT'S WEAKNESSES!
TOMMY... WHY DO YOU THINK I DITCHED MY CAPE?
AAHHH!

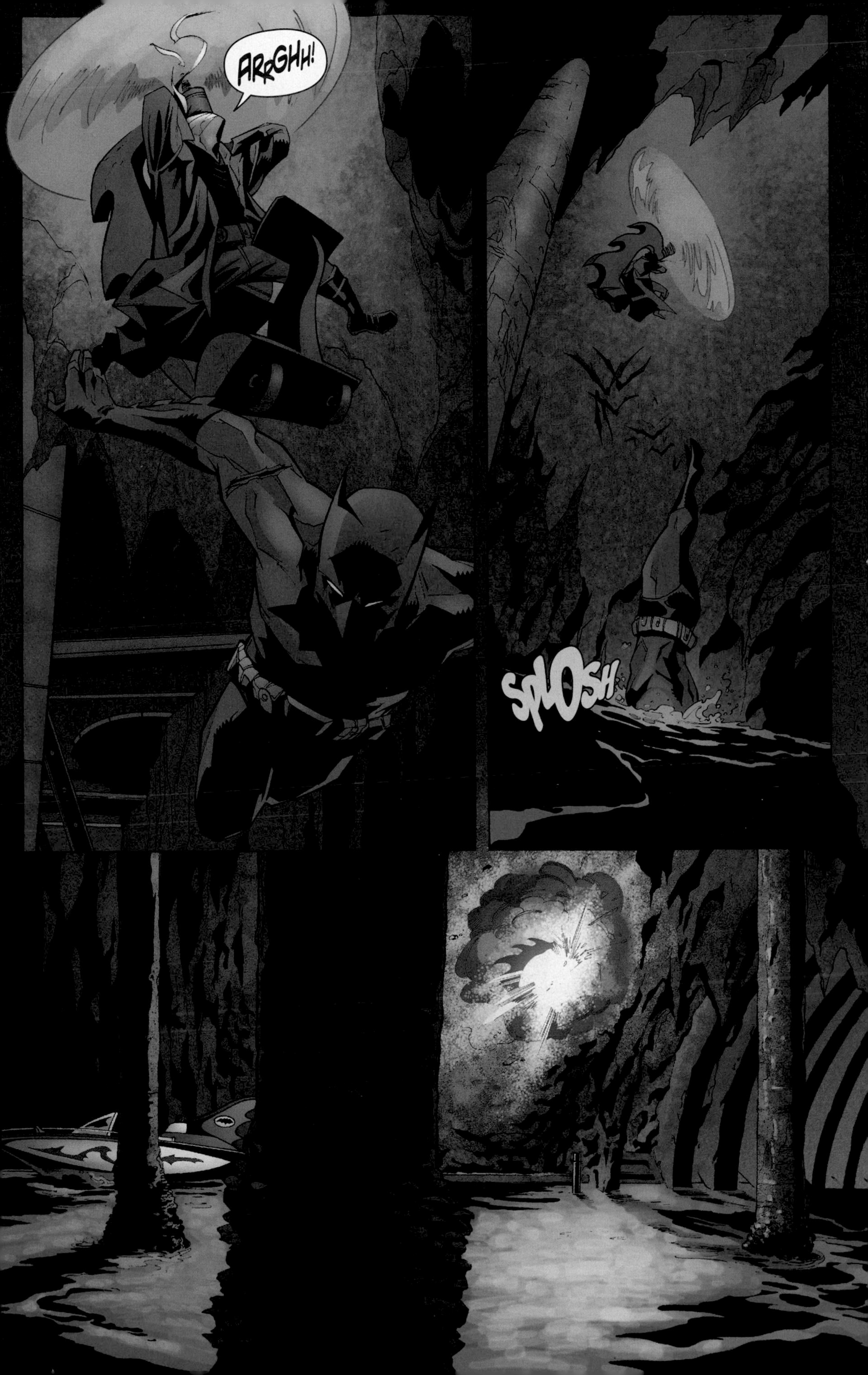
ARRGHH!
SPLOSH

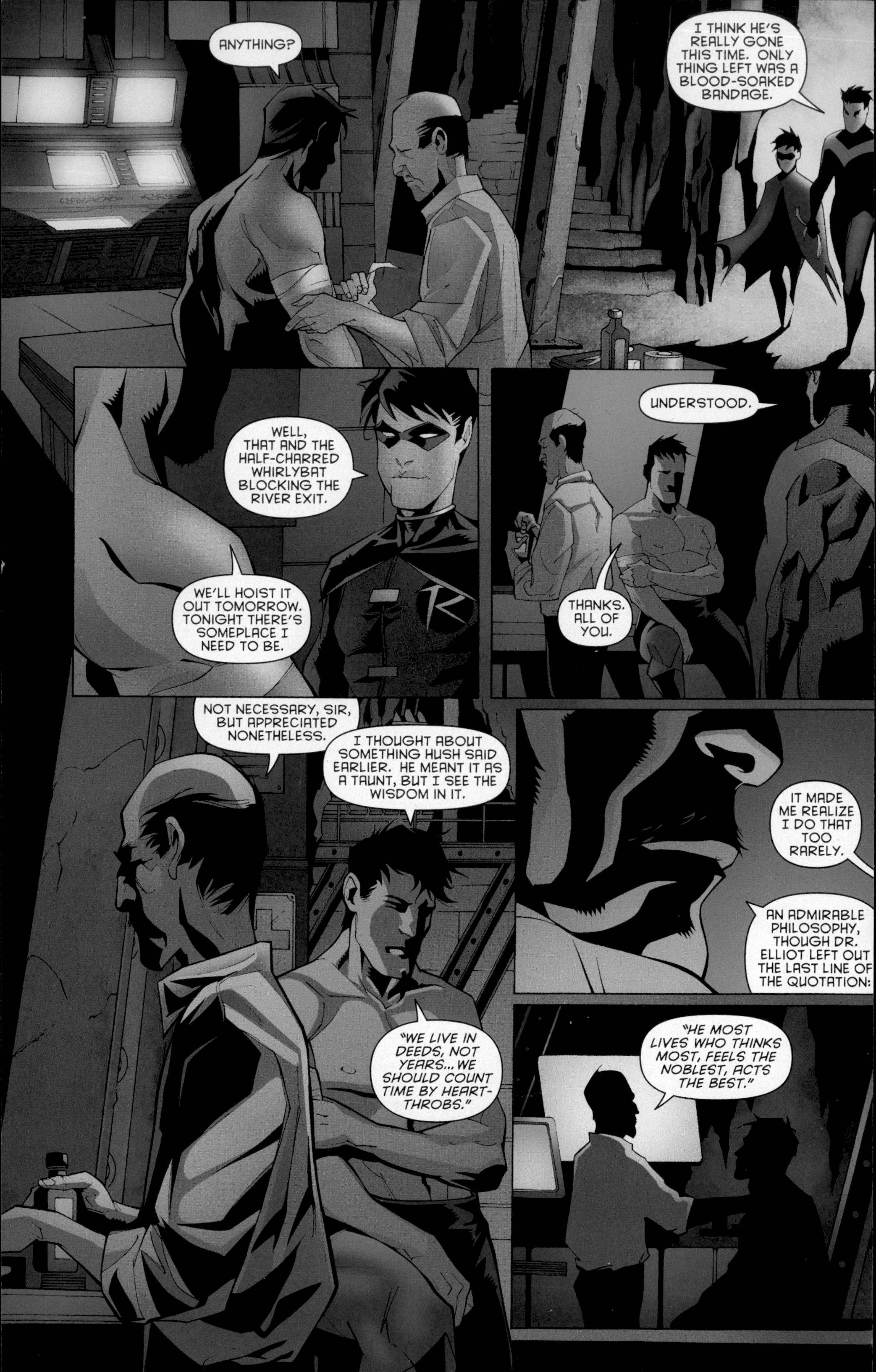
ANYTHING?
I THINK HE'S REALLY GONE THIS TIME. ONLY THING LEFT WAS A BLOOD-SOAKED BANDAGE.
WELL, THAT AND THE HALF-CHARRED WHIRLYBAT BLOCKING THE RIVER EXIT.
WE'LL HOIST IT OUT TOMORROW. TONIGHT THERE'S SOMEPLACE I NEED TO BE.
UNDERSTOOD.
THANKS. ALL OF YOU.
NOT NECESSARY, SIR, BUT APPRECIATED NONETHELESS.
I THOUGHT ABOUT SOMETHING HUSH SAID EARLIER. HE MEANT IT AS A TAUNT, BUT I SEE THE WISDOM IN IT.
"WE LIVE IN DEEDS, NOT YEARS... WE SHOULD COUNT TIME BY HEART-THROBS."
IT MADE ME REALIZE I DO THAT TOO RARELY.
AN ADMIRABLE PHILOSOPHY, THOUGH DR. ELLIOT LEFT OUT THE LAST LINE OF THE QUOTATION:
"HE MOST LIVES WHO THINKS MOST, FEELS THE NOBLEST, ACTS THE BEST."

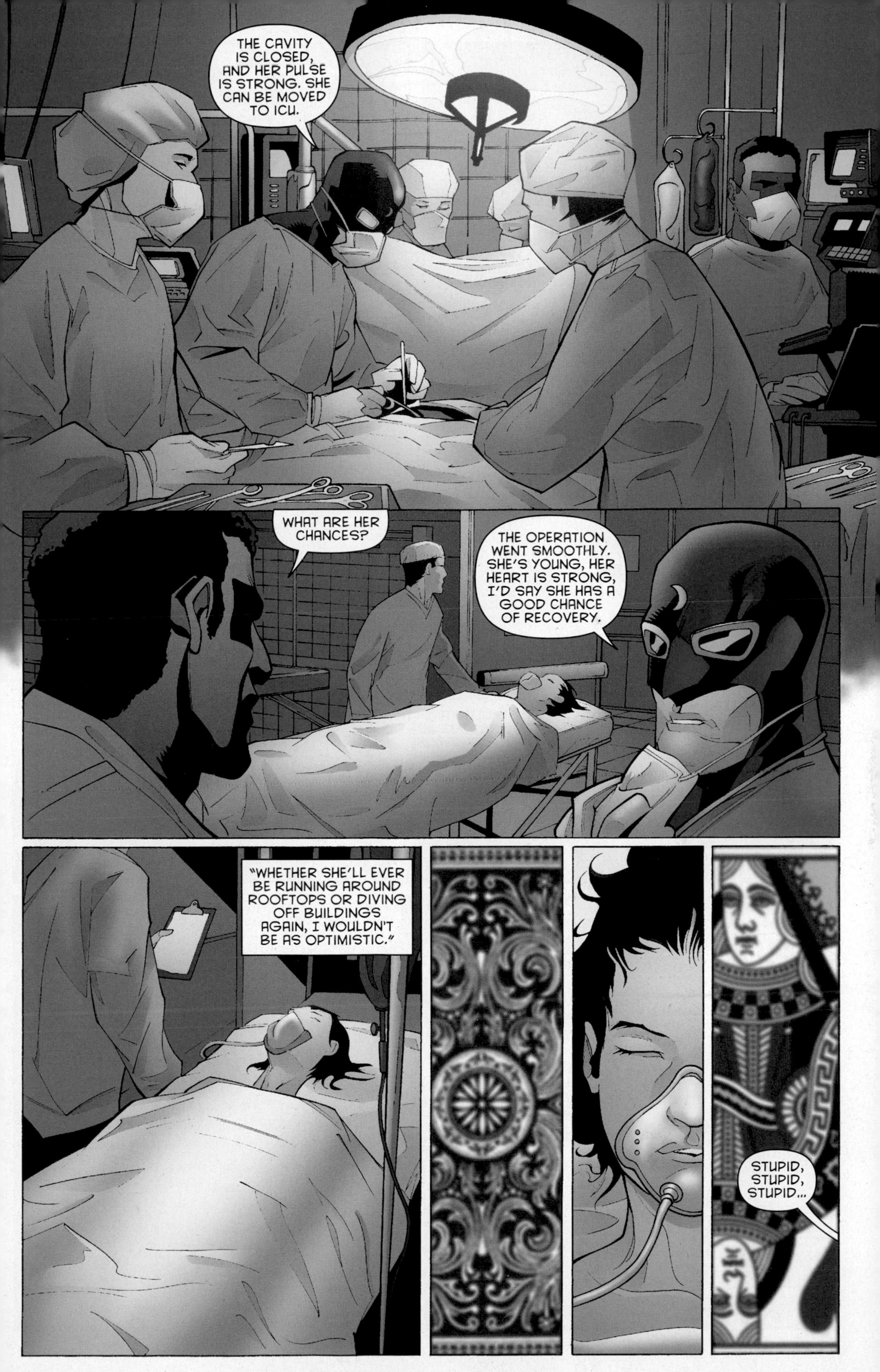
THE CAVITY IS CLOSED, AND HER PULSE IS STRONG. SHE CAN BE MOVED TO ICU.
WHAT ARE HER CHANCES?
THE OPERATION WENT SMOOTHLY. SHE'S YOUNG, HER HEART IS STRONG, I'D SAY SHE HAS A GOOD CHANCE OF RECOVERY.
"WHETHER SHE'LL EVER BE RUNNING AROUND ROOFTOPS OR DIVING OFF BUILDINGS AGAIN, I WOULDN'T BE AS OPTIMISTIC."
STUPID, STUPID, STUPID...

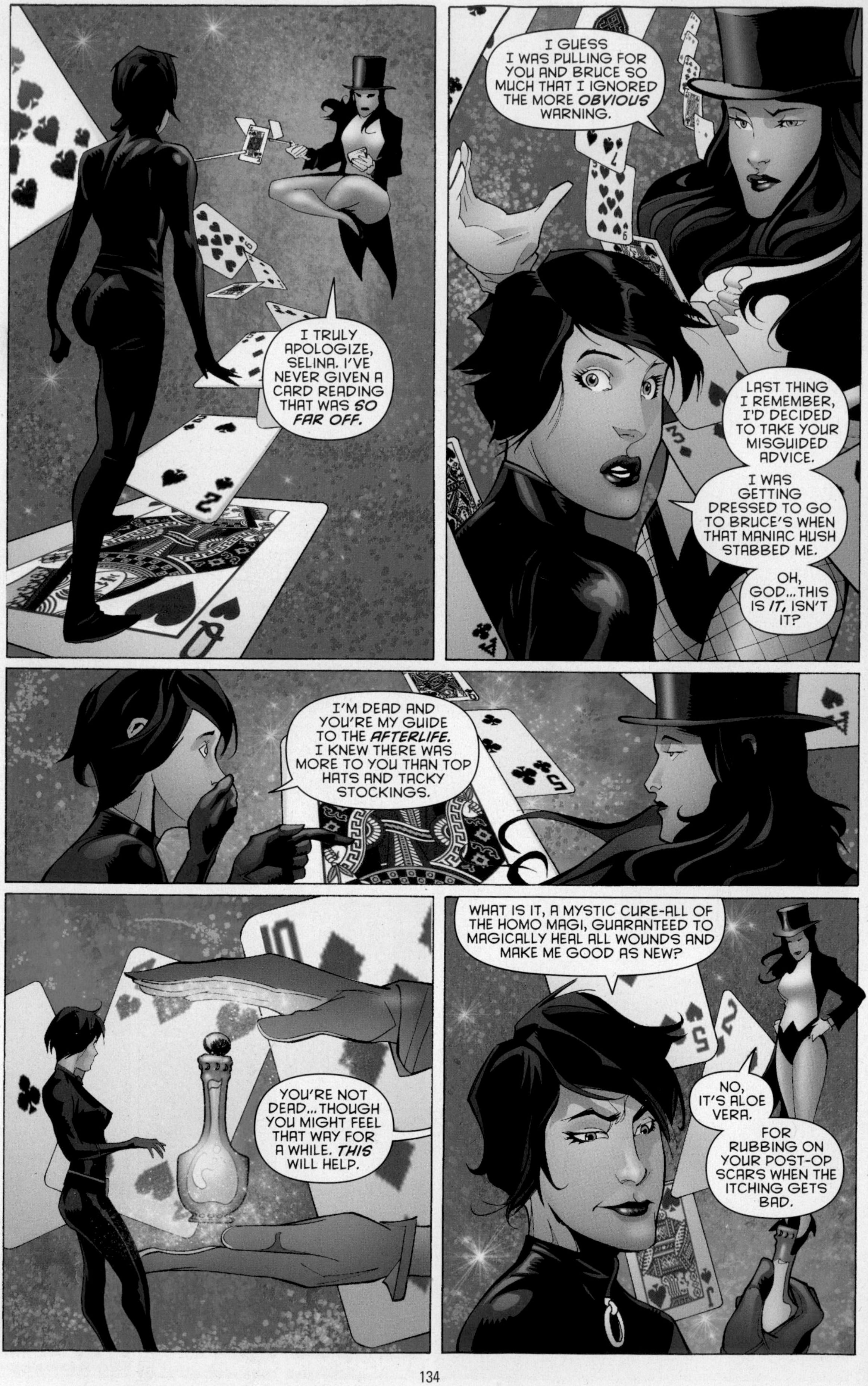
I TRULY APOLOGIZE, SELINA. I'VE NEVER GIVEN A CARD READING THAT WAS SO FAR OFF.
I GUESS I WAS PULLING FOR YOU AND BRUCE SO MUCH THAT I IGNORED THE MORE OBVIOUS WARNING.
LAST THING I REMEMBER, I'D DECIDED TO TAKE YOUR MISGUIDED ADVICE.
I WAS GETTING DRESSED TO GO TO BRUCE'S WHEN THAT MANIAC HUSH STABBED ME.
OH, GOD... THIS IS IT, ISN'T IT?
I'M DEAD AND YOU'RE MY GUIDE TO THE AFTERLIFE. I KNEW THERE WAS MORE TO YOU THAN TOP HATS AND TACKY STOCKINGS.
YOU'RE NOT DEAD... THOUGH YOU MIGHT FEEL THAT WAY FOR A WHILE. THIS WILL HELP.
WHAT IS IT, A MYSTIC CURE-ALL OF THE HOMO MAGI, GUARANTEED TO MAGICALLY HEAL ALL WOUNDS AND MAKE ME GOOD AS NEW?
NO, IT'S ALOE VERA.
FOR RUBBING ON YOUR POST-OP SCARS WHEN THE ITCHING GETS BAD.

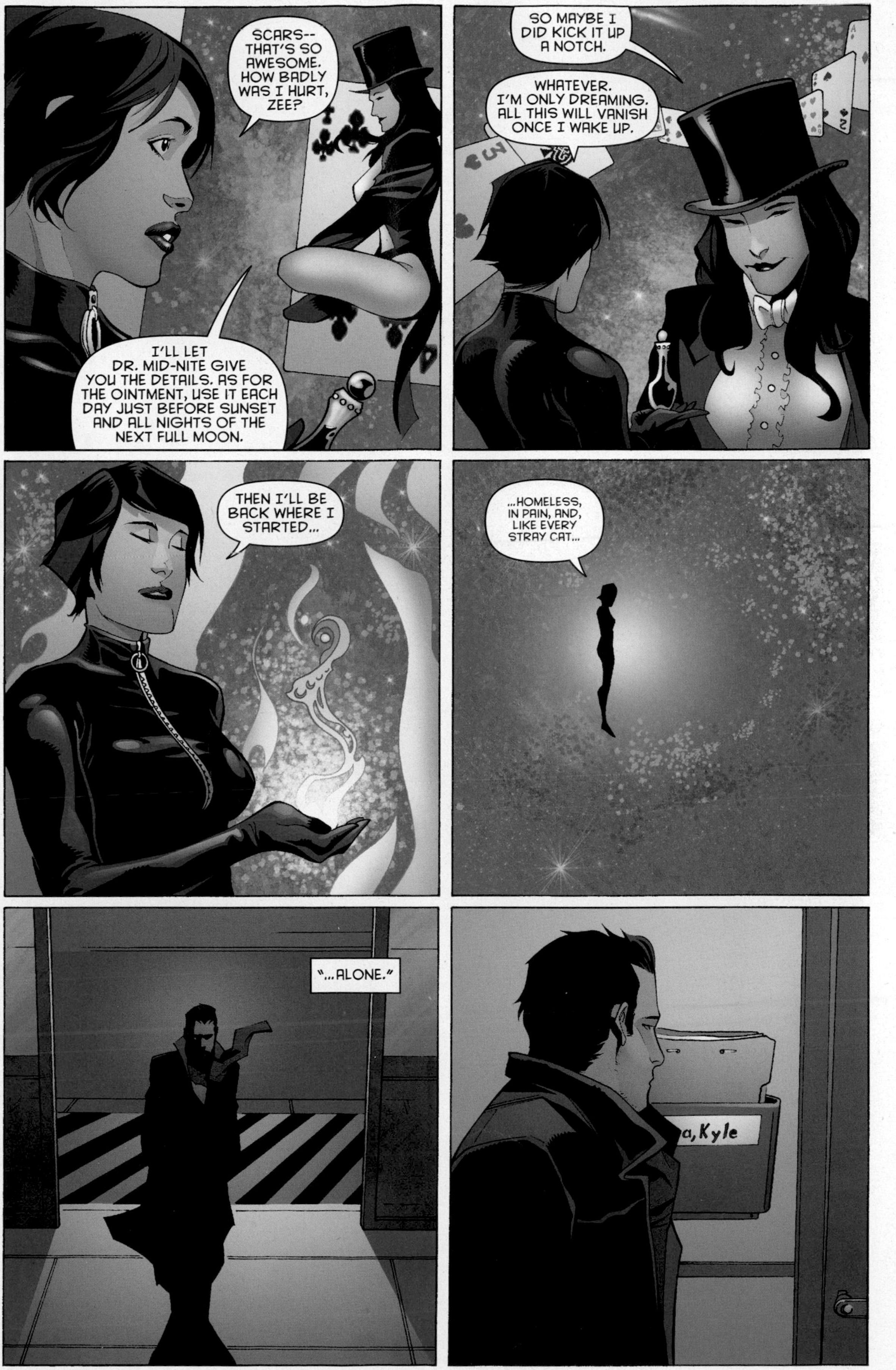
SCARS-- THAT'S SO AWESOME. HOW BADLY WAS I HURT, ZEE?
I'LL LET DR. MID-NITE GIVE YOU THE DETAILS. AS FOR THE OINTMENT, USE IT EACH DAY JUST BEFORE SUNSET AND ALL NIGHTS OF THE NEXT FULL MOON.
SO MAYBE I DID KICK IT UP A NOTCH.
WHATEVER. I'M ONLY DREAMING. ALL THIS WILL VANISH ONCE I WAKE UP.
THEN I'LL BE BACK WHERE I STARTED...
...HOMELESS, IN PAIN, AND, LIKE EVERY STRAY CAT...
"...ALONE."
a, Kyle

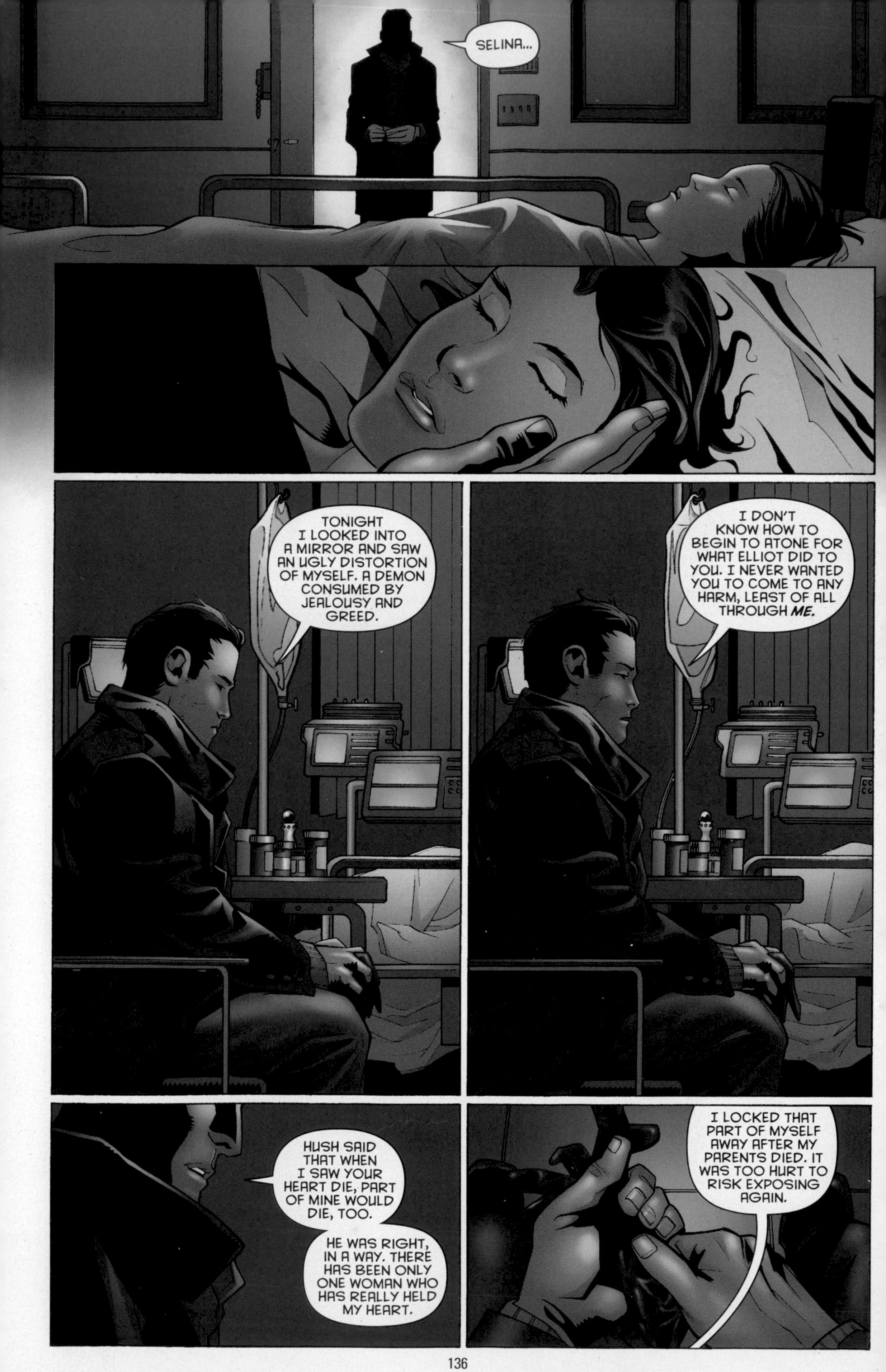
SELINA...
TONIGHT I LOOKED INTO A MIRROR AND SAW AN UGLY DISTORTION OF MYSELF. A DEMON CONSUMED BY JEALOUSY AND GREED.
I DON'T KNOW HOW TO BEGIN TO ATONE FOR WHAT ELLIOT DID TO YOU. I NEVER WANTED YOU TO COME TO ANY HARM, LEAST OF ALL THROUGH ***ME.***
HUSH SAID THAT WHEN I SAW YOUR HEART DIE, PART OF MINE WOULD DIE, TOO.
HE WAS RIGHT, IN A WAY. THERE HAS BEEN ONLY ONE WOMAN WHO HAS REALLY HELD MY HEART.
I LOCKED THAT PART OF MYSELF AWAY AFTER MY PARENTS DIED. IT WAS TOO HURT TO RISK EXPOSING AGAIN.

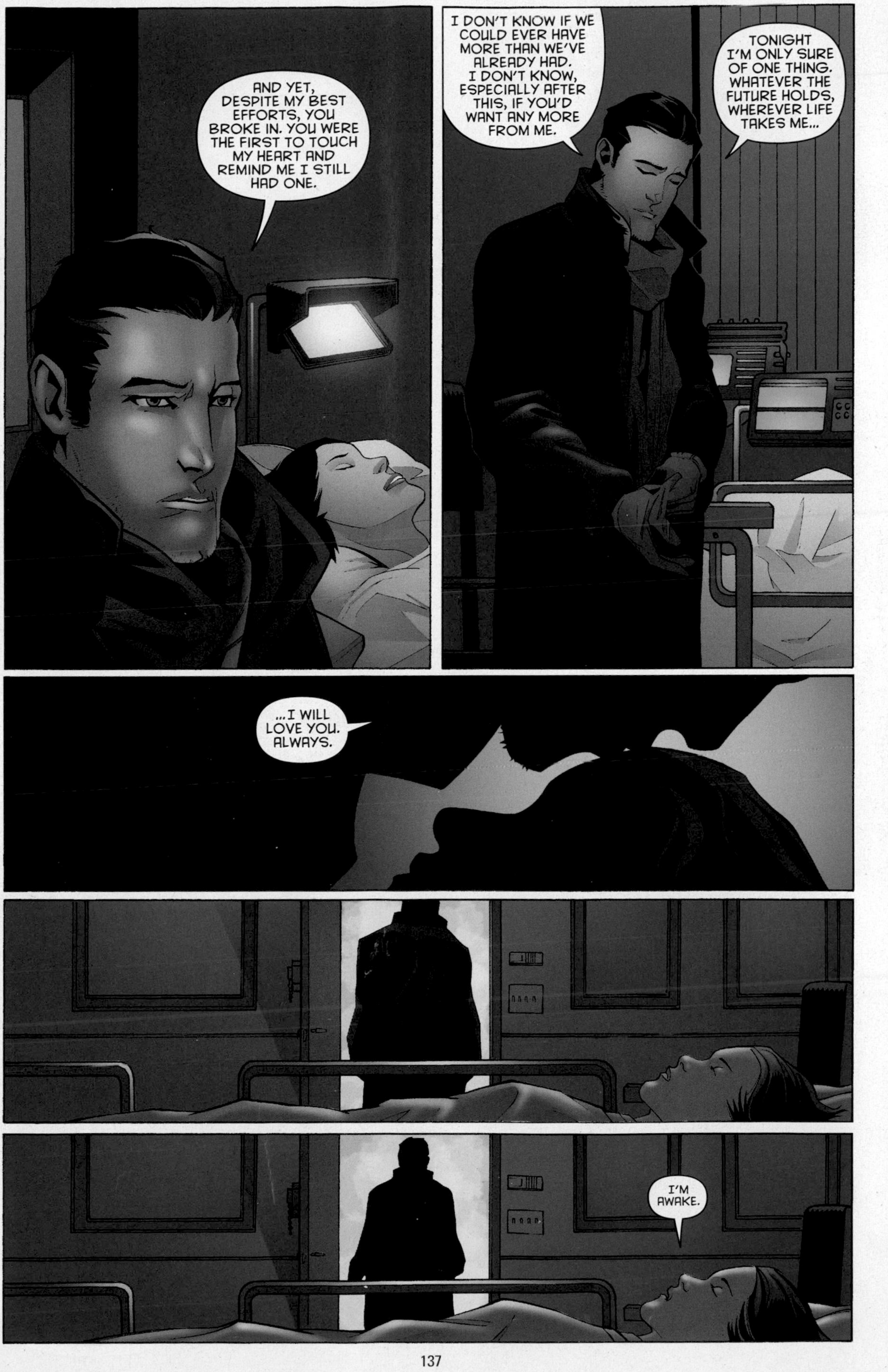
AND YET, DESPITE MY BEST EFFORTS, YOU BROKE IN. YOU WERE THE FIRST TO TOUCH MY HEART AND REMIND ME I STILL HAD ONE.
I DON'T KNOW IF WE COULD EVER HAVE MORE THAN WE'VE ALREADY HAD. I DON'T KNOW, ESPECIALLY AFTER THIS, IF YOU'D WANT ANY MORE FROM ME.
TONIGHT I'M ONLY SURE OF ONE THING. WHATEVER THE FUTURE HOLDS, WHEREVER LIFE TAKES ME...
...I WILL LOVE YOU. ALWAYS.
I'M AWAKE.

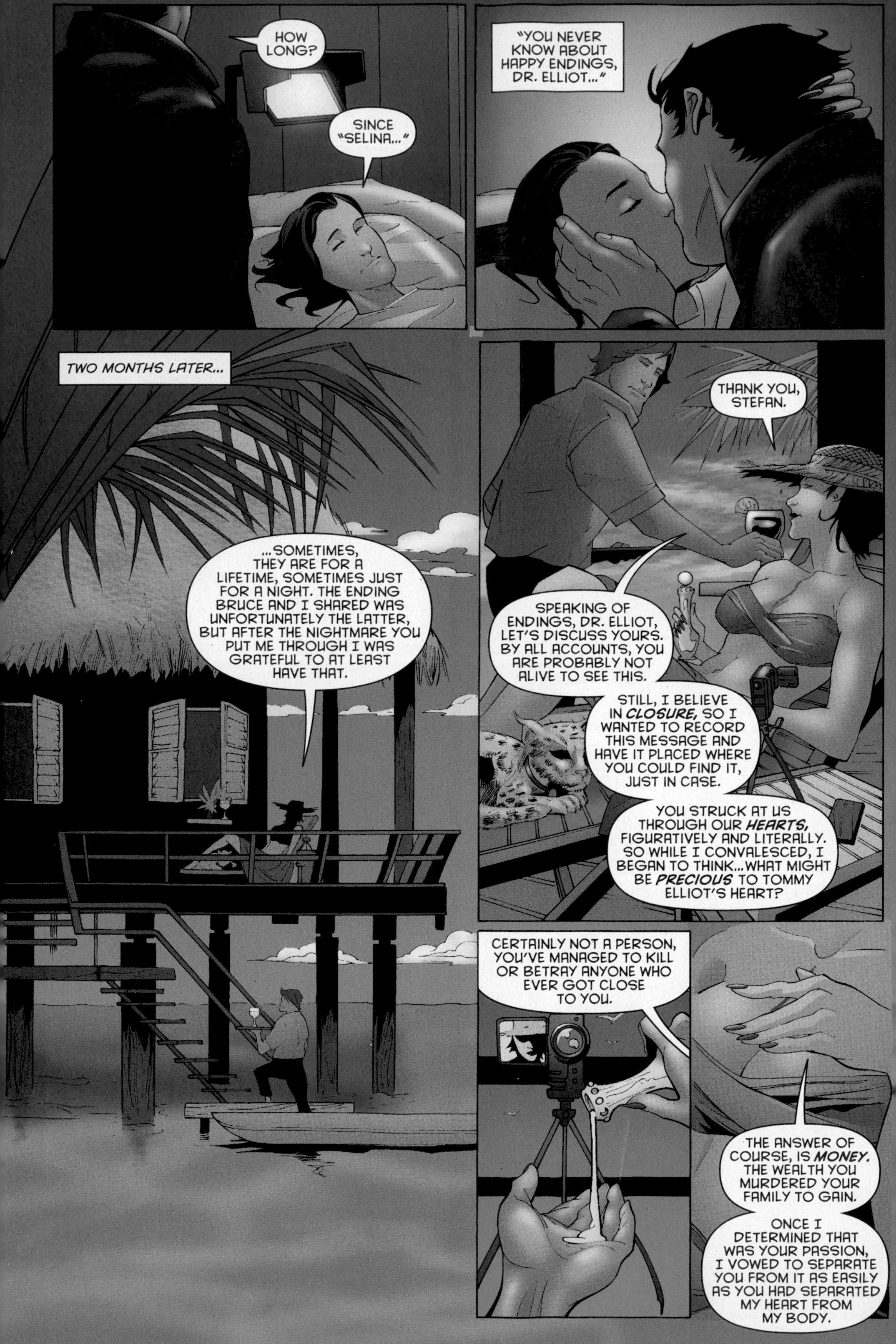
HOW LONG?
SINCE "SELINA..."
"YOU NEVER KNOW ABOUT HAPPY ENDINGS, DR. ELLIOT..."
TWO MONTHS LATER...
...SOMETIMES, THEY ARE FOR A LIFETIME, SOMETIMES JUST FOR A NIGHT. THE ENDING BRUCE AND I SHARED WAS UNFORTUNATELY THE LATTER, BUT AFTER THE NIGHTMARE YOU PUT ME THROUGH I WAS GRATEFUL TO AT LEAST HAVE THAT.
THANK YOU, STEFAN.
SPEAKING OF ENDINGS, DR. ELLIOT, LET'S DISCUSS YOURS. BY ALL ACCOUNTS, YOU ARE PROBABLY NOT ALIVE TO SEE THIS.
STILL, I BELIEVE IN *CLOSURE,* SO I WANTED TO RECORD THIS MESSAGE AND HAVE IT PLACED WHERE YOU COULD FIND IT, JUST IN CASE.
YOU STRUCK AT US THROUGH OUR *HEARTS,* FIGURATIVELY AND LITERALLY. SO WHILE I CONVALESCED, I BEGAN TO THINK...WHAT MIGHT BE *PRECIOUS* TO TOMMY ELLIOT'S HEART?
CERTAINLY NOT A PERSON, YOU'VE MANAGED TO KILL OR BETRAY ANYONE WHO EVER GOT CLOSE TO YOU.
THE ANSWER OF COURSE, IS *MONEY.* THE WEALTH YOU MURDERED YOUR FAMILY TO GAIN.
ONCE I DETERMINED THAT WAS YOUR PASSION, I VOWED TO SEPARATE YOU FROM IT AS EASILY AS YOU HAD SEPARATED MY HEART FROM MY BODY.

"MY FIRST STEP WAS CALLING IN FAVORS FROM *OLD FRIENDS.* SOME OF THEM HAD BEEN DUPED INTO YOUR SERVICE BEFORE, AND THEY WERE HAPPY TO HELP ME GET EVEN."

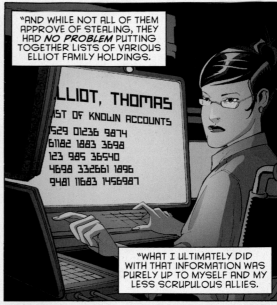

"AND WHILE NOT ALL OF THEM APPROVE OF STEALING, THEY HAD *NO PROBLEM* PUTTING TOGETHER LISTS OF VARIOUS ELLIOT FAMILY HOLDINGS.

LLIOT, THOMAS
ST OF KNOWN ACCOUNTS
529 01236 9874
61182 1883 3698
123 985 36540
4698 332661 1896
9481 11683 1456987

"WHAT I ULTIMATELY DID WITH THAT INFORMATION WAS PURELY UP TO MYSELF AND MY LESS SCRUPULOUS ALLIES."

"UNDER MY DIRECTION, SOME USED CHARM AND FORGED DOCUMENTS TO *SIPHON AWAY* YOUR FORTUNE.

"WHILE OTHERS I COACHED ON A MORE *HANDS ON* APPROACH.

"USING ALL THE TRICKS IN OUR ARSENAL, MY *KITTENS* AND I FOUND EVERY *CENT* IN EVERY ONE OF YOUR HIDING PLACES.

"I SHOULD ALSO MENTION THAT WHEN OUR MUTUAL FRIEND *SLAM BRADLEY* HEARD YOU WERE RESPONSIBLE FOR MY PREDICAMENT, HE WASTED NO TIME IN SHAKING DOWN HIS UNDERWORLD CONTACTS FOR YOUR WHEREABOUTS.

"EVEN WHEN YOU WERE A KID THE DETECTIVE HAD YOU PEGGED AS A *PSYCHO,* AND HE'S BEEN ACHING FOR ANOTHER SHOT AT YOU."

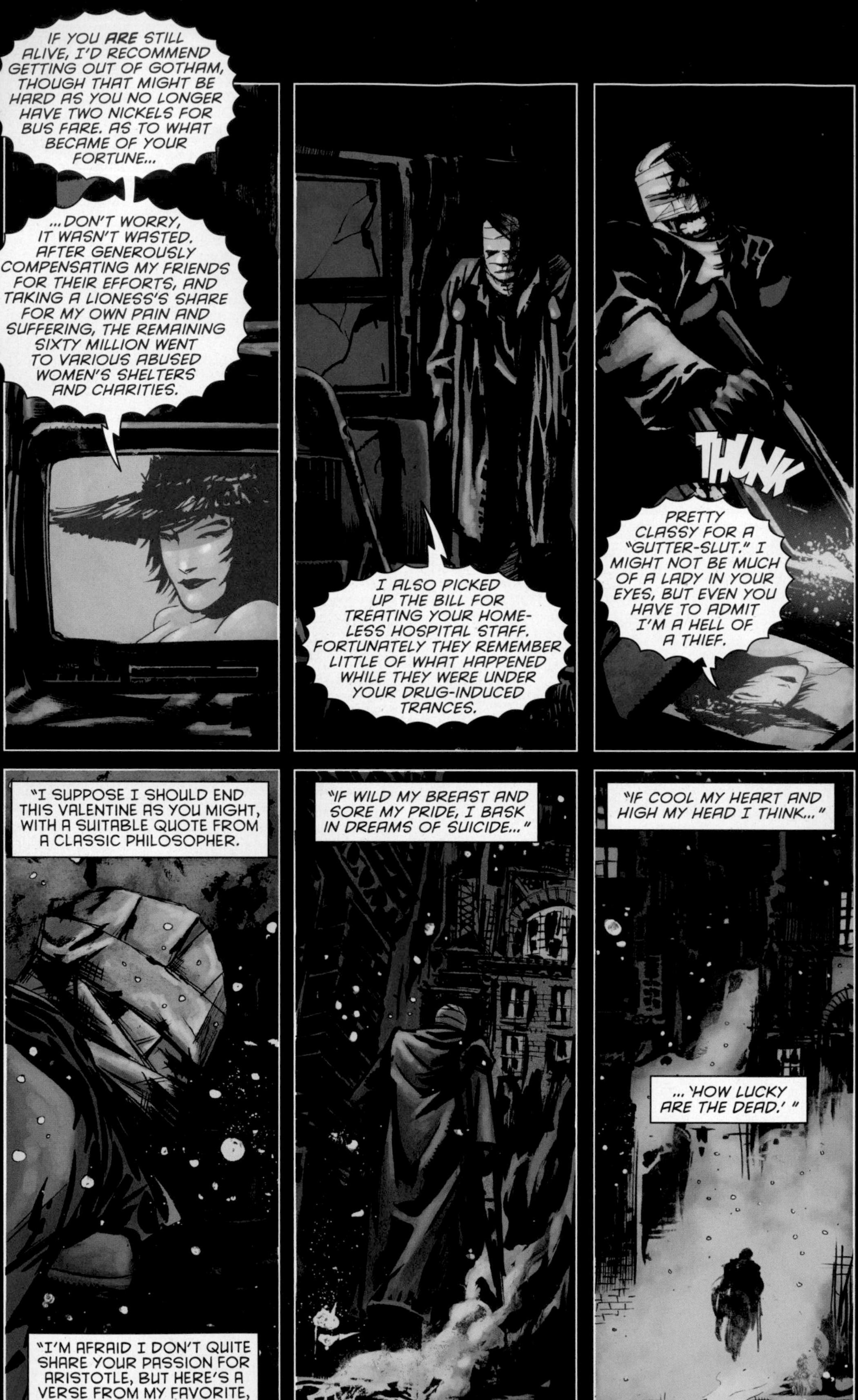
IF YOU ARE STILL ALIVE, I'D RECOMMEND GETTING OUT OF GOTHAM, THOUGH THAT MIGHT BE HARD AS YOU NO LONGER HAVE TWO NICKELS FOR BUS FARE. AS TO WHAT BECAME OF YOUR FORTUNE...
...DON'T WORRY, IT WASN'T WASTED. AFTER GENEROUSLY COMPENSATING MY FRIENDS FOR THEIR EFFORTS, AND TAKING A LIONESS'S SHARE FOR MY OWN PAIN AND SUFFERING, THE REMAINING SIXTY MILLION WENT TO VARIOUS ABUSED WOMEN'S SHELTERS AND CHARITIES.
I ALSO PICKED UP THE BILL FOR TREATING YOUR HOME-LESS HOSPITAL STAFF. FORTUNATELY THEY REMEMBER LITTLE OF WHAT HAPPENED WHILE THEY WERE UNDER YOUR DRUG-INDUCED TRANCES.
THUNK
PRETTY CLASSY FOR A "GUTTER-SLUT." I MIGHT NOT BE MUCH OF A LADY IN YOUR EYES, BUT EVEN YOU HAVE TO ADMIT I'M A HELL OF A THIEF.
"I SUPPOSE I SHOULD END THIS VALENTINE AS YOU MIGHT, WITH A SUITABLE QUOTE FROM A CLASSIC PHILOSOPHER.
"I'M AFRAID I DON'T QUITE SHARE YOUR PASSION FOR ARISTOTLE, BUT HERE'S A VERSE FROM MY FAVORITE, DOROTHY PARKER, FOR YOU TO RUMINATE UPON:
"IF WILD MY BREAST AND SORE MY PRIDE, I BASK IN DREAMS OF SUICIDE..."
"IF COOL MY HEART AND HIGH MY HEAD I THINK..."
... 'HOW LUCKY ARE THE DEAD.' "

The End

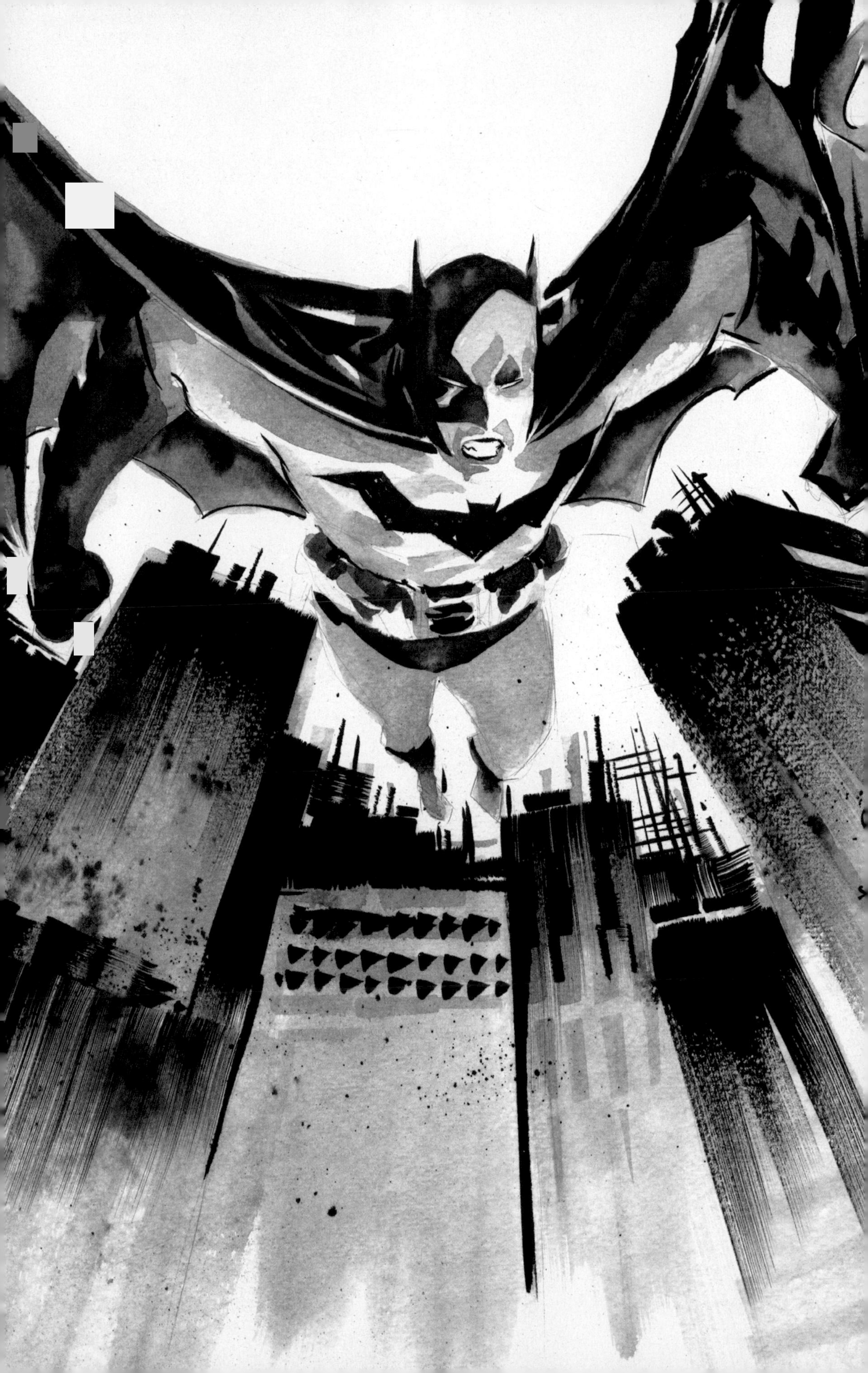

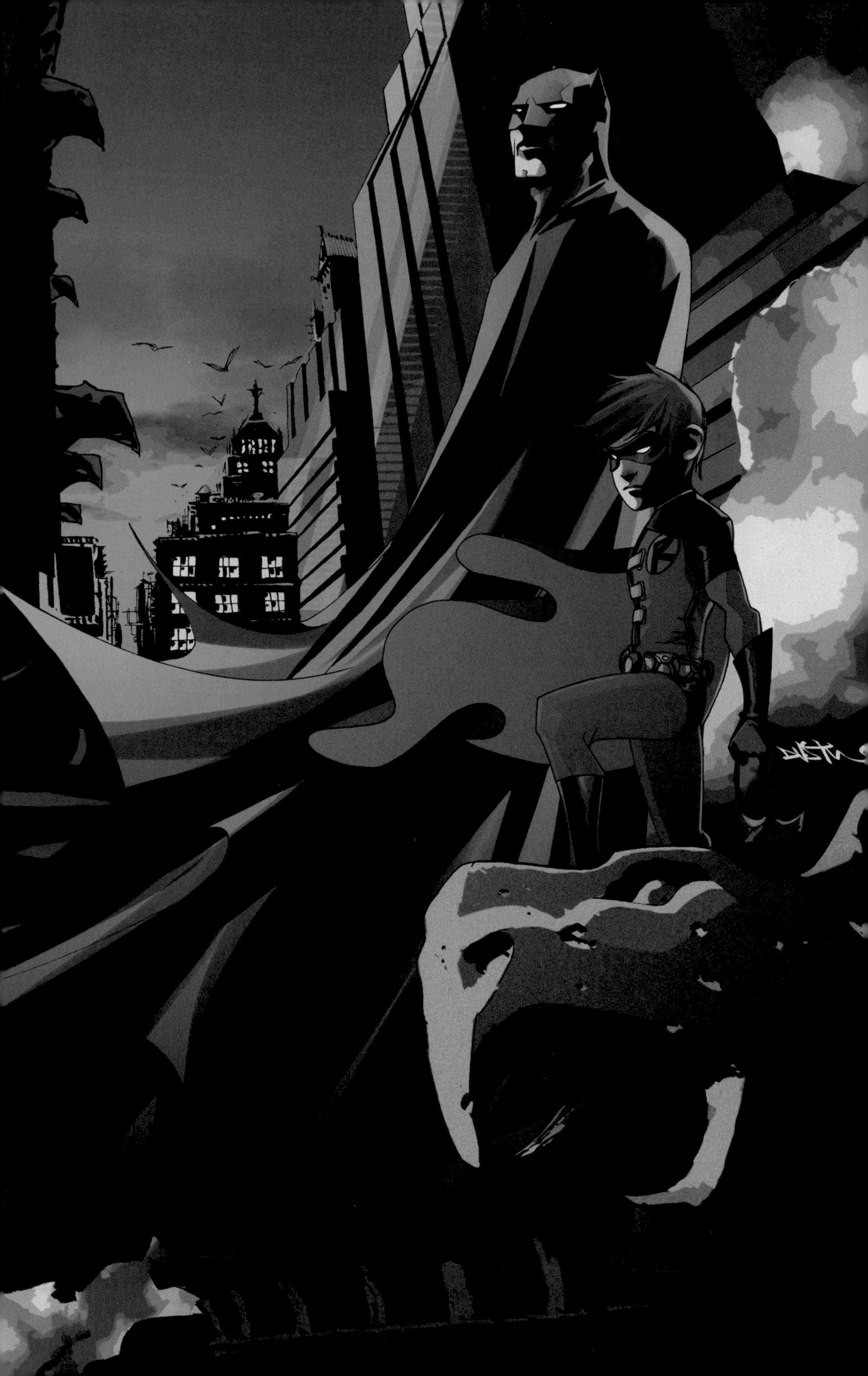

MORE CLASSIC TALES OF **THE DARK KNIGHT**

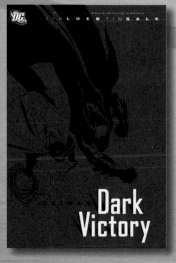
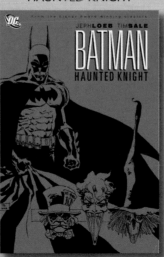
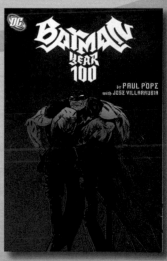